Sebastian Buckle gained his PhD in History and LGBT Studies at the University of Southampton. He is a blogger, writer, and researcher on British queer history.

THE WAY OUT

A History of Homosexuality in Modern Britain

SEBASTIAN BUCKLE

Leabharlann Shráid Chaoimhín
Kevin Street Library
Tel: 01 222 8488

I.B. TAURIS
LONDON · NEW YORK

Published in 2015 by
I.B.Tauris & Co. Ltd
London • New York
www.ibtauris.com

Copyright © 2015 Sebastian Buckle

The right of Sebastian Buckle to be identified as the author of this work has been asserted by the author in accordance with the Copyright, Designs and Patents Act 1988.

All rights reserved. Except for brief quotations in a review, this book, or any part thereof, may not be reproduced, stored in or introduced into a retrieval system, or transmitted, in any form or by any means, electronic, mechanical, photocopying, recording or otherwise, without the prior written permission of the publisher.

References to websites were correct at the time of writing.

International Library of Twentieth Century History 77

ISBN: 978 1 78453 183 6
eISBN: 978 0 85773 738 0

A full CIP record for this book is available from the British Library
A full CIP record is available from the Library of Congress

Library of Congress Catalog Card Number: available

Typeset in Garamond Three by OKS Prepress Services, Chennai, India
Printed and bound by CPI Group (UK) Ltd, Croydon, CR0 4YY

'There are as many ways to live as there are people in this world, and each one deserves a closer look.' – Gully
Harriet the Spy, dir. by Bronwen Hughes (Paramount Pictures, 1996)

CONTENTS

Acknowledgements	viii
List of Acronyms	x
Preface	xii
Introduction	1

Section 1: Gay Liberation
1. Early Optimism — 17
2. Early Images — 37
3. 'Ostentatious Behaviour and Public Flaunting' — 66

Section 2: A Visible Subculture
4. Political Backlash — 91
5. Conflicting Public Images — 120
6. Gay Space — 146

Section 3: Joining the Mainstream
7. 'An End to Unjustifiable Discrimination' — 165
8. Real Lives in the Media — 189

Conclusion — 213

Notes — 224
Bibliography — 246
Index — 259

ACKNOWLEDGEMENTS

A book, by its very nature, can only have one author. But it would be wrong to think it is the work of only one person. Many people have helped make this possible, but my main thanks must go to Professor Mark Cornwall. Mark offered a great deal of advice and constructive criticism when this research was first undertaken as a PhD project. His feedback helped guide this project and improve it beyond measure; without his support it simply would not exist. So too, I thank Dr Joan Tumblety for her support and advice – not just during the candidature of my PhD, but throughout my time at the University of Southampton, including as an undergraduate not always so dedicated to learning.

I have relied on the help of many people, both directly and indirectly, in gathering the source material for this book. Particular thanks must go to those who are quoted directly: Waheed Alli, Ben Summerskill, and Edwina Currie. Thanks too must go to the staff of the British Library, the British Film Institute, and the Hall-Carpenter Archives at the London School of Economics and at the Bishopsgate Institute. The speed and professionalism with which they dealt with my queries and requests saved me a huge amount of time and difficulty – a welcome relief while researching in an archive. Special thanks must also go to the countless people involved in creating these treasure troves of information in the first place, as though preparing for my future research.

Similarly, there are others who have contributed in less tangible, but no less meaningful, ways. Without my friends to encourage me, distract me, and be there for me, I would never have embarked on this research. So, thank you to Mark Aldridge, Kieran Ellis, Lucie Harvey, Georgina Searle, Kevin O'Donovan, James Laidler, Alex Duffy, Matt Hurst, Richard Carruthers, Elle Williams, Michael Griksaitis, Jamie Parkhouse, Dan Byrne, Adele De Mello, and Claire Evans. Further thanks are also due to my contemporaries Charles Smith, Mike Everett, and Tom Plant for motivation, support, and advice.

As a historian my final thanks must go to the people who have come before me and who made my life and countless others easier through their hardship. So, to those who are the subject of this research, I offer my sincerest gratitude.

LIST OF ACRONYMS

Act-Up	AIDS Coalition to Unleash Power
CHE	Campaign for Homosexual Equality
GLC	Greater London Council
GLF	Gay Liberation Front
GMFA	Gay Men Fighting AIDS
HLRS	Homosexual Law Reform Society
ILEA	Inner London Education Authority
LLGRC	Legislation for Lesbian and Gay Rights Campaign
MANDFHAB	Male and Female Homosexual Association of Great Britain
MRG	Minorities Research Group
NIGRA	Northern Ireland Gay Rights Association
NWHLRC	North-Western Homosexual Law Reform Committee
OLGA	Organisation for Lesbian and Gay Action
SLRS	Sexual Law Reform Society
SMG	Scottish Minorities Group
THT	Terrence Higgins Trust

TORCHE	Tory Campaign for Homosexual Equality (previously the Conservative Group for Homosexual Equality)
TUC	Trades Union Congress
USFI	Union for Sexual Freedoms in Ireland
WLM	Women's Liberation Movement

PREFACE

Homosexuality has always existed. It may have been called by different names, been celebrated by society or condemned by religion, but it has been an ever-present feature in all human life. To suggest otherwise – claiming it is a modern invention – is both illogical and demonstrably wrong. But modernity has influenced homosexuality. We live in a world where people are classified based on their sexuality, and where their sexual identity becomes the defining feature of their personal and public life. The characteristics that inform and define these identities are not innate, but are constructed in our society.

The Way Out: A History of Homosexuality in Modern Britain is a unique book. It takes the reader through an accessible and in-depth analysis of the history of homosexuality in post-war Britain. It tells the modern history of homosexuality through the lens of identity, charting the growth of a public discourse on sexuality. Indeed, the history of homosexuality in Britain during this period cannot be told without reference to the rise of a system of classifying people based on their sexuality. In exploring this system, it examines a public discourse influenced by images of homosexuality from the media, politics and the law, and the social lives of gay men and lesbians. It shows how ideas about identity – which became synonymous with homosexuality – were constructed from the 1940s onwards. It explains how our very modern ideas surrounding homosexuality developed within living memory, and continue to do so.

The Way Out also tells the compelling and often tumultuous history of homosexuality in Britain. Before 1967 men could be sentenced to life in prison if convicted of homosexual offences. Throughout the twentieth century men and women could face the prospect of invasive, humiliating and mentally scarring psychological treatment, to 'cure' them of their homosexuality. But after 2004 those same men and women could enter into civil partnerships – sharing in almost all the legal rights afforded to heterosexual couples through marriage. This journey from criminality and discrimination to the centre of mainstream life took place in just 37 years. *The Way Out* tells that story.

INTRODUCTION

Writing in 1992, Antony Grey – the long-term homosexual rights campaigner and Secretary of the Homosexual Law Reform Society (HLRS) – noted that the Gay Liberation Front (GLF) had 'implanted a new stereotype of "gayness" in the public mind'. He claimed the group, which had emerged in the 1970s to challenge his discreet tactics and middle-class respectability, had also instilled this image,

> in the minds of a new generation of homosexuals: the image of the blatant, flaunting, determinedly iconoclastic, far-out, far-Left sexual rebel, despising and challenging all society's accepted values and scornful of those homosexuals – the majority – who kept their heads down.[1]

Coming from a man who achieved notable success with the (albeit limited) reforms of the Sexual Offences Act, this statement illustrated what he saw as the power of images to influence or block change. Decades later the recognition of the power of images in influencing ideas about identity remained stronger than ever. One young gay man, speaking in 2012, commented:

> I didn't visit a gay bar until 2004 – all my perceptions up 'til then had been formed by watching *Queer as Folk* (late at night, with subtitles only so the family couldn't hear!) so I was certain

they were all seedy and obsessed with having sex. And the first bar I visited was just like that – it wouldn't be until several years later that I would find out that gay men weren't all promiscuous and sex obsessed![2]

Homosexuality in modern Britain is wrapped up in these images and ideas. Taken as a whole – through political, social, and cultural factors – they inform a public discourse on homosexuality which creates a sexual identity, defining what it means to be a gay man or lesbian.

But sexual identity is not sexuality. The latter is a complicated psychology of sexual attraction, which is never as simple as the gender of your sexual partner, but includes every conceivable characteristic. Sexual identity, on the other hand, is a historically constructed category. It can be dependent on time, location, class, ethnicity, religious background, and gender. It is constantly evolving, but seemingly without contradiction is often assumed to be timeless and unchanging. Sexual identity is more than just the labelling of desires; it is about constructing an identity on to those desires, and using the ideas, images and, often, prejudices in society to inform them. As a concept, its origin is within living memory, as society became more open about discussing sex, and whom you desired became an integral part of your personal and public identity. Modern Britain has created a sexual order out of a disparate series of likes and dislikes, as has Western society. Within this sexual order homosexuality has emerged as a category of identity, where ideas, images, and actions have influenced the creation of the personal 'social identity' and the publicly-perceived 'group identity'. But what people assume to be the innate 'gay' and 'lesbian' identity – either of themselves, or others – are, in fact, very modern constructions. They have their genesis in the late 1960s and early 1970s, when a gay/straight binary started to be understood by the majority of people, which categorised people based on their sexuality, and for homosexuals, created a group identity through the assimilation of images in society.

This book is thus a study of the representations of homosexuality in the public arena that have been integral to the creation of sexual identity. Individual gay men and lesbians have drawn on different images in society (depending on their exposure to them) and internalised them – as have straight people – creating their ideas about sexual identity. By exploring the political, media, and social changes taking place in relation to homosexuality between 1967 and 2004, this book chart the evolution of a public discourse on a gay and lesbian community and identity – which are increasingly used synonymously – as well as of binary definitions of sexuality more generally. In doing so it discusses the origins and nature of homosexual social and group identities in order to recognise the historical construction of all identities. Between the political rhetoric and actions of government, the visibility of gay men and lesbians, the incidence of homophobic hate crime, and other homophobic hate crime, change was far from linear in this period. However, there is tangible evidence that public perceptions changed. The exploration of attitudes towards gay men and lesbians is vital in understanding the development of this identity over those 37 years. These perceptions, from both society and from self-identified homosexuals, through the political, media, and social spheres, provide the framework for understanding the creation of the contemporary gay man and lesbian in Britain.

Situating the history

There is a strong body of historical writing that has focused on the history of sexual identity in the United Kingdom. Jeffrey Weeks is the preeminent British historian of sexual identity in Britain, having written widely on the subject. His first book, 1977's *Coming Out*, began by asserting that changing words to describe homosexuality reflected broader cultural changes. He wrote that '[t]hey are not just new labels for old realities: they point to a changing reality, both in the way a hostile society labelled homosexuality, and in the way those stigmatized saw themselves', before going on to claim that:

> The focus of historical inquiry therefore has to be on the developing social attitudes, their origins and their rationale,

for, without these, discussion of homosexuality becomes virtually incomprehensible. And as a starting-point we have to distinguish between homosexual behaviour, which is universal, and a homosexual identity, which is historically specific – and a comparatively recent phenomenon in Britain.³

By examining sexuality this way he distinguished his work from other histories, which had sought either to reinsert homosexuality into the past or to simply tell a history of it. Instead, he concentrated on combining the two in examining the nature of homosexuality and its 'historically specific' nature. His work on the post-1967 period focused, therefore, on the emergence of a new reality for homosexuality, with the advent of the contemporarily understood gay and lesbian social and group identities. He claimed,

> [t]he early 1970s mark the turning-point in the evolution of a homosexual consciousness. The homophile organizations that tiptoed through the liberal 1960s were superseded in the 1970s by a new type of movement which stressed openness, defiance, pride, identity – and, above all, self-activity.⁴

Indeed, his work has been characterised by an exploration of the roles homosexual men and women have created for themselves in what he described as a 'democratisation of everyday life'.⁵ He also sought to study the underlying causes of these historical shifts, in particular his premise that 'we cannot understand homosexuality by studying homosexuality alone'.⁶ His work on the rise of the 'moral right' in the 1980s, for example, drew on the changes taking place in relation to identity in the 1970s.⁷

Weeks' work has also focused on the study of 'the forces, ideas and social practices that have elevated sexuality into a prime focus of social concern over the past two hundred years'.⁸ However, his later work has sought to challenge the homogenisation of sexual labels, which have often overlooked individual experiences and masked important historically-specific differences in sexual identity. While the 1970s onwards created the idea of a gay identity and community in Britain, he claimed that this 'tends to reaffirm the sense of separateness and unity of the category of "the homosexual" which gay liberation sought to challenge, and which the realities of contemporary sexualities make untenable'.[9] Indeed, this pre-empts later queer theory, which has challenged the idea of fixed and binary sexual labels. His work has tended to emphasise the role of the individual, claiming '[t]he significant shift is that those who were talked about in the pioneering works of the sexologists are now speaking openly for themselves, in a variety of voices, and are changing the nature of the debate.'[10] This is at the expense of ideas and images created by other sources, however, which have influenced the development of social and group sexual identities that this book addresses.

Rebecca Jennings has examined a similar post-war period in the history of the development of a specifically lesbian identity in Britain. While her book, *A Lesbian History of Britain,* offers an overview of lesbian experiences throughout the last 500 years, its later chapters exploring life from the 1960s onwards provide a similar focus on how social organisations and political change have influenced the creation and development of contemporary ideas surrounding sexual identity.[11] Similarly, in *Tomboys and Bachelor Girls* Jennings argues that the immediate post-war period was vital in the creation of this new lesbian identity:

> The ambiguities and contradictions in post-war notions of femininity afforded women a surprising degree of flexibility in the expression of alternative gender and sexual identities. Concepts such as 'tomboy', 'bachelor girl' and 'career woman' enabled women to forge social identities as single, economically independent and active women and to deploy these identities to express same-sex desire.[12]

Likewise, Hugh David's *On Queer Street* explored the evolution of a 'gay community' in Britain through oral testimony of men who were part of this hidden world, but without any serious look at public perceptions.[13] Additionally, Ken Plummer's *The Making of the Modern*

Homosexual, published much earlier in 1981, is typical of a number of early writings, working from the premise that 'the homosexual' is a historical construction.[14] Presenting a sociological background, and then expanding this theory with empirical examples of the changes that were taking place in relation to the homosexual identity, it reflected important work that was being carried out on sexual identity in Britain in the 1980s. More recently, Matt Cook's chapter in a recent synthesis of gay history is the latest attempt at addressing the relative absence of work on the emergence of a gay identity in the United Kingdom after 1967, while also challenging a progressive narrative in gay British history.[15] These histories, therefore, show how far the study of homosexuality in Britain has developed. They point to the post-war period as being vital to the creation of contemporary sexual identities, and they offer a valuable contribution in understanding the nature of constructed identities. They invariably concentrate on self-created labels, however, while earlier work advanced the now widely accepted premise that sexual identities are a social construction. More recent work has sought to challenge the homogenisation of these labels, but lacks a focus on the role of a public discourse on homosexuality in creating sexual identities, and the impact of images in society that have contributed to that discourse.

From reform, to regression, and back to reform again

Histories of homosexuality have often, although not always, separated the experiences of men and women for obvious reasons. Criminality, separate social spheres, and historically-specific gender roles, among other reasons, have combined to ensure that men and women experienced their sexual lives in very different ways in the past, and to an extent through modern changes, continue to do so. Historians of sexuality are simply reflecting reality by segregating their experiences. But during this period there is a strong sense of the interconnectedness of male and female homosexual lives, especially in the public discourse. The GLF brought homosexual men and women together for the first time under a new 'gay'

INTRODUCTION

identity, and through many political and social organisations since their lives have been linked. A public discourse on homosexuality thus often combines ideas about men and women, and a study of that discourse would not be complete without an analysis of that interconnectedness. But for every example of common experiences in the creation of a public discourse, there is another showing the separation of lives. Feminism, HIV/AIDS, publications, and media representations all demonstrate the gendered dimension to the construction of sexual identity. It is important, therefore, to understand and explore the different ways male and female homosexuality has been constructed in the public arena, and how they interact. Integral to this is the recognition of the different approaches necessary. Men and women read different magazines, were represented in different films and TV shows (although there was some cross-over), and socialised in different circles. A history of homosexuality needs to be aware of the differences and similarities in these gendered lives when exploring the public discourse, especially when negative images can feed a homophobia which affects both men and women, regardless of gender. Indeed, binary definitions of sexuality are just that, and the modern phenomenon of categorising people based on their sexuality, equally, if not to a greater extent than gender, requires a study of both men and women.

Existing work has pointed to this post-war period as being vital in our understanding of the development of a public discourse surrounding (homo)sexuality, and the subsequent desire to classify individuals and groups based on their sexual identity. Houlbrook writes how,

[f]or many observers, the rapid social changes unleashed by the war seemed to have rendered Britain's stability problematic, destabilizing the critical interpretative categories – of masculinity, youth, and nationhood – within which narratives of sexual difference and danger were framed. When established notions of Britishness seemed more threatened from every direction, queer urban culture was viewed as ever more

dangerous, assuming a central symbolic position in the postwar politics of sexuality.[16]

For women, meanwhile, the war gave them 'opportunities in the workplace, political power, and a degree of personal freedom', which afforded them the opportunity to 'take up these new definitions [of sexual identity] and deploy them to make sense of their own experiences', in the post-war period.[17] By the 1970s the GLF emerged as part of a broader countercultural and socially revolutionary movement in Britain. For Sandbrook, this period marked a critical moment, when the social changes fought for in the 1960s 'gathered momentum'.[18] Indeed, the significance of the war in shifting social attitudes cannot be overstated. Displacing families who had lived in the same location for generations, exposing people to new ideas and cultures, and fighting a total war, meant that British society was irrevocably changed when peace was declared. The post-war consensus on the construction of a welfare state is the most obvious example of the change that society demanded. For the next generation, coming of age in the 1960s and 1970s, gay liberation and a new openness is discussing sex and sexuality were some aspects of these new social movements born out of the changes taking place.

Political change is fundamental to this history, in particular its influence on the lives of individual homosexual men and women, and also on the wider public, whose attitudes affected those same lives. The self-identified nature of modern sexual labels owes its origins not only to a desire for social acceptance, but – particularly for men – political change. It is thus integral to an understanding of sexual identities, and crucially how they were understood by the wider public, that political change is discussed. But these events are rarely ordered. At different times and at different speeds, political reform was spearheaded by a variety of actors. Sometimes more representative, and sometimes less, these groups never fully reflected the lives of the people they were trying to 'improve'. Similarly these reforms have at times sought to define homosexuality, while at other times they have been defined by it.

But as much as politicians would like to believe the power of their own influence, the media has provided a hugely influential forum in which ideas, attitudes, and perceptions of homosexuality have developed. At different times during this period a gay group identity has been promoted, denied, defamed, or even reluctantly accepted. The media, separated broadly into the gay media (given licence to exist after 1967), the press (sometimes pushing for gay rights and writing positively about gay men and lesbians), and television and film (often pushing the boundaries of what the public were prepared to watch), have created an increasing public perception of homosexuality in Britain and, in doing so, helped define a gay identity. Like political change, however, these distinct aspects of the media have had, at different times, often opposing agendas. But, crucially, for men and women growing up after World War II in a society gradually becoming more at ease with talking about sex and sexuality, these images of gay men and lesbians were often the only representations they had in constructing their own identities.

The social lives of gay men and lesbians have also been key to the creation of a discourse on homosexuality. These people were the principle actors in the emergence of this new identity, and have, at times deliberately, and at times inadvertently, contributed to its evolution. Through their public visibility – in a society that had previously hidden homosexuality from view – they created and recreated an image of homosexuality, which informed not only public perceptions, but also the lives of individual homosexual men and women coming to terms with their own sexuality.

The journey from Wolfenden to *Queer as Folk*

Section One 'Gay Liberation' explores the period from the 1950s through to the middle of the 1970s, when some of the first public images of homosexuality developed. Chapter One begins by exploring the early post-war political landscape and the circumstances leading to both the publication of the Wolfenden Report and the subsequent introduction of the Sexual Offences Act in 1967. It looks at the formation and work of the Homosexual Law Reform Society (HLRS) and the role of parliamentarians in campaigning for legal change throughout the 1950s and 1960s. In conjunction with this it studies the images being presented by Parliament and the law, and how they influenced a public discourse on homosexuality. It then moves on to study the political work of the GLF in the 1970s, its ideology, and public visibility, and the role of the Campaign for Homosexual Equality (CHE) and its efforts to secure future legal reform throughout the 1970s. Chapter Two explores the role of the media in presenting some of the first public images and ideas of homosexuality to the broader public. In particular, it discusses the press and its response to the Wolfenden Report after 1957, including how many newspapers used their editorials to support the campaign for reform, while others remained opposed. It then moves on to look at the reaction to Gay Liberation in the early 1970s, highlighting the changing response of the press after law reform was secured. It also looks at the role of the early gay media and how they debated and explored their own emerging homosexual identity, both before and after law reform. It ends with a study of films and television programmes including the films *Victim* and *The Killing of Sister George,* and the television dramas *Girl* and *Bermondsey* that contributed to a growing public debate about law reform and the 'realities' of a homosexual life. Chapter Three examines the emergence of homosexual social organisations and how they contributed to a visible public identity, and a personal identity among their members. It focuses on the lesbian organisation the Minorities Research Group (MRG), the mixed sex (but male-dominated) CHE, and the GLF. In a period where the role of women was often hidden, the GLF provides an important opportunity to explore the role of feminism as part of a lesbian identity, and the often misogynistic role of men – even in these counter cultural organisations. As a result, this chapter ends by looking at the lesbian political scene, in particular Greenham Common and a 'separatist' agenda that defined many people's idea of lesbianism in this period.

Section Two 'A Visible Subculture' focuses on the period from the middle of the 1970s through to the early 1990s, when a clear gay subculture developed in Britain. In contrast to the previous section, Chapter Four explores a political backlash that developed against homosexuality from the late 1970s onwards. It looks at failed attempts to achieve further law reform after the success of 1967, in particular the 1976 attempt to have the provisions of the Sexual Offences Act extended to Scotland, the 1977 attempt to lower the age of male consent, and the unsuccessful 1979 struggle to secure law reform in Northern Ireland. It then studies the introduction of section 28, which banned the 'promotion of homosexuality', suggesting that, while damaging, the protests against it led to the emergence of Stonewall – a modernised campaigning organisation – to lobby on behalf of middle-class gay people, who had been largely ignored by the more radical protestors in the 1970s and 1980s. Chapter Five explores media representations in a period when attitudes towards homosexuality were hardening, but also when gay men and lesbians were forming a visible subcultural identity. In contrast to the earlier gay media, this period witnessed publications with increasing confidence in what they stood for, and what they gay community they served represented. For the majority of the mainstream press, however, this was a period of explicit homophobia, brought about initially in its reporting of the HIV/AIDS crisis, with some newspapers either suggesting that homosexual sex between men should be recriminalised, or that the disease was punishment from a disapproving God. With links to the previous chapter's focus on section 28, this chapter also shows how the impetus for legal change was brought about through the efforts of newspaper editors arguing that children were being indoctrinated into homosexuality in some schools in London. For television and film, however, this was a period when more nuanced storylines and characters were being developed. Looking at the film *My Beautiful Laundrette*, the two-part television dram *Two of Us*, the television magazine series *Out On Tuesday*, and the television dram a *Oranges Are Not the Only Fruit*, it shows how programme makers were moving away from the earlier guilt-ridden images of the 1960s and 1970s towards stories that included happy endings, and magazine series produced specifically for gay men and lesbians. Chapter Six looks at two distinct aspects of gay social life in the 1980s that contributed to a public image of homosexuality: firstly, the development of the gay social scene, in particular the clubs and bars that emerged in the London and Manchester gay villages; secondly, the development of HIV/AIDS among gay men, and the impact this had on individual lives, the interactions between men and women, and public ideas about homosexuality. Highlighting the personal tragedy of the crisis, it explores the lingering images of death and disease that many people associated with homosexuality – in particular through a comparison with the previous chapter's focus on newspaper accounts.

Section Three 'Joining the Mainstream' focuses on the period between the early 1990s up until the middle of the 2000s, when a gay identity became increasingly mainstream – particularly through legal change. Chapter Seven examines the gradual liberalising of the law, in particular the legislative battle to secure a lower (although still unequal) male age of consent in 1994, and then the raft of legal changes brought about after the election of the Labour government in 1997, including: the repeal of section 28, the equalisation of the age of consent, the Adoption and Children Act, banning discrimination in the delivery of goods and services, and the Civil Partnership Act. As well as explaining the origins of these legal changes, this chapter also argues that these liberal reforms began a process of presenting a new, positive image of homosexuality into the public discourse, while acknowledging how the, at times, vitriolic debate itself contributed to continuing negative stereotypes. Chapter eight explores the contrasting images being presented in the media during this period of political change. It looks at the gay media's move towards a lifestyle focus – replicating non-gay publications, and exploring an evolving identity that was increasingly mainstream and integrationist, showing how these magazines were becoming aware of the diversity in their readership and in gay life more generally. Looking at the mainstream press, it shows how newspapers remained preoccupied with the legal changes that were taking place. It demonstrates how, gradually, as each piece of legislation was introduced, the press became less interested in fighting legal reform, and more interested in presenting a balanced report on gay men and lesbians. In terms of television and film, the chapter looks at the television soap opera *Brookside* as an example of the move towards exploring the emotional development of 'normal' characters, who just happened to be gay, while the film *Beautiful Thing* will provide an example of a young gay love story with a happy ending. Television magazine series *Gaytime TV,* meanwhile represents a defiantly different and non-apologetic example of homosexuality. Similarly, the television series *Queer as Folk,* in telling the story of promiscuous men in Manchester, including the relationship between one of the main (adult) characters and a 15-year-old boy, felt able to present gay life on gay terms, which would not have been possible only a decade earlier.

SECTION 1
GAY LIBERATION

CHAPTER 1

EARLY OPTIMISM

On 27 July 1967, after almost a decade of campaigning, the HLRS celebrated the royal assent of the Sexual Offences Act, partially decriminalising sex between consenting men in England and Wales. However, despite their success the Act was a compromise. It did not apply to Scotland or Northern Ireland; it only applied to men over the age of 21, in private, with no more than two people present; and it did not apply to those in service in the armed forces or the merchant navy. In addition, the main sponsor of the bill (and high-profile advocate of reform) Lord Arran had issued a stark warning to those he had helped emancipate:

> I ask those who have, as it were, been in bondage and for whom the prison doors are now open to show their thanks by comporting themselves quietly and with dignity. This is no occasion for jubilation; certainly not for celebration. Any form of ostentatious behaviour; now or in the future any form of public flaunting, would be utterly distasteful and would, I believe, make the sponsors of the Bill regret that they have done what they have done. [...] Lest the opponents of the Bill think that a new freedom, a new privileged class, has been created, let me remind them that no amount of legislation will prevent homosexuals from being the subject of dislike and derision, or at best of pity.[1]

Despite this warning, the Act created an almost instant impetus to campaigners who hoped to achieve legal parity between homosexuality and heterosexuality. The on-going political debate the Act created, rather than ended as its sponsors had hoped, helped structure how homosexuality was understood in Britain during this period of post-law reform.

The early pioneers of the HLRS had been well aware that the realities of individual behaviour were secondary concerns to the perceptions of society. In a world where homosexuality was mostly hidden, innuendo, gossip, and the bigotry of newspaper editors, as well as the overarching power of the statute book, were the principle means for the general public to gather facts about homosexuality. Thus it was their job to ensure that a different view prevailed, one that would be more acceptable to the public, but most importantly to the law makers whom they were attempting to influence.

The post-war social landscape had already provided these men and women with a unique combination of circumstances that provided the space in which to pursue law reform. On 24 March 1954, Lord Montagu, his cousin Michael Pitt-Rivers, and the journalist Peter Wildeblood, had been found guilty of 'conspiracy to incite certain male persons to commit serious offences with male persons' and were sent to prison. Montagu was sentenced to 12 months, and Pitt-Rivers and Wildeblood to 18 months each.[2] When they left court Wildeblood recalled a crowd of people who 'tried to pat us on the back and told us to "keep smiling"'.[3] Crucially, the trial was an example of middle- and upper-class adult men engaged in consensual sex in private, which had only come to light following a police investigation and the testimony of their working-class lovers, on the condition that they would not then face trial themselves.[4] Following the conviction of the three men, *The Sunday Times* published an editorial entitled 'Law and Hypocrisy':

> The law, it would seem, is not in accord with a large mass of public opinion. That condition always brings evil in its train: contempt for the law, inequity between one offender and another, the risk of corruption of the police [. . .]. The case for a

reform of the law as to acts committed in private between adults is very strong. The case for an authoritative enquiry into it is overwhelming. An interim report under the auspices of the Moral Welfare Council of the Church of England has recently given that case clear support.[5]

At the same time political attention was increasing. The Conservative MP Sir Robert Boothby (whose bisexuality was well-known in Westminster) and the Labour MP Desmond Donnelly had raised the issue of homosexual law reform in the Commons in December 1953, and asked for the Government to set up a Royal Commission to examine the laws surrounding homosexual offences. The then Home Secretary, Sir David Maxwell-Fyfe, had responded that the matter was under consideration, while offering his personal view that 'homosexuals in general are exhibitionists and proselytisers'.[6] The following year Donnelly again tried to get a commission to examine the law, and on 19 May 1954 the House of Lords held its first debate on homosexuality.[7] On 24 August, five months after the Montagu trial had ended, the Home Secretary responded to the demands for a Royal Commission by setting up a lesser departmental committee to examine the laws surrounding both homosexuality and prostitution. Maxwell-Fyfe hoped this would enable him to better control the committee, while serving to move the issue into the long grass.[8]

In what Weeks describes as 'a crucial moment in the evolution of liberal moral attitudes', the Report of the Committee on Homosexual Offences and Prostitution (Wolfenden) was published in September 1957, and recommended that 'homosexual behaviour between consenting adults in private should no longer be a criminal offence'.[9] In a further sign that the public were closely following these events, the report's initial print-run of 5,000 sold out within hours and had to be reprinted, unheard of for a government report.[10] A year earlier, the Church of England had pre-empted these findings in its own report 'Sexual Offenders and Social Punishment', which had recommended a universal age of consent of 17 for both homosexual and heterosexual couples, claiming that,

[t]he fact that certain homosexual acts committed in certain circumstances may be penalized by statute or condemned by religion and morality does not imply that the homosexual condition, *per se*, is immoral or culpable.[11]

It would prove to be the cumulative weight of these two influential reports that would add to the growing calls for law reform. Indeed, the future members of the HLRS, made up of mostly well-educated heterosexual men and women, seized the opportunity the Wolfenden report provided, and used it as the basis for their future campaign. In March 1958, a letter was published in *The Times* from '33 distinguished figures' and organised by a 29-year-old homosexual university lecturer, A. E. Dyson:[12]

The present law is clearly no longer representative of either Christian or liberal opinion in this country, and now that there are widespread doubts about both its justice and its efficacy, we believe that its continued enforcement will do more harm than good to the health of the community as a whole.[13]

Dyson had felt compelled to act because of the resurgence in chain prosecutions for homosexual offences – where prosecutors used the evidence of convicted men to charge others they had been in contact with. The signatures to this letter were then convinced by Dyson to form the Homosexual Law Reform Society as members of an honorary committee, and campaign for the implementation of the Wolfenden proposals. A smaller executive committee was also set up, chaired by the sexologist Kenneth Walker, who through his work had a similar interest in law reform.[14]

By aligning themselves with the recommendations of Wolfenden, they attempted to create the image of a conservative respectability surrounding homosexuality, which represented the type of man they wanted to help. In doing so, their message corresponded with that of another conservative homosexual, Peter Wildeblood, who, as well as giving evidence to the Wolfenden Committee, had written in his influential book, *Against the Law*, that he was not making the case for 'the corrupters of youth, not even the effeminate creatures who love to make an exhibition of themselves'.[15] Houlbrook has identified this 'respectable' homosexual as key to the emergence of the Sexual Offences Act, in particular the creation of a certain kind of homosexual man who was not immoral:

> [T]he 'homosexual' was constituted through and within broader matrices of sexual difference, defined through his distances from places, practices, and people repudiated as abject, immoral, and dangerous.[16]

However, the Wolfenden Report also reflected a competing framework of negative sexual identities by associating homosexuality more broadly with rape and unlawful sex, and working from the premise that the law was there to protect the vulnerable from homosexual men:

> We believe that it is part of the function of the law to safeguard those who need protection by reason of their youth or some mental defect, and we do not wish to see any change in the law that would weaken this protection. Men who commit offences against such persons should be treated as criminal offenders.[17]

And it would be its association with paedophilia that would endure:

> [T]here are two recognisably different categories among adult male homosexuals. There are those who seek as partners other adult males, and there are paedophiliacs, that is to say men who seek as partners boys who have not reached puberty.[18]

This would remain a key argument in future debates – particularly on the age of consent, and section 28 – where the protection of children was considered paramount. The safeguards the report put in place, however, including an unequal age of consent and privacy constraints, ensured that if the Government acted on its recommendations, it would only ever be emancipating the 'homosexual' and the respectable identity that represented, including discretion and middle-class values, and not all men who engaged in homosexual acts more generally:

> It has to be borne in mind that there are many homosexuals whose behaviour never comes to the notice of the police or the courts, and it is probable that the police and the courts see only the worst cases; the more anti-social type of person is more likely to attract the attention of the police than the discreet person with a well-developed social sense.[19]

This debate over the respectable and unrespectable homosexual would continue throughout future parliamentary debates on law reform. The respectable, middle-class, and private homosexual man did not need to be criminalised since his sexual behaviour was always in private with men of his own age, while the unrespectable homosexual could be characterised by his public identity, disrespect for the law, and in some cases paedophilia.

The HLRS spent the next ten years building up a case for reform. It began its lobbying campaign by sending out its pamphlet 'Homosexuals and the law' to every MP. This coincided with the distribution of Wildeblood's *Against the Law* and Dr Eustace Chesser's *Live and let live*, which led to 'a parliamentary outcry by opponents of reform that the Commons was being subjected to the attentions of a "rich and powerful lobby of perverts"'.[20] Despite these set-backs, the society's secretary Anthony Grey – himself homosexual – continued campaigning around the country with a series of debates and lectures, ensuring the reform movement was kept alive.[21] He visited the Dutch COC (*Cultuur en Ontspanningscentrum*, or Centre for Culture and Leisure), building up a relationship between them, the Albany Trust – the counselling wing of the HLRS – and also the French organisation *Arcadie*, who shared his ideas about discreetness and respectability. During this time the HLRS also built up relationships with sympathetic members of the Lords and the Commons. No political party had an official policy on homosexuality, despite the views of individual politicians, so instead legal change would be through a free vote. As a result, on 12 May

1965, the hereditary peer Lord Arran introduced a one-clause Sexual Offences Bill: 'A homosexual act in private shall not be an offence provided that the parties consent thereto and have attained the age of 21 years.'[22] Arran later claimed that his reasons for getting involved with homosexual law reform were complex:

> Exhibitionism? Because I went to Eton and I knew what it was all about? A hatred of injustice...? I do not know my own motives anymore. Most probably my – or Parliament's – liberation of the male homosexual here and elsewhere derives from my unhappiness at that time over a purely domestic matter (nothing to do with homosexuality). I have known more than one man in his distress turn to matters which give him a new anxiety.[23]

Abse, however, suggested that Arran's involvement owed more to the alleged homosexuality of his own brother:

> I met a man who for many years had been the lover of Arran's older brother: then it was all clear. This older brother, who over many years had received psychiatric aid, died tragically only a matter of days after becoming Earl. Arran succeeded to the title: it must have brought him much guilt. But it brought him, too, the opportunity to make a massive and brave act of reparation.[24]

Arran's bill passed its second reading by a margin of 94 to 49, with members of the House of Lords making repeated claims that they wanted the public to see the Lords as a reforming chamber. At the same time the Labour MP, Leo Abse, in the House of Commons, was attempting to garner support to introduce a similar change in the law. In May, under the ten-minute rule, which gives the House an opportunity to debate the proposed introduction of a bill, Abse encouraged MPs to support some measure of homosexual law reform. Unlike the Lords, however, his motion failed with a final vote of 159 to 178.[25] The following year in February, however, the Conservative

MP Humphry Berkeley (another whose homosexuality was well-known in Westminster) introduced Arran's completed bill to the Commons. Berkeley had won the opportunity to do this on the private member's ballot. Directing his argument against those who said that the public were not yet in favour of reform and the time was not right, Berkeley claimed that a Gallup poll and a National Opinion poll both showed that 63 per cent supported a change in the law along Wolfenden recommendations.[26] The bill passed its second reading by 179 to 99, and was committed to a standing committee. The following month, however, the Prime Minster, Harold Wilson, called a general election in an effort to shore up his majority of four in the Commons, and all incomplete bills were lost.

Unsure when the next ballot would take place for the introduction of a Private Member's Bill, or even if the successful MP would be willing to support homosexual law reform, Lord Arran reintroduced his bill after the election to ensure that the reform agenda was kept alive. It again passed all its stages, but with little chance of success, until Leo Abse, in July 1966, introduced a similar private member's bill in the Commons. The first reading was carried with a vote of 244 to 100. In what was widely regarded as behind the scenes Government support, time was found for the bill to have its second reading, some five months later on 19 December.[27] Indeed, decades later when the Commons debated an Order of Council to bring the benefits of the Sexual Offences Act to Northern Ireland, Leo Abse confirmed,

> [t]he Bill that I introduced was in collusion with the 1966–70 Labour Government, to their credit. It was done on the initiative of a Ten-Minute Bill when the House expressed its view, following which the Cabinet made the decision that full time should be given so that in accordance with the wishes of the House the Bill could reach the statute book. The Home Secretary actively participated in every stage and there was full co-operation from the Government.[28]

Thus while officially the Labour Government had no policy on law reform, they instead offered this tacit support in order to avoid any potential repercussions. After amendments, the final debate, which took place a further six months later on 3 July 1967, saw the bill pass its third reading by 99 votes to 14 with the final debate lasting until after 4am. Once in the Lords, it progressed through all its stages relatively quickly, and became law the same month.

Grey subsequently wrote that he believed 'a better piece of legislation could have been achieved' if Arran and Abse had concentrated on securing 'concessions from the Home Office' rather than 'placating the implacable'.[29] Abse's later comment that the bill was full of 'compromises and blemishes' necessary to secure the passage of the legislation suggests he too was not happy with the final Act.[30] Moreover, ten years later, Arran would also attempt to lower the age of consent, while supporting another measure to extend the provisions of the Act to Scotland. It was in this climate of opinion that the HLRS met in 1968, and at an executive committee meeting,

> those Committee members present agreed that further legal reform would ultimately be necessary, especially in view of the likely lowering of the age of majority to 18, forecast in the recent report of the Latey Committee.[31]

They therefore agreed to continue working as part of the HLRS, at least 'for the immediate purpose of preparing and submitting a Memorandum of evidence to the Criminal Law Revision Committee' in order to achieve a more liberal law in the future.[32] Their reliance on the will of Abse and Arran, however, exposed the weakness of their approach; their public campaigning had perhaps helped change public opinion, but they were still powerless to affect change in Parliament. Indeed, the final Act meant many legal restrictions remained. By decriminalising sex between men over the age of 21 when it occurred it private, the Act left the crimes of sodomy and 'gross indecency' on the statute book (not to mention its inapplicability in Scotland, Northern Ireland, the armed forces, and the merchant navy). Thus both parties in a sexual relationship where one was under 21 could be prosecuted, as could sex in public, while kissing or holding hands in public could also be prosecuted under public indecency laws. Obscenity laws, meanwhile, ensured that publications – including the underground *International Times* homosexual personal advertisements – could be deemed obscene.[33] In addition, soliciting and importuning remained criminal offences, meaning that it was illegal to offer or ask for sex, or introduce two men for the purpose of sex. Scotland, meanwhile, retained the crimes of sodomy and gross indecency. James Adair, the former Procurator-Fiscal (public prosecutor) for Glasgow, who had been a member of the Wolfenden Committee, had written his own reservations into the final report disagreeing with the decision to decriminalise male homosexual sex. Combined with the view that Scotland (like Northern Ireland) was a more socially conservative part of the United Kingdom, and the existence of a long-standing agreement of the Scottish Procurator-Fiscal not to prosecute private acts between consenting adults, was enough to ensure that the act would only apply to England and Wales.

Furthermore, the homosexual identity the HLRS and others had been projecting in order to achieve law reform was never representative of all homosexual men in Britain. But it was only through this categorisation that law reform in the 1960s was ever achievable. This became clear in parliamentary debates, which, for example, encouraged the image of the homosexual as a man driven to paying a blackmailer to ensure he could maintain his position in society. Rather, it was an attempt to define in law a specific homosexual identity in a society that was, since the late 1950s, increasingly defined individuals by their sexuality, and polarised these identities between homosexuality and heterosexuality.[34] For many members of Parliament who had voted against the bill, these new freedoms already went too far – legalising immoral behaviour, threatening further social decline, and endangering children – while for those who had supported them, the creation in law of a type of homosexual represented a conclusion to homosexual law reform. However, rather than mark the end of the matter, and the cementing of a distinctly respectable homosexual identity, the law instead granted licence for all kinds of homosexual men to emerge publicly, and for the first time begin to join with female homosexuality in an attempt to create their own public identity and campaign for greater law reform.

Arguably the most significant of the new political organisations to emerge from the freedoms of the Sexual Offences Act was the Gay Liberation Front. While the Stonewall riots are often claimed as the 'birth' of gay liberation, its genesis in American culture is more complicated.[35] But despite this, the GLF was an American invention, and arrived in Britain in 1970 at the London School of Economics with the help of Aubrey Walter and Bob Mellors (a 19-year-old sociology student) who had met at the 'Revolutionary Peoples' Constitutional Convention' in Philadelphia, organised by the Black Panther Party. Gay Liberationists had attended to show their solidarity with the Black movement, and were, in turn, offered support by the leader of the Black Panthers, who famously declared that gay people were probably the most oppressed in society, and potentially the most revolutionary.[36] According to Walter, 'the first sparks of the new gay consciousness were already beginning to fly in Britain'.[37] Indeed, Gay Liberation reflected a changing cultural landscape in the United Kingdom, with connections to a broader protest movement – both in the United Kingdom and across the Western world – linked by their 'rejection of convention and authority.'[38] Indeed, the GLF's American links to the Black Panthers predicted future associations with Marxist, feminist, and union campaigns. It is clear, also, that Gay Liberation would have arrived with or without the new freedoms of the Sexual Offences Act, although this undoubtedly made life a lot easier for them. The militant tactics they brought back to the United Kingdom ensured that the image of respectability created by the predominantly heterosexual HLRS would be usurped by a self-declared 'gay politics':

> Those gay men and lesbians who had constructed a comfortable niche for themselves in the conventional 'straight gay' closet, soon began to get very disturbed by all these out, militant gay liberationists. They really hated GLF for rocking their boat. It was already clear to us at the time, however, that we were having a very real effect on the gay community, and were even pushing

the uptight traditional gay organisations towards a more militant stand – we were challenging them to come out.[39]

Writing in 1980, however, Walter appears to be constructing his own view of the past. He describes homosexual men and women as 'gay men and lesbians', as well as talking about a 'gay community' which is a problematic concept when ideas about a gay social and group identity were still developing. Indeed, this no doubt came from what he saw as the permanency of the 'gay community' in 1980s Britain, before the dual threats of HIV/AIDS and political hostility developed. Despite this anachronism, the use of the term 'gay' was a significant symbol of the change that the GLF represented. Taken from the United States (revealing the on-going influence of American ideas), Weeks claims it drew its strength from being self-adopted. Since it came from the concept of gay pride it suggested a rebellion against the medicalised and derogatory terms that had been so prevalent in the public discourse.[40]

After their initial meeting on 13 October 1970 (attended by 19 people, only one of whom was a woman), the GLF drew up a list of basic demands, later published as a leaflet, which they distributed to areas of West London where they knew many homosexual men and women lived; it helped bring in hundreds of new recruits.[41] It would be a year later before their 16-page manifesto was published. Unlike the HLRS Constitution, which committed the organisation to work towards 'conduct[ing] research into the problems of homosexuality', and to 'secure reform of the law relating to homosexual behaviour in accordance with the recommendations contained in the [Wolfenden] Report', the GLF manifesto was far more radical.[42] Under the subtitle 'The way forward' it declared,

> [t]he long-term goal of the London Gay Liberation Front, which inevitably brings us into fundamental conflict with the institutionalised sexism of this society, is to rid society of the gender-role system which is at the root of our oppression. This can only be achieved by the abolition of the family as the unit in which children are brought up.[43]

Crucially, this attack on the 'gender-role system' recognised not just what they saw as the root of homosexual oppression, but also the oppression of women, which, according to Weeks, suggested a future linkup between gay liberation and feminism.[44] Indeed, the feminist historian Sheila Jeffreys claims that '[t]he commitment to support women's liberation was more than empty words and does seem to have been central to gay-liberation theory'.[45] In attacking society's proscribed regulations they positioned themselves in opposition to groups such as the HLRS, which they saw as part of the problem for propagating the image of the discreet homosexual, while they represented the visible and traditionally 'unrespectable' homosexual.

The chief tactic in achieving their political aims was through protest, which reflected other protest movements throughout the 1960s and 1970s, including, for example, the CND movement, and the anti-war protests surrounding Vietnam. Indeed the left-wing and student-focus of the GLF meant that GLFers were often simultaneously part of these other social and protest groups, borrowing those tactics and sharing similar ideology. Maintaining relations with GLF groups across the globe, moreover, they borrowed ideas from each other and regularly reported on new developments through their international liaison group and with publications in their newspaper, *Come Together*.

To create public visibility, they organised the first Gay Pride rally in London in 1972 in which 1,000 people marched from Trafalgar Square to Hyde Park for a picnic and party, and 'zaps', or stunts, directed at the authorities, businesses, and religious groups whom they regarded as homophobic.[46] The most successful of these, in September 1971, was code-named 'Operation Rupert' and was directed at the Christian Festival of Light. The organisation had been formed by two Christian missionaries in May, and had attracted the GLF's attention through its overt homophobia. Their three-week national event in London was subjected to a coordinated sabotage at its opening ceremony in Central Hall, Westminster, with GLFers gaining inside access to the Festival, stealing tickets and forging their own copies.[47] In a choreographed attack, GLFers variously threw stink bombs, released white mice across the floor, unfurled a banner from the balcony declaring 'Cliff for Queen' (Cliff Richard was one of the official attendees), and invaded the stage in drag and dressed as nuns, vicars, and bishops.[48] The organisation of this 'zap' ensured that individual groups were each responsible for a different element of the protest, and were not sitting near each other; thus as soon as the conference organisers had restored order, the protest would begin again. The protesters succeeded in their attempt to use humour to expose what they saw as the bigotry of those they were protesting against, but in some cases were assaulted as a result. Janet Winter remembers: 'this woman started hitting me over the head in a frenzied manner with her handbag, yelling "Jesus loves you" again and again', while others recall stewards beating people.[49] The GLF, however, considered it a success, and in his 1972 book on the organisation, one Festival of Light supporter grudgingly acknowledged:

[T]he media in general and the national newspapers in particular must stand condemned for their inadequate reporting of the Festival. When asked by one of the Festival organizers what he knew about the Festival of Light, an ordinary man in the street replied, 'Isn't it something to do with mice and people dressed up as nuns?'[50]

Yet the GLF was short-lived. Although in February 1972 women were the first to leave the organisation, citing the need for a separate women's movement, other conflicts had already developed. Weeks lists these as: 'between the activists and the feminists; between the socialists and the counter culture; and, most damagingly, between the dreams of the GLF and the real possibilities of 1972'.[51] For others, the GLF lacked the roots among homosexual men and women in Britain, which had held it together in the United States, and was instead transported from across the Atlantic.[52] Many members, however, were merely reconciled that 'it was a product of the time and the time had passed':

GLF was like a comet – it wasn't going to continue. At the beginning, what we had in common was much more important than all the differences between men and women, between socialists and radical feminists and everything else – people who were interested in cottaging and people who weren't, people who wanted to concentrate on women's issues and people who didn't, there was an enormous difference [...] By the time the initial excitement of being together and coming out had finished, we were all thinking about different things. People wanted to do different projects and go in different directions.[53]

Although it brought people together for political reasons, it lacked any concrete aims beyond its ambition for a social revolution, and was thus doomed to failure. Instead, its success lay in changing people's ideas about their own homosexuality; these social aspects of the organisation overshadowed anything it was able to achieve politically (as we shall see). For earlier campaigners, however, as well as older men and women, the GLF was an unwelcome counter cultural group that did not represent the homosexual majority in Britain.[54]

Meanwhile, the HLRS, on achieving its goal of law reform broadly along Wolfenden lines, was contemplating its future. In March 1970 it agreed to reconstitute itself as the Sexual Law Reform Society (SLRS), to campaign 'to secure those reforms of the law as it regulates or affects sexual behaviour which are considered by the Society's Executive Committee from time to time to be necessary'.[55] It recognised that in addition to the laws surrounding homosexuality, all laws concerning sexual behaviour needed modernising. In doing this, it marked a move away from the cause of homosexual law reform, and confirmed its position as an organisation that never sought fundamentally to alter the relationship between homosexuality and society. When, in 1975, the Home Secretary Roy Jenkins announced that the Criminal Law Revision Committee would be reviewing the laws relating to sexual offences with the help of a policy advisory committee, the SLRS concentrated its efforts on preparing a detailed report for their consideration. Their minor success came when, six years later in 1981, the Policy Advisory Committee on sexual offences recommended lowering of the age of consent to 18, confirmed in the final report of the CLRC in 1984.[56] This was some way off their own proposed age of consent of 14, however, and was never acted on by Government.[57]

While the GLF was confronting urban, and predominantly London, society with gay pride, and the SLRS was attempting to alter the law's relationship towards sex more generally, another organisation meanwhile was busy constructing a nationwide structure. The North-Western Homosexual Law Reform Committee (NWHLRC) had been formed by Labour councillor Alan Horsfall and Church of England senior social worker Colin Harvey in 1964, initially hoping to operate as a regional version of the HLRS, which was increasingly looking London-centric. Horsfall had written a letter to the *Bolton Evening News* complaining about the law surrounding homosexuality and was encouraged to form the group from the replies he received.[58] From the outset it had had a fractious relationship with its London counterpart:

> Relations between the two organisations were equivocal from the beginning. London seemed to embrace us or reject us according to the mood of the moment. [. . .] They had taken the view that any new organisation was necessarily going to corner a proportion of finite financial support which had hitherto been at their exclusive disposal, and as a consequence weaken them.[59]

More likely, however, was that the HLRS were concerned that an organisation made up of mostly homosexual men left them open to prosecution if any evidence of their sex lives became public.

After 1967, the committee – which included the owner of a Manchester club for homosexuals, further reflecting its distinction from the HLRS – was faced with a decision:

> When the Sexual Offences Bill was enacted in July of last year, the Committee was faced with a difficult decision. Should it disband? Or should it continue and work towards a solution of the many varied personal and social problems which remain. It was decided to do the latter.[60]

With a predominantly homosexual membership, it was inevitable that with a measure of law reform in place they would be keen to pursue policies which would address these 'personal and social problems'. Principally, this referred to tackling the isolation felt by many men and women in England and Wales, but also to developing educational programmes to address prejudice and help younger people deal with their own sexuality. Building up a network of local groups, in 1969 it became the Committee for Homosexual Equality and in 1971 the Campaign for Homosexual Equality (CHE). While it initially concentrated on providing safe ways for men and women to meet (although it remained a male-dominated organisation) through local groups that would meet in members' homes, it later attempted to capitalise on its size as the largest homosexual organisation in England to build up a political wing.

Its first campaign 'for better sex education at all levels of the education system' was launched at the Cardiff National Council in September 1973. It was an attempt to coordinate what had previously been '70 local groups doing 70 different things in 70 different ways'.[61] Two years later, however, the Annual Report of 1975 was only able to state that '[m]ost of the national work has been done concerned with the production of an educational study kit, which is presently being printed'.[62] They launched similar campaigns throughout the decade, concentrating variously on trade unions, social services, armed forces and medical services, primarily by providing information on the needs of their constituents – principally older homosexual men – but never matching the (albeit limited) success of the HLRS.

Perhaps their biggest political campaign was the launching of a draft Homosexual Law Reform Bill in July 1975, jointly with the Scottish Minorities Group (SMG), and the Union for Sexual Freedom in Ireland (USFI). They had held a rally in Trafalgar Square the previous November to launch the official opening of the campaign, attended by 3,000 people, and had received prominent media attention.[63] The bill included provisions to,

> achieve complete equality at law, to give proper respect to the protection of the public from unacceptable displays of sexual

behaviour in public, to protect homosexuals from harassment and persecution from the police in instances where equivalent heterosexual behaviour would not be offensive, and to nullify the effects of court decision about the publication of homosexual literature and advertisements.[64]

The commitment to protecting the public reflects CHE opposition to GLF tactics, and their desire to be seen as a more respectable organisation. It was less than two weeks later that Roy Jenkins announced that the Criminal Law Revision Committee would begin a legal review of sexual offences, which undoubtedly must have been influenced by the publication of the draft bill. By the time the committee issued its findings, however, CHE had lost much of the support it previously enjoyed, and the final report completely failed to meet their proposals.

CHE's political ambitions were never realised, despite taking over the mantel of homosexual rights from the HLRS after 1967. According to Weeks, it,

never seemed capable of taking full advantage of the new opportunities. [...] [It] became notoriously concerned with 'structure', revising its constitution in 1971 and 1974, with new proposals in 1976, and displayed a constant preoccupation with *how* to do things rather than *what* to do.[65]

Indeed, in August 1980, its conference would vote to split the organisation in two between the political campaigning arm and the grassroots groups, and while it still exists to this day, it never regained the success enjoyed in the 1970s, when it boasted over 4,500 members.[66]

While these organisations undoubtedly advanced the social aspect of homosexual life in the United Kingdom – by providing older homosexual men and women with places to meet and activities that had previously been denied them – their political success was far more limited. Indeed, while these groups campaigned, lobbied, and protested, the centres of power in Britain – including police, councils, MPs, and members of the House of Lords – were increasingly distressed by what they were witnessing. It soon became clear that the law, which ultimately codified the Government's – and to an extent the country's – attitude towards homosexuality would not be amended any time soon, evident through the failure to achieve any further legal change, reinforcing a disparity in law, and a continued second-class status in society.

Despite the fundamental legal change that the Sexual Offences Act had implemented, it soon became apparent that homosexual men remained a target for some police officers who had retained their negative pre-reform attitudes towards homosexuality. 'Between 1967 and 1976 the recorded incidence of indecency between males doubled, the number of prosecutions trebled and the number of convictions quadrupled.'[67] Indeed, importuning and soliciting remained criminal offences, so it was possible for a man to be found guilty of offering or asking for sex with another man, or introducing men for the purpose of homosexual sex, in addition to the limitations that the Sexual Offences Act had introduced. It seemed that the law was only prepared to accept a limited 'private' version of homosexuality; anything that transgressed into the public realm remained a threat to morality and, where legally possible, would be prosecuted.

Indeed, in their 1968 bulletin, in which the NWHLRC had taken the decision to maintain operations, they had also asked their supporters to continue submitting newspaper cuttings 'to build up a broad picture of the way in which the law is being applied'. Suggesting that 'the spirit of the act is not being observed', they used the following example to reinforce their decision to work for further change:

> A number of Staffordshire teenagers have been successfully prosecuted and sentenced for PRIVATE homosexual acts which took place in the autumn of last year. Another of them, nineteen years old, hanged himself in a cell at Risley remand centre while awaiting trial on a similar charge.[68]

Throughout this period, the political and legal emphasis remained on adult men, and what was widely believed to be their corrupting influence on youth. Much of the debate on legal change leading up to 1967 had linked male homosexuality with paedophilia, which resulted in an age of consent of 21, and (as in the case above) anyone subsequently found guilty of homosexual sex under that age being sent to Borstal, ostensibly for their own benefit. Despite the attempts of groups like the SLRS to make the public aware of the difference between homosexuality and paedophilia, this view prevailed in Parliament, challenging the image of respectability that their forerunners had worked so hard to establish. Aided by the national press, it led to further failed attempts at law reform, and culminated in the passing of section 28 of the Local Government Act 1988.

During this early era of gay law reform there were clear examples of competing homosexual identities projected by various elements of the political establishment, campaigners, and the law. The HLRS, although predominately heterosexual, represented the first attempt at presenting a political homosexual identity, both in lobbying Parliament and campaigning around the country. Although this was not an identity that the majority of homosexual men could identify with – predicated on respectability and discreetness – it nevertheless represented the first public political identity that presented homosexuality in a partially positive light. The restrictions of the Wolfenden Report and the subsequent Sexual Offences Act were themselves a product of earlier attitudes towards homosexuality and reflected another aspect of the homosexual in which he was considered predatory and criminal, seen principally through the Report's focus on children. It was not until the emergence of the GLF that homosexual women were given any kind of political/legal identity through their own campaigning and subsequent visibility. Along with men, they rejected the middle-class respectability that had been created for them, and instead reflected a visible counter-cultural identity that they believed would ensure the overthrow of the gender system that had caused their own oppression. In doing so they established their own political model of homosexuality – now a 'gay' identity – which was visible, left-wing, counter cultural, and allowed earlier prejudices towards homosexuality to reappear and grow stronger.

CHAPTER 2

EARLY IMAGES

The gay liberation era signified a time of huge change for representations of homosexuality in the media. Largely absent before, films, television programmes, newspapers, and gay publications gradually emerged that presented some of the first widespread images of what it meant to define someone as homosexual in Britain. Their appearance was a consequence of a broader social shift taking place in British society, with a political move to the left and a gradual liberalising attitude. With a desire to explore social problems and a greater ease in talking about sex, publications felt able for the first time to shed light on the subject.

For the majority of people not interested in law reform or political debate, this was by far the most important way they gathered their impressions of this, until then, relatively hidden group. While these images reflected the emergence of a public discourse on the subject of homosexuality – in a sense the gay liberation of the media – their attitudes varied greatly, through time, medium, and topic. But together they reflected a shift. They represented the arrival of images and examples of identity; they represented what people thought of them; and they represented what self-identified homosexuals thought themselves. Although it is clear that sexual identities are never static, in this period they were particularly fluid – as the heterosexual and homosexual public grappled with the new sexual world order, and where sexuality increasingly defined identity.

Before 1967, there were few publications written specifically for a British homosexual reader. While imports from America and mainland Europe often appeared, home-grown publications were noticeable by their absence.[1] The lesbian organisation Minorities Research Group (MRG) was the first to challenge this, beginning publication of their magazine, *Arena Three*, in 1964.[2] The women had been drawn together initially by the publication of the article 'A quick look at lesbians', in the current affairs journal *Twentieth Century*. Written by Dilys Rowe, it frustrated a number of women, including Diana Chapman, who had her reply to the article published in the following issue. Esme Langley, who had been interested in setting up a magazine, wrote to Chapman, while at the same time making contact with Antony Grey of the HLRS to enquire whether he had any contacts among other lesbians who would be interested in creating a magazine. He introduced her to Cynthia Reid and Julie Switsur, and along with 'Paddy' Dunkley, they formed the MRG and produced the first edition of *Arena Three* the same year.[3] Like other magazines that appeared in this 'gay liberation' period, it sought to discover its own identity — as well as that of its lesbian readership — when there were few concrete ideas about specific sexual identities. Beginning life as little more than a newsletter for MRG, and with a total circulation never exceeding 2,000, it gradually became a glossy magazine, before folding in 1972.[4]

In a period in which lesbians were relatively isolated from each other, and there were few images of lesbianism in the public arena, it devoted a significant proportion of its column inches to readers' correspondence. Jennings claims this helped 'open [...] up a dialogue between different readers' in which the *Arena Three* community could offer advice and comment on each other's experiences'.[5] This forum provided a snap-shot of self-identified lesbians' own views about their identity. J. Purvis, for example, in a letter entitled 'happy homosexual' claimed,

> like the non-militant students, the non-Zionist Jews and the Anglicized West Indians, we don't want our cause to be fought, because we don't have one.

You don't hear about us because we have settled in quite happily with the rest of the world.[6]

Indeed, in the same issue, M.S. Midlands wrote,

what we need to do, in a non-aggressive and reasonable way, is to show society that we, too, are normal human beings. We only differ from them in as much as our emotional and sexual needs are fulfilled by members of our own sex. [...] I am heartily against GLF's slogan 'GAY IS GOOD'. It isn't, neither is it bad. It just IS.[7]

These letters are typical of a magazine – and an organisation – that gained a middle-class reputation, and was similar in outlook to Antony Grey's respectable HLRS. In a later edition, however, another reader implored lesbians to 'join GLF':

GLF provides the jab in the arm a queer needs to become a homosexual, in the same way that people like Angela Davis and the Black Liberation Movement provide the jab a nigger needs to become black.[8]

Language aside, the inclusion of this letter implies that there was an on-going debate about what it meant to be a lesbian, and what kind of public role a lesbian identity should have.

Moreover, articles published by the magazine confirm this apparent desire for definition. In a review of the book, *Love Between Women*, by Dr Charlotte Wolfe, J. Forster implied that *Arena Three* and its readership were looking for validation:

For once, we are not just a medical case history of deviants vis-a-vis 'normals', but are women of involvement with society, family, lovers, jobs, clothes, minds, dreams, ambitions, achievements and faults. [...] The great power of understanding invested in this book 'Love Between Women' certainly expresses what we *really* are.[9]

Despite these more inclusive ideas about a lesbian identity, the magazine nevertheless perpetuated stereotypes, while ostensibly trying to defeat them. In the article 'The Butch – an examination of a stereotype', and under the sub-heading 'Maturation', the author claimed,

> [i]n my experience, once 25 is achieved, the butch has reached a fair degree of maturity [...] [she] has probably worked through the earlier tendencies towards petty antisocial behaviour which may or may not have resulted in a period in an all-female institution.[10]

This perhaps, again, owed its origins to the magazine's middle-class authorship, while its efforts to forge an identity independently of the relatively public homosexual male ensured the inclusion of the article 'Notes of a Militant Lesbian' from a New Zealand publication:

> [T]he basic difference between the pattern of male and female homosexuality: men are more flamboyant, public and outgoing. Their relationships generally physical and short term. Women, on the other hand, are more confined, 'invisible', and the Sapphic relationship frequently lasts a long time, tending to develop into an emotional interdependence.[11]

This reflected the perceived differences between male and female homosexuality in pre-law reform England, as well as a stereotypical gender divide and a desire for their image of the discreet middle-class lesbian not to be associated with (promiscuous and criminal) male homosexuality. Moreover, the inclusion of an article from New Zealand shows how debates about identity were taking place across the Western world, with influences travelling both ways.

Arena Three also contained stories that reflected the lives of ordinary lesbians, including storylines such as childhood crushes and female friendship (often confirming common experience), as well as reports on the media, analyses on social groups in Europe, political lines on issues such as custody rights for women, and the promotion of local groups in the United Kingdom, although these were all very small in number. This early lesbian magazine thus helped establish the beginnings of a common identity for its readership (which they claimed was often wider than the sales figures suggested, since women were likely to pass on the magazine to friends). Its middle-class and London-centric bias, however, as well as its limited circulation figures, meant it was never fully representative of all lesbians living in Britain during its years of publication. Despite this, it was the only British-made magazine for lesbians and thus represented a visible and public discourse on lesbianism and a lesbian identity, albeit almost entirely among its lesbian readership.

In contrast, early male homosexual magazines, appearing after 1967, seemed to have less interest in what it meant to define a man as homosexual, and more interest in the physical act of male homosexual sex. *Jeremy*, launched in 1969, was one of the first of this new generation of magazines. In its first edition, under the headline 'Who cares about sex?', the magazine explained its philosophy:

> If sex is for enjoyment as well as procreation within a marriage, it is also part of every person's basic need to relax, whether tied by the bond of wedlock or not, and express physically emotions which, denied that outlet, will lead to acute frustration and an inevitable deterioration in a relationship between two people.
>
> And those two people are as likely to be male and male or female and female as boy and girl.
>
> Human nature cannot be regiments and not everybody's need is alike. Discipline is necessary in any ordered society but this should be voluntary and self-imposed, not enforced by legislation. Morality concerns us all but private morality is the concern of the individual.[12]

Indeed, the managing director explained *Jeremy*'s editorial policy in the *Daily Mirror*: '*Jeremy* will be designed to appeal to gay people and bisexuals. It will not be at all crude, but very sophisticated and camp, and its motto will be: "Who cares about sex".'[13] The use of the word 'gay', both here and throughout the magazine, suggests its readership understood the term, and that it had begun by some to be used interchangeably with 'homosexual', reflecting American publications and culture which had originated its use. Indeed, in describing a type of person, rather than an attribute of a person, the inclusion of the word 'gay' reflected the changes taking place in British society, and the beginnings of the establishment of a gay social and group identity from 1969 onwards.

As well as including pictures of semi-naked men, and sections on grooming, books, film, music, cuisine, celebrities, stories, and a 'gay guide', it also presented a political line with articles including 'Gay Power!':

> Gays of the world unite! And take inspiration from the new militance that has been stirring in America this summer. The New York Review of Sex reports on the gay demonstrations that followed a recent attempt by a police raiding party to close down The Stonewall Bar, one of the favourite haunts of New York gays.[14]

Apparently trying to build a similar subculture that had enabled the Stonewall riots, the magazine was aware that male homosexuality, however more free since the Sexual Offences Act, nevertheless remained constrained. It also points to the role of America, and American ideas, in the development of a new 'gay' movement in Britain. In contrast to female homosexuality, however, which had never been legally restricted, this image of gay male identity in these magazines seemed to be predicated on sex. The magazine nonetheless shared a similar concern with lesbian publications in trying to establish exactly what being a gay man meant, especially since the magazine presumed the identity existed.

Meanwhile *Timm,* described as 'the international male magazine', and, in 1969, as 'Europe's leading male magazine', offered a similar mix of fashion, stories, articles, and semi-naked pictures of men.[15] Its emphasis on suits in a substantial fashion section, as well as an advert for the Albany Trust, suggests that – pictures of semi-naked men aside – it was attempting to cater for a more middle-class readership.[16] Like *Jeremy* it was exploring exactly what a magazine catering for gay or homosexual men should be. Notably, it included an article exploring homosexuality and psychiatry, in which the author, David Dane, underwent various aversion therapies in order to understand how psychiatry treated homosexuality. In concluding that he thought success possible, Dane claimed he wrote the article,

> out of bitterness that homosexuals are felt by definition, (that is the rub) to be neurotic, inferior, even morally degenerate; bad little boys who have to be smacked for playing with themselves; instead of men who are marginally different from others in enjoying and submitting to sexual experiences which differ from those of the majority.[17]

This again reflected the on-going debate surrounding what it meant to define a person as either homosexual or gay when the freedoms of the Sexual Offences Act were just being explored.

Spartacus was another of these new magazines that emerged after 1967, and 'catered openly for homosexual men'.[18] It contained full-frontal pictures of naked men, as well as many semi-naked pictures and explicit sex references. Like other magazines, it included the usual mix of stories, features, pictures, travel, and a personal advertisements section entitled 'trading post'. Again trying to establish the basis of an identity, the magazine's use of language reflected this debate:

> [V]ery few ordinary men working in offices and factories would have the courage to be honest with their closest friends and say 'I am a Homosexual'. [...] We are men and we should have the courage of men and be prepared to admit and fight for the fact that we are homophie [sic] men [...] If every gay doctor, lawyer, accountant, MP, factory worker was to be as honest about being gay as his married colleagues are about being heterisexual [sic]

society would have to accept us. [...] Let's shake off the image we still have in many minds of being camp mincing ladies [sic] hairdressers. Camp is not funny any more – it merely makes us our own worst enemies.[19]

This was in contrast to *Jeremy* whose managing director had said it would be a camp magazine, exposing the competing ideas about what constituted this gay social and group identity. But apparently aware that stereotypes in society were the primary means by which many homosexual – and heterosexual – people were informed about homosexuality, this editorial reflected their desire to change that. The confused language, however, suggests that it was not yet sure about the nature of these emerging identities, beyond a labelling of sexual desires. Indeed, in a later edition, under the headline 'Words, words!' Roger Baker addressed this use of language:

> In recent years, the word that has come very much to the fore is 'gay'. Most certainly it has been used extensively in American and has only recently been taken up in any general way over here. The Gay Liberation Front has helped to propagate its usage amongst all sorts of people. [...] It is, surely, preferable to hear about a new 'gay bar' than a new 'queer bar' as they were called in the 1950s. It also has the advantage of being equally applicable to women as well as men.[20]

Baker acknowledged how this new name had developed in America, and been adopted in Britain, suggesting that homosexual men and women were seeking out new ideas about sexuality and sexual identity from wherever they could find them. Like other magazines – both for men and for women – *Spartacus* appeared engaged in trying to define its market, and its product. They all contained stories, pictures, articles on fashion, food, etc., which were geared towards a homosexual audience – some, like *Arena Three*, even attempted to explore the science of sexuality. In doing so they reflected a period in which ideas about sexual identity were just beginning to emerge. Although these were often conflicting, they nevertheless reflected a desire to think about, create, and project what it meant to be homosexual in Britain.

With these magazines in place, establishing a gay media for the first time in the United Kingdom – albeit London-centric – the objective shifted towards reporting on this established gay group identity and culture through these publications. Although never a professional newspaper, GLF's *Come Together* managed to shape the debate around exactly what a 'gay' publication should be, and instigated a move towards a greater journalistic style, in particular by reporting on specific events and how they affected gay men and lesbians. Under the title 'Who we are', in the first edition of *Come Together*, the editorial board made it clear it was going to be different:

> We would like to say right now, that all the so-called gay mags, such as *Jeremy*, are just a load of absolute bullshit and an outright insult to gay people. They just try to foist a 'closet-queen' mentality on to us; they think that all we are interested in are the secret life of closeted pseudostars and the latest in rip-off bourgeois fashions. Some of us are just about pissed-off with this shit and are beginning to say – 'NO MORE. From now on gay people in Britain are going to write their own history.'[21]

Overtly political, deliberately amateur in style (in contrast to earlier magazines), and with a greater sense of their own gay identity – predicated on their visibility and counter cultural outlook – *Come Together* was able to offer gay news for the first time. Invariably reporting on their own stunts, they nevertheless provided a model of what a gay newspaper/magazine could include. When the GLF began its own decline, beginning in 1972, the collective responsible for *Come Together* ensured that their work continued with the foundation of *Gay News* – the UK's first professional gay newspaper. While this early gay liberation period witnessed only the beginnings of the emerging gay publication market, it pointed to the continued expansion of the gay media into the 1980s, which would increasingly focus on lifestyle and on reporting events that impacted gay men and lesbians.

Meanwhile, the press was grappling with the issue of homosexuality its own way. Unlike the emerging homosexual media, these newspapers had traditionally ignored the topic in favour of a more veiled approach to reporting. While this veil had temporarily lifted during the trial of Oscar Wilde in 1895, with every newspaper bar the *St James Gazette* reporting on the salacious details of the court case, it was not until the 1950s that newspapers ended their self-censored relationship with homosexuality. Indeed, Houlbrook claims 'it was exceptionally rare for any newspaper to investigate queer London independently between the end of the First World War and the early 1950s. [...] Unless engaged with the apparatus of the law, queer lives remained hidden from readers.'[22] This situation had changed under the leadership of *The Sunday Pictorial*, and its editor, Hugh Cudlipp. Through a series of articles collectively entitled 'Evil Men', in 1952, he observed,

> [t]he natural British tendency to pass over anything unpleasant in scornful silence is providing a cover for an unnatural sex vice which is getting a dangerous grip in the country [...] a number of doctors believe that the problem would be best solved by making homosexuality legal between consenting adults. This solution would be intolerable – and ineffective. Because the chief danger of the perverts is the corrupting influence they have on youth. Most people know there are such things – 'pansies' – mincing, effeminate young men who call themselves queers. But simple decent folk regard them as freaks and rarities. [...] If homosexuality were tolerated here, Britain would rapidly become decadent.[23]

With the topic now fit for discussion – albeit with the stereotyped associations of paedophilia, proselytising older men, and the corrupting influence on society – the events of the 1950s, culminating in the publication of the Wolfenden Report in 1957, gave newspaper editors licence to debate the 'social problem' of homosexuality.

While it is tempting and easy to dismiss all newspapers of this era as bigoted and homophobic – especially when judged against more modern liberal criteria – there is, in fact, a much more complicated picture. Editorial policies changed (as did editors); articles could be damning in their condemnation, while others could be surprisingly tolerant. Crucially, newspapers that presented a negative image of homosexuality on one issue at one particular time could then promote a much more liberal image on another issue – and vice versa. It is therefore of little use to talk broadly about specific newspapers' relationship to homosexuality, but rather to different events, and how they were covered by the popular press. Indeed, Adrian Bingham, in his book, *Family Newspapers?* maintains that,

> it is inaccurate and unproductive to dismiss all popular journalism as cynical, trivial, and routine, or to reduce it to a tool for the maintenance of the existing social order. [...] Newspapers were more complex, diverse, and unpredictable than many critics have admitted, and they provided challenging, well-written, and informative material as well as undemanding entertainment. They were not invariably reactionary and negative, but could be progressive and generous; [...] they undermined stereotypes as well as consolidated them.[24]

Wolfenden provided a unique situation for newspaper editors. Indeed, Bingham quotes the Home Secretary Maxwell-Fyfe as claiming that a 'dispassionate survey by a competent and unprejudiced body might be of value in educating public opinion, which at present is ill-informed and apt to be misled by sensational articles in the press'.[25] This early recognition of the power of the press to create and reinforce a public perception of homosexuality in Britain is important. Even though the situation where newspapers discussed homosexuality openly had only begun in the 1950s, it was already providing a tangible effect on ideas of what it meant to be homosexual in 1950s Britain.

The *New Statesman* and *The Observer* had both supported the decriminalisation of homosexuality for a number of years, but when the Wolfenden Report was published in 1957, *The Times* and *The Manchester Guardian* joined them in backing its proposals. Popular dailies had been almost entirely unreceptive to legal change, but the *Daily Mirror* became the first to back the report from its publication in September.[26] In contrast to articles on the problem of homosexuality, commentaries were appearing that suggested the beginning of a more tolerant approach. *The Times* wrote that '[a]dult sexual behaviour not involving minors, force, fraud or public indecency belongs to the realms of private conduct and not of the criminal law', while the *Daily Mirror* described Wolfenden as 'a sensible and responsible report'.[27] Earlier, *The Sunday People* had written that the Montague trial – itself a prelude to the Wolfenden Report – had 'exposed the complete failure of our so-called "civilisation" to find any remedy for sexual perverts to replace cruel and barbaric punishment [...] society must realise that imprisonment is no cure for abnormality'.[28]

Despite this, the *Daily Express*, *Sunday Express*, *The Daily Telegraph*, *London Evening Standard*, and the *Daily Mail* consistently opposed reform. The *Daily Express* claimed that it was the Home Secretary's 'duty to see that family life remains protected from these evils'; the *Sunday Express* branded it 'the pansies' charter'. The *London Evening Standard* said simply, that '[o]n no account must the Wolfenden recommendations be implemented. They are bad, retrograde and utterly to be condemned.' The *Daily Herald* was initially non-committal, claiming that '[h]omosexual vice – or weakness – is so abhorrent to normal minds that public opinion will be slow to accept such a change'.[29] Indeed, their arguments seemed to focus on morality, the degradation of society, and a general opposition to 'perversion', which included veiled references to paedophilia. Over the next ten years, these newspapers almost all came round to the idea of law reform, with only the *Daily Express* remaining opposed.[30]

But it would be naive to assume this change of heart on one particular issue – namely the tentative reforms offered by the Wolfenden Report (which was offering nothing like legal equality) – represented a broader change in the press's overall relationship with homosexuality. As Bingham has noted, 'prejudice and hostility against homosexual men certainly did not disappear from the popular press in the 1960s. [...] Even the more sympathetic writers only offered "toleration" and "pity" for homosexual men rather than genuine understanding or acceptance.'[31] The decision by the press to support legal change that would stop homosexual-inclined men being criminalised did not mean they suddenly condoned their lifestyle; indeed, homosexuality was still treated as an illness to be tolerated, and not encouraged. For homosexual men and women, these images were still broadly negative − if not explicitly so, then at least implicitly − where the reader was left with the impression that homosexuality was wrong, unnatural, and shameful. The continued reporting of crimes such as soliciting and importuning, as well as the more insidious association between homosexuality and paedophilia − reinforced through the assertion that homosexual men corrupted youth, and 'by reporting sexual offences involving adults in a similar style to those involving adults and children' − meant that a hugely influential medium in the creation and maintenance of a public discourse on homosexuality remained broadly negative.[32] The continued discussion of homosexuality, however, had the effect of establishing a binary narrative in the public discourse, where people were either homosexual or heterosexual, each with a set of ideas and images that defined them. This served to pave the way for the emergence of gay liberation the following decade, including female homosexuality in a real sense for the first time.

Central to the success of the GLF in the United Kingdom was their visibility. During the 1970s, some newspapers reported events involving gay liberation protests in an objective way, thereby helping to establish ideas surrounding the creation of an openly gay social and group identity in Britain. Indeed, even articles that included a negative undertone nevertheless helped spread the idea that being gay was not something that necessarily had to be hidden or felt ashamed of. They also showed that sexuality and sexual identity could now be discussed openly in Britain. But readers still needed to have these ideas explained to them. The *London Evening Standard*, for example, under the heading 'The other Lib group on the march today', wrote, gay is angry, read the inscription on the Harley Street pavement, puzzling many an honest citizen. Gay in this case means homosexual, and homosexuals are angry with the psychiatrists who describe homosexuality as a sickness and undertake to cure it. [...] They are united in a desire to remove the stigma from homosexuality, and in the case of having a sexual liaison with a man under 21, the fear of prosecution and imprisonment. [...] The freedom to kiss and hold hands in public may not seem very precious, but the GLF see it as a perfectly reasonable thing to ask. Twenty-five per cent of their membership, incidentally, is female.[33]

Meanwhile, *The Observer*, under the title 'Putting a gay front on things' profiled the new GLF:

Brian is a member of the Gay Liberation Front, who are trying to do for homosexuals – both men and women – much what Women's Lib are trying to do for women. One main aim is to liberate their 'brothers' and 'sisters,' the 'closet queens,' who now hide their homosexuality or live double lives. 'Out of the gay ghettos and into the straight world, that's half the battle,' said Brian. [...] At these meetings, which are earnest and democratic, a list of demands was argued out and voted on. 'GAY IS GOOD' – all power to oppressed people!' reads the resultant leaflet, which lists eight aims, these range from a call for the ending of 'all discrimination against gay people, male and female, by the law, by employers, and by society at large' to the demand that 'gay people be free to hold hands and kiss in public, as are heterosexuals.'[34]

These articles, written without a negative undertone, presented a positive image of homosexuality to a mainstream readership. Explaining the term 'gay', as well as suggesting fairly uncontroversial aims of gay liberation – including the 'freedom to kiss and hold hands in public' as well as to have their sexuality not seen as a mental health issue – they offered a relatively tolerant approach to homosexuality that could then be taken on board by homosexual and heterosexual readers in creating their own internal ideas about a gay sexual identity.

But there were also explicitly negative representations of homosexuality as well – often in the guise of thoughtful calls for tolerance – and even in the same newspapers. *The Observer* published an opinion-piece by the columnist Thomas Carter in February 1972, in which he claimed

> there are solid grounds for opposing the teaching and public demonstration of homosexual relations as being entirely normal, because it is just as clear that we are designed for heterosexual rather than homosexual relations as that we are designed to walk on two limbs rather than four.[35]

In *The Daily Telegraph* in 1976, moreover, under the title 'Homosexuals on the march', it was claimed that the Sexual Offences Act had established a 'public propaganda in favour of homosexuality':

> Much of the controversy which preceded the legalising, in 1967, of homosexual acts between consenting adults hinged on one precisely defined question: would such legislation open the way to public propaganda in favour of homosexuality as a way of life. [...] Now, almost a decade after the contentious legislation was passed, it is possible to say with certainty that, in this respect at least, its opponents were wholly right. There is now a vigorous movement in favour of homosexual liberation. [...] Such demonstrations are doubtless within the law, but it cannot be denied that they constitute something approaching a sustained campaign for homosexuality as a way of life. This is certainly not what Parliament or the public intended, and it surely has some important lessons to teach about the relationship between law and morals.[36]

These articles left the reader in no doubt about the subordinate place of homosexuality – and an emerging gay group identity – in 1970s

Britain. Indeed, they preceded a much more vitriolic press during the 1980s at the height of the HIV/AIDS epidemic, when these morality-led pieces became front-page headlines, effectively demonising homosexuality.

But there were explicit press champions of the gay liberation movement. Nicholas de Jongh, one of the first openly gay journalists in Britain, used his arts brief to write objectively about the blasphemy trial against *Gay News* – launched by the self-declared morality campaigner Mary Whitehouse. Under the headline, 'Margaret Drabble to the defence of Gay News', for example, he wrote,

> Gay News, the fortnightly homosexual newspaper, was a 'thoroughly responsible' and 'well written' journal which did not encourage its readers to perform illegal sexual acts, Margaret Drabble, the novelist and literary critic, and Bernard Levin the journalist and theatre critic, told a jury at the Central Criminal Court yesterday.[37]

Thus the 1960s and 70s witnessed a complicated picture in relations between the press and homosexuality. On the one hand they appeared to broadly support the Wolfenden proposals in order to see the end of prosecutions for private consensual acts. But on the other they had not changed their overall impression of homosexuality. For these papers pity dominated any sympathetic story, with warnings that further toleration might lead to future moral decline and an increase in homosexuality – something that had to be avoided. While not explicitly negative, the concern regarding the growth of Gay Liberation and the continued visibility of homosexuality preceded a greater press backlash against homosexuality in the 1980s.

Meanwhile, on television and in film, images of homosexuality were emerging for the very first time. While Vito Russo's *The Celluloid Closet* has revealed a hidden world of homosexual characters in cinema pre-dating this period, the early images he explores are not explicitly homosexual.[38] Instead, their homosexuality is implied: through their actions, their behaviour, and their (often dire) personal circumstances. In contrast, the films and television programmes explored here are chosen because they present (for the first time) openly homosexual characters. They are also 'firsts': the first British film on the topic of male homosexuality; the first lesbian sex scene. It is impossible to provide a complete history of every example of homosexuality in television and film that a British man or woman might have seen in this period. Instead, exploring a snap-shot of important examples, while looking only at British-made productions, can provide a sample of what this medium – itself primarily an art form – considered important, sometimes in an effort to educate the public, sometimes to represent real lives, and sometimes just to tell a compelling story.

Victim, released in 1961 – five years after the publication of the Wolfenden Report and at the beginning of this 'gay liberation' period – has achieved an iconic status in both early cinematic portrayals of homosexual men and its impact on public opinion towards law reform in the United Kingdom. Based around the character Melville Farr – a respectable, married barrister – the film tells the story of how he is drawn in to a world of blackmail in order to assuage his guilt at the suicide of a man he was romantically (but not physically) involved with. Farr, it is revealed, had a history of homosexuality that he put in his past after his marriage to his wife Laura, but he nevertheless became attached to the young Jack Barratt. Indeed, in a powerful scene when Laura confronts him about the relationship, he replied passionately: 'I stopped seeing him because I wanted him, do you understand? Because I wanted him!'. Barratt, we learn, was being blackmailed in order to prevent the release of incriminating pictures with Farr, which apparent showed the two looking longingly at each other. After his arrest for stealing from his employer to pay the blackmailer, and failing to get help from Farr, Barratt commits suicide, precipitating Farr's involvement in discovering who the blackmailer is.[39]

One of the film's aims was to present a sympathetic image of the homosexual man in pre-law reform Britain. Andy Medhurst described it as a 'watershed moment' in British cinema: 'pre-gay queers [those on film before *Victim*] are almost always ludicrous, villainous, monstrous, shadowy, pained, paranoid, edgy, guilty, doomed, or mocked'.[40] Indeed, Russo expands this point:

Victim's stark portrait of the pressures caused by hiding and the sense of despair of the homosexuals in the film (including the noble Farr) removed it from the category of films that dealt only with harmless, amorphous sissies; it made gays real. Farr's insistence on being both a homosexual and a real person mirrors the producers' insistence on using candid language in the film. On the one hand, the film was a regrettable legitimization of social issues perceived to be distasteful', on the other, it was a validation of the existence of homosexuals who were not comic relief for the majority.[41]

The reviews on its release were mixed. Leonard Mosley, of the *Daily Express,* claimed '[i]t is almost certainly the most controversial film ever made by a British studio'.[42] Alexander Walker, of the *London Evening Standard,* said that the film's writer, Janet Green, had turned her attention as a social commentator 'grippingly to that parasite of perversion – the blackmailer', while Dilys Powell of *The Sunday Times* called the decision to make the film 'brave'.[43] Indeed, Green had previously written the 1959 film, *Sapphire,* which dealt with race relations in 1950s London. But *The Times Educational Supplement* was less impressed: 'Victim is simply one more example of the habit British film makers have of disinfecting a topic and then imagining they have dealt with it.'[44]

Dirk Bogarde's performance as Farr – including his decision to play the part – proved an important aspect of the film's success. In pre-law reform England, the decision of a well-known actor to move into a potentially damaging role helped legitimise the film. Moreover, as Rosso says, Farr is a fully-formed character, with only his sexuality separating him from 'ordinary' men. Indeed, turning these men into victims ensured that the viewer sympathised with the cause, and the film employs minor characters throughout to emphasise its message. In one scene, for example, Sergeant Bridie bemoans homosexual men for not reporting blackmail, while Detective Inspector Harris presents a more sympathetic opinion:

Harris: If only these unfortunate devils would come to us in the first place.
Bridie: If only they led normal lives they wouldn't need to come at all.
Harris: If the law punished every abnormality we'd be kept pretty busy sergeant.[45]

While the film undoubtedly presented a more realistic image of homosexual men – who were just like everyone else – it did so at the expense of other homosexual men who might not so easily lend themselves to sympathy. Like the HLRS, only respectable men were shown, and the almost apologetic portrayals, which never sought to challenge the basic assumption that homosexual men were often sad and lonely figures, maintained a particular idea of homosexuality that characterised film and television in the 1960s and 1970s. Despite this, it offered a sympathetic portrayal of male homosexuality between the publication of the Wolfenden Report and the introduction of the Sexual Offences Act. But homosexual men watching the film at the time interpreted it in different ways. Terence Davies, then a 15-year-old clerk in Liverpool, remembers seeing the film as 'one of those moments in one's life where you just feel that something profound has happened to you', although as a Catholic he went on to remark how it 'really frightened me. I sort of decided that I would probably be celibate for the rest of my life – and I have been.'[46] Another reported that 'several members of the public walked out of the cinema complaining', while others were more positive, claiming 'a watershed in my awareness of gay life', and that 'we felt some kind of breakthrough had been achieved'.[47] For John Coldstream, meanwhile, writing about the impact of *Victim*, it was, simply '[a] movie that truly mattered'.[48]

Seven years later, in 1968, *The Killing of Sister George* was released. Huge changes had taken place in cinema since *Victim's* release. The old American production code system had been dismantled, which meant that much racier and more violent films were coming across from Hollywood. For Britain, this had a similar effect, and may have made the making of *The Killing of Sister George* more palatable to a studio. Either way, it was a very different film, but like *Victim* presented fully-formed homosexual characters, albeit ones who were flawed:

> Whilst on one level the film can be seen as an important contribution to British queer cinema by the very nature of its long overdue existence, the mixed critical response that the film has received since its release has revealed a very real uneasiness with the ambivalent way in which it tended to construct "the lesbian" as pathological, and as marking the boundary of the sinister and bizarre.[49]

Indeed, while *Victim*'s agenda appeared to be sympathy, it nevertheless presented homosexuality as inherently damaged. *The Killing of Sister George* took this further in exploring an abusive intergenerational lesbian relationship, and the gradual emotional breakdown of June Buckridge, precipitated by her dismissal from her job as 'Sister George' in a BBC soap opera, and culminating in her smashing the studio where it was filmed, and mooing like a cow.

Buckridge, a middle-aged woman, plays the part of a popular character in the fictional soap 'Applehurst' – a pastiche of the BBC radio series *The Archers,* the doyen of middle-class respectability in England. She is quickly presented as a butch, tweed-wearing alcoholic with serious mood swings, living with her partner, Childie, a childishly naive younger woman with whom she has a fractious relationship. Seemingly unwilling to hide her sexuality, she has instead developed an aggressive persona that she employs to devastating effect towards anyone who crosses her. It is this tempestuous attitude that finally forces the writers to kill off her character, with producer Mercy Croft telling her of the decision at the famous Gateways nightclub (filmed on location there). Croft had already witnessed Buckridge lose her temper with Childie, and appeared interested in the younger woman. Indeed, after Buckridge's leaving party at work, during which she got drunk and argued with her colleagues, Childie and Croft leave together. Back at the flat Croft seduces Childie in a scene designed to appear both predatory and dangerous. Buckridge discovers the pair, and after Childie and Croft leave together, she goes back to the set where she moos in reference to the only new role she has been offered – as a talking cow on a children's show.[50]

While it is possible to look back and see a film that explores the emotional decline of a woman so used to being able to manipulate others, its subject matter meant that its contemporary reception was less forgiving. Despite Beryl Reid being nominated for a Golden Globe for her performance as Buckridge, Ian Christie, writing in the *Daily Express* under the title 'The Boredom of Sister George', described it as 'vulgar, repetitive, over-long and boring':

> [I]nstead of taking a considered sympathetic look at the unnatural relationships, the film aims at sensationalism. There can be no other reason for the drawn-out bedroom scene of Miss Browne seducing Miss York.[51]

Gay Times, meanwhile, claimed it 'presents the lesbian world as a grotesque collection of the sick and the predatory'.[52] Lesbians who saw the film at the time were similarly unimpressed. Maria remembers that,

> The film came out around the time I was a teenager and first falling in love with other girls. We just knew about it even though we didn't get to go and see it. The image I had was of a very masculine older woman dressed in tweeds and the film being about her. This was jumbled up in my mind with the general image I had of 'lesbians' which at the time was daunting and off-putting to me! I was a longhaired purple flare-wearing hippyish young person and I couldn't relate to Sister George at all! My other impression was that it all ends in tears and the character is miserable![53]

Catherine, who saw the film in 1975 aged 21, remembers that the 'lesbian club appeared sad and unusual [...] that it created conflict and uncomfortable feelings for me, – [I] did not want to be part of that world, but knew that I would.'[54]

Russo claims that the film reflected negative contemporary ideas about sexuality:

> Because of what Mercy Croft calls George's 'refusal to conduct herself in a decent, civilized manner,' the Sister George character is killed off on the BBC [...]. Croft then seduces Childie away from George, leaving her without a job and without a relationship. Yet the final indignity is the theft of her openness. The only job offered the aging actress is the part of an animal on a children's series [...]. The options are invisibility, assimilation or ostracism.[55]

Indeed, the film continued a tradition during this period which presented homosexuality as a pathology and part of a broader theme of isolation and depression. The scene of the older Buckridge punishing Childie by making her eat the butt of a cigar, moreover, lent itself to the contemporary view that mature homosexuals manipulated younger men and women psychologically, physically, and sexually. With both Buckridge and Croft both preying on the weak Childie, the assumption, while not fully explored, is that these women have been able to influence her sexuality for their own ends.

Similar negative depictions were also appearing on television in this period. In 1967, the BBC had broadcast two editions of its documentary and current affairs series *Man Alive*. The first, *Consenting Adults: The Men*, was shown on BBC2 on 7 June 1967, a month before the Sexual Offences Act received royal assent. The documentary included a series of interviews by the presenter Jeremy James, characterising homosexual men as lonely, promiscuous, and lacking the protection of the law. Beginning with an interview with a woman who married a man she later discovered was homosexual, James tells the viewer how, [t]wice during their marriage he was arrested for importuning. The second time he killed himself rather than face the punishment of a court and the disgust of his friends.[56]

Setting the scene for the remaining 30 minutes, James goes on to stereotype homosexual men as artistic, sensitive, and, in particular, promiscuous. When interviewing a hairdresser, for example, he repeatedly points out that all his relationships had been short-term, even after the man explicitly says he wants a long-term relationship, but has not been able to find one since his last relationship ended four years earlier. Discussing the threats these men face – including the story of one man who had been severely beaten while soliciting for sex in a toilet – the programme highlighted what James saw as the loneliness of a homosexual life. In particular, when interviewing a couple who acknowledged that they were not in love, despite being together for 26 years, he commented:

> Most homosexuals dread getting old, dread losing their looks, fear in particular the final loneliness of living without a companion. Like men needing wives, they search for someone with whom they can establish a lasting relationship, which includes warmth and protection as well as sex.[57]

The programme ends with another man, his back to the camera, telling James that he is searching for 'someone with whom I can share a life with. That's all I need. But it seems that it's wrong.'[58] Although the men chosen appear respectable enough – they are well dressed and politely spoken – the image they present to the viewer cannot be misinterpreted: homosexual men are inherently unhappy, through the persecution of the law, the attitude of society, and their own innate inability to form long-term relationships.

The second episode, *Consenting Adults: The Women*, was broadcast a week later on 14 June. Presented by Angela Huth, it showcased a cross-section of women and begins with an acknowledgement of the different – but equally difficult – place of lesbians in 1960s British society:

> For women who love women unqualified acceptance by our society still does not exist. We are heterosexually geared; naturally propaganda for love, for sex, for conformist lives is all aimed at women with men. The idea of two women feeling about each other in the same way as a normal couple disturbs

that happy concept and so lesbians receive the minority treatment: intolerance, suspicion, often disgust. That they're legally free to live as they like makes little difference.[59]

Despite its focus on lesbians, one of the main interviewees – a young woman calling herself 'Steve Rogers' – describes a textbook case of gender dysphoria: 'I'd do anything I could to be a man. I think it could make me more happier if I was a man.'[60] In particular, she recounts an adolescence spent pretending to be a boy and taking girls on dates:

> When I was sixteen I met this girl and I was with her for six months and I got engaged to her. I really forgot that I was a woman. And she thought she was pregnant because there's some things a lesbian can use and I got away with using them and she didn't know the difference.[61]

While the viewer cannot help but sympathise with her situation, her own confusion with her gender identity and sexuality does not help define nascent ideas of lesbianism in British society. Instead, the viewer is left to assume that lesbians (at least those who looked or behaved in a masculine way) coveted the role of men in courtship and society.

But unlike the previous programme, the episode also includes what Huth called 'a happy, and lucky and well-adjusted couple'. Cynthia Reid and Julie Switsur – the founders of the lesbian group MRG – are interviewed in their house in Wandsworth, where they deliberately describe ordinary domestic life together. When asked what they would like to see done to improve attitudes towards lesbians, Reid replies: I think many lesbians could help themselves by ceasing to be obsessed with their own lesbianism – that is, regarding it as simply a part of their personality and not the whole of it.[62]

Indeed, an earlier interviewee seems to suggest the same, putting the emphasis on women to 'come out' to help change society: 'I think if people had to courage to do that [come out] [...] it would be much much better because people would become accustomed to the fact that we're ordinary people.'[63] But despite the inclusion of stories of more contented women, the episode ends in the same way as the first, this time with a married woman with her back to the camera. She tells the viewer how she has been left heartbroken after her girlfriend (with whom she was planning on running away with) backed down at the last minute, fearing that she would eventually go back to her husband: 'So suddenly I find myself again with empty hands, wondering why the hell I was ever born, and there isn't anything I can do. [...] nothing but wilderness, without love.'[64]

The reviews tended to reinforce the message of sympathy that the two programmes sought from viewers. *Birmingham Post* reviewer Linda Dyson wrote that, [t]he strongest impression received of this wide assortment of personalities was a deep underlying loneliness, brought about [by] the difficulty they experienced in meeting fellow homosexuals and achieving long-term friendship.[65]

The *Reading Evening Post* meanwhile described it as 'the most sensible probe into the social problem ever to be screen on television'.[66] The *Morning Star* went even further, with the reviewer lamenting the treatment of homosexual men in society: 'One can only hope that we shall soon shave some legislation which will put an end to the prosecution of consenting adults.'[67] The programmes also offered critics the opportunity to reflect on the state of the law and society. The *Daily Mail*'s Peter Black wrote that,

> [homosexual] life is clearly one of horrible inconvenience, secrecy and menace, thanks to laws that reflect a kind of mania which the large body of society no longer shares.
>
> To suppose anyone chooses it out of sheer wickedness seemed hardly sane.[68]

Philip Purser of the *Sunday Telegraph,* however, wrote that the first programme 'offers no solutions' and that '[h]ad the programme editors so chosen, they could perhaps have tipped the thing quite the other way by tracking down some louche, child-molesting pederast'.[69] Reviewing the second programme, John Dodd of *The Sun*, claimed,

> Angela Huth [...] sounded like a priest comforting bereaved widows. She kept trying to drain the last bit of emotion out of the lesbians' plight, faced, she said, as they were with 'intolerance, suspicion and disgust.' You could have fooled me. I thought most of them looked full of the joys of spring.[70]

Dodd ended his review by asking '[w]hen are the BBC going to get round to that ridiculed, slandered, misunderstood persecuted minority, the heterosexual male'.

In addition to documentaries, the BBC was also producing some of the first fictional representations of homosexuality on television. *Girl*, first broadcast on BBC2 in February 1974, included the first lesbian kiss on British television and came with a warning about its content from the controller of BBC2.[71] It tells the story of Jackie Smithers, who, as the drama begins, is waiting to be discharged from the army. Intelligently written, the back-story is gradually revealed to the viewer as we discover she has been raped and is leaving the army because she is pregnant. Before she leaves she talks at length with her army superior, Corporal Harvey (a more stereotypical lesbian in contrast to the feminine Smithers), who it transpires was her secret lover for a short time. Harvey broke up with Smithers without reason, and appears to have a history of doing the same with others. Smithers repeatedly asks Harvey why she broke up with her, at one point almost begging: 'I still don't understand. I loved you. With all my heart I loved you.'[72] Harvey never answers. Just before Smithers leaves, the couple sing and dance to a song, and then kiss passionately, before being interrupted. Smithers then leaves, and Harvey is left alone in the room looking regretful, smoking a cigarette. Like *The Killing of Sister George*, the story is a fascinating insight into these two characters, although the length of the programme (only 30 minutes) prevents such an in-depth exploration. But like *Sister George*, the representation of lesbians is negative and melancholic. While only one of the characters could be considered stereotypical (although there is an obvious butch/femme dimension to their relationship), both are presented as inherently unhappy. Indeed, the resolution, that Harvey could never offer anything more than a short physically relationship because she is unable to deal effectively with her emotions, and that Smithers is left heartbroken and as a single mother, leaves the viewer in no doubt about what the writers saw as the sad realities of living a homosexual life. Either because of the nature of homosexuality, or the way homosexuality is viewed publicly, a long-lasting relationship was not open to them. Moreover, the decision to detail the rape of Smithers as the reason for her pregnancy and subsequent discharge from the army also points to the difficulties lesbians face, aside from their sexuality. Harvey's image as a strong and almost aggressive woman may in part be explained as a defence against the kind of men who were able to attack the more feminine Smithers. As with *The Killing of Sister George,* some viewers may even have wondered about the nature of their relationship, and whether Harvey, with a reputation for heartbreak, had been preying on weak women in an effort to influence their sexuality.

A similar 30-minute drama was broadcast on the BBC in 1973. *Bermondsey* was one of a series of four 'Thirty Minute Theatre' productions written by John Mortimer. It tells the odd story of the upper-class Pip, who spends his Christmases with his old army friend Bob, Bob's wife Iris, and their children, in their pub in Bermondsey. Like *Girl* it is set entirely in one room (the living room behind the bar), and the back-story is gradually revealed, telling the viewer that Pip and Bob were lovers. Bob has since become an alcoholic unhappy with life. This, and his feelings for Pip, are revealed when he puts his hand on his shoulder and says: 'I'm in a bit of a rut here Pip', before they kiss passionately, parting when Bob's wife comes in.[73] The plot twist arrives when it transpires Iris is actually aware of Pip and Bob's relationship, telling Pip 'I'm not a complete bloody idiot, I do know what's going on. He's your boyfriend, isn't he?'[74] Iris then implores Pip to help prevent Bob from leaving with the new barmaid, Rosemary, asking him to tell her about their relationship. However, after Rosemary persistently asks why Pip keeps visiting, it is Bob who relents and says:

One Christmas Eve, a change came. Pip asked me back to his mother's house. And he played the piano [...] and we drank whiskey out of a decanter. And we got pissed, bloody senseless. On the way home we climbed on a haystack. It was all hard with frost and we saw each other's breath in the moonlight. And suddenly, for no good reason, we grabbed each other like we was both drowning. And we proceeded to have it away as if that side of life had just been invented. I regret to tell you, Rosemary, it didn't stop then; it's been going on ever since.[75]

To add to the peculiarity of the story, they then casually start practising a Christmas carol, while Rosemary puts her coat on and leaves.

Although unique in actually presenting a bisexual character, together with a plot resolution that he will stay with his wife and keep seeing Pip, these characters are still left unhappy. Pip can never have Bob permanently. Bob is still unhappy with life, and Iris has had to negotiate a complicated terrain in order to keep her family together. Like *Girl, Bermondsey* seems to conform to a particular style of presenting homosexuality on television and in cinema in the 1960s and 1970s, which leaves the cause of their melancholy unresolved, even if the viewer is meant to feel sympathy for their situation. For people either growing up with homosexual feelings, or learning about homosexuality for the first time, these are strong emotions to contend with, and make sense of. It would be another decade before homosexual characters on television were presented as happy, and even then this was not always the case.

The early gay liberation period, then, was one of contrasts. Although almost all newspapers came to offer their support for the Wolfenden proposals, these were themselves limited reforms which would naturally fit within the conservative framework of the majority of the British press at the time. When gay liberation exploded into life in the 1970s, some newspapers reverted back to printing morality pieces that questioned the decision to pass the Sexual Offences Act. But not all of the press was negative. Crucially, even discussing homosexuality was a change from life before the 1950s, when homosexual men and women could be left isolated by their sexuality, and the 'heterosexual majority' could assume that homosexuality either did not exist, or was limited to so minor a section of society as to have no impact on their own lives. So too, the gay media not only presented a more visible front for these emerging identities, but also engaged in discussions about what homosexuality meant in terms of personal identity, building the foundations for a gay media to grow and become an integral part of life in 1980s Britain. The more positive ideas and images in these publications were only ever really available to self-identified homosexual men and women who bought them, however, who had thus either come to terms with their sexuality or were in the process of doing so. Film and television, meanwhile, seemed engaged in producing more fully-formed homosexual characters for the first time, including more realistic scenes of intimacy between couples. This often happened at the expense of the types of persons presented, however. Characterised by loneliness, pity, and unhappiness, while their visibility was a welcome change, it did not present a positive image of homosexuality to either a heterosexual or homosexual audience. Nevertheless, taken together, this greater visibility had the effect of making homosexuality a topic fit for discussion in the developing public discourse, with the characters' homosexuality often presented as an unchangeable part of their make-up. If not wholly positive, these representations at least presented images of homosexuality that were at times tolerant, sympathetic, and liberal, which then fed into emerging public ideas about increasingly binary sexual identities in Britain.

CHAPTER 3

'OSTENTATIOUS BEHAVIOUR AND PUBLIC FLAUNTING'

While political and media changes were projecting very visible ideas about emerging sexual identities in Britain, an increasingly open social world was also developing. Unlike the social scene of pre-war Britain, which was largely hidden from the public discourse, this mixture of organisations, support structures, and networks of people gradually became more visible. Indeed, the late 1960s and early 1970s was a period of huge social change in the United Kingdom, with the political move to the left providing the space for the rise of many subcultural and counter cultural groups. Through their visibility they began shaping personal ideas about identity, creating community structures for homosexual men and women, and − like political and media impressions − presenting public and visible images of homosexuality. Often intimately linked to the political climate, these social changes reflected the real lived experiences of homosexual men and women in 1960s and 1970s Britain. As with the competing images of homosexuality, however, the experiences of these people were equally diverse as they tried to define what their homosexuality meant to them. The result was complex, overlapping, and oppositional identities in a period when a public discourse surrounding sexual identity was just developing.

1967 was a watershed moment in English and Welsh legal history. For the first time since the Labouchere Amendment had outlawed all male homosexual sex acts in 1885, the law was now permitting homosexual sex, albeit in restricted circumstances. For many men, this legal change had huge social implications. Bernard Dobson remembers: 'When the law was reformed we were very pleased – we thought it was a marvellous thing to happen, that you weren't considered to be a criminal anymore in the eyes of the law.'[1] Indeed, the private lives of countless homosexual men over the age of 21 changed from hidden and at risk of prosecution, to gradually more relaxed and open. But for others, however, the legal change made little difference:

> I remember reading in the paper about something called the *Wolfenden Report* on homosexuality but was not very curious about it. And certainly unaware of the political agitation in 1967, the campaign to change the Act. It didn't seem to register much in my mind. I thought, oh well, it's legal now, you know. If this had happened years ago I wouldn't have been convicted. I'm not a political animal and, once the conviction had happened in Leicester, I think I was so bruised by it that I didn't want to know. Probably somewhere I think, deep down, I didn't want to know about sex even.[2]

Indeed, for many homosexual women, the Sexual Offences Act made little difference to their lives as social and support structures had already been established. Three years before the Act, in 1964, the lesbian organisation MRG had been founded by five women, initially with the aim of publishing a lesbian magazine, but growing to include a pastoral role. In a memorandum entitled 'Social Organisations for Homosexuals' circulated in May 1968 to members of the Albany Trust, Grey described how, in addition to *Arena Three*, MRG also,

> organises social functions both in London and the provinces, refers members in need of help to appropriate professional aid, participates in University and other research projects, and puts its members in touch with one another by means of advertisements and correspondence.[3]

Indeed, in the first edition of *Arena Three* MRG listed its aims as:

> [T]o conduct and to collaborate in research into the homosexual condition, especially as it concerns women; and to disseminate information and items of interest to universities, institutions, social and educational workers, writers, poets, editors, employers, and, in short, all those genuinely in quest of enlightenment about what has been called 'the misty, unmapped world of feminine homosexuality'.[4]

Pre-dating the work of the CHE, the group organised social meetings, initially at each other's houses, and then at the Shakespeare's Head pub on Carnaby Street, Soho; these meetings were later extended to other areas of the United Kingdom in an effort to construct a country-wide social network.[5] By organising these events MRG provided homosexual women with a way to meet and construct social lives for themselves, and in the process construct a common identity based on their sexuality. While these were small groups that largely hid their sexuality from the public, they nevertheless represented a first step in developing public identities — albeit among themselves — that would later become more visible. Crucially, however, as the name suggests, this was a group dedicated to understanding the 'homosexual condition' and not to either the progression of legal or social change, despite the social functions they organised. Its links to the HLRS, moreover, reflected its middle-class and respectable nature, replicating the image that the HLRS was promoting.

Despite not being limited by the illegality of female homosexuality, these women were nonetheless restricted in their activities through fear of prosecution, and the overall place of women in society. Oram and Turnball note how,

> [t]he emergence of lesbian identities, roles and subjectivities at particular historical moments depends on the material possibilities open to women; on the degree of economic independence they can muster within and away from the family, for example. Not least important is the individual

woman's agency in the shaping of a sexual self in the context of (but also often despite) the social, cultural and economic circumstances of her life and times.[6]

Indeed, after advice from Anthony Grey that there might be potential legal difficulties in allowing married women to subscribe to *Arena Three*, for example, the magazine's founders decided to require the written consent from the husband of any married woman requesting a subscription. This had the effect of preventing many women from subscribing, since many did not feel able to ask their husband's permission. The magazine subsequently received many letters from women complaining about the situation.[7] These restrictions undoubtedly prevented women throughout the United Kingdom from reading the magazine, or attending the social functions, as did the widely perceived middle-class bias of the group, which early on debated excluding women dressed in men's clothes, since it did not fit with the image of respectability they were trying to project.[8]

MRG was able to use the publicity surrounding the Wolfenden Report and subsequent debate about a change in the law, in an attempt to shape opinion on lesbianism. Articles appeared in a number of newspapers and magazines, which often took the MRG's view that lesbians were no different from other women – other than in the gender of their sexual partner – replicating what many readers were saying in their magazine. They were also invited, and accepted, an invitation to appear on an edition of *This Week* – a current affairs programme that had previously focused on male homosexuality in one of its broadcasts. The journalist responsible, Bryan Magee, attended MRG meetings, and some members appeared on the programme.[9] Seemingly happy with how they had been presented, MRG agreed to another programme in the *Man Alive* series, although they were less happy this time, noting,

> a very long drawn out interview with Steve Rogers – a youthful 'Colonel Barker' whose over-riding compulsion is to pass as a male, even to the point of 'courting' and getting engaged to another girl and using an artificial penis.[10]

As previously discussed, Steve Rogers was by all accounts telling the story of someone dealing with gender dysphoria, and not sexuality, confusing what it meant to describe someone as a lesbian. For MRG, while sometimes successful in putting their middle-class and respectable image across, they were battling with a male construction that understood lesbians as women who fundamentally wanted to be men.

MRG faced internal arguments early on when tensions developed between the magazine, which Langley edited throughout and guarded preciously, and the social role of the group, ultimately leading to a split. Diane Chapman remembers how,

> Kenric was formed in 1965. I walked out on Esme that year and that precipitated a crisis. People who formed the basis of the Kensington and Richmond group then said, Esme's being difficult about all this and we'll form a new group and call it Kenric. I think people wanted to help and take over a bit and Esme just wanted to keep it all herself and she made *Arena Three* into a limited company.[11]

Kenric also gained the reputation of a middle-class and inward looking organisation, but nonetheless helped build the foundations of lesbian groups in Britain for the first time. Their exclusion of working-class and masculine-looking women, moreover, reflected their own attempts to construct a particular public sexual identity, predicated on respectability. At a similar time, however, another group formed, initially to produce a magazine to replace *Arena Three* but which also took over part of its social role. Sappho is remembered as a diverse organisation – including a large number of black and working-class women:

> I remember the first night I went there, I sat with my back to the wall and I looked around the room and I was absolutely amazed. I thought if you'd gone along Oxford Street and taken one woman in every ten, you'd have that range of women there. I'd got no idea so many different women were lesbians.[12]

These organisations were vital in providing the opportunity for women to meet each other and discover what their sexuality meant to them in the construction of their social sexual identity.

But 1967 did prove crucial for what would become the Campaign for Homosexual Equality. In the pamphlet 'after the Act...' published in 1968, the North-Western Homosexual Law Reform Committee, which had been campaigning for the decriminalisation of male homosexual sex, included in its aims a commitment to 'support the inauguration of new social centres where homosexuals and others can meet in congenial surroundings'.[13] This was initially proposed as a network of Esquire Clubs, run as an independent company, which would operate as an alternative to the hidden bars that operated in some towns and cities. Although they listed the vice-presidents as the respectable figures of Antony Grey, Revd Basil Higginson (the national general secretary of the Samaritans), and Revd George Honshaw (the director of the Manchester Samaritans), the idea provoked strong opposition.[14] In response to a letter from the HLRS about the clubs, Leo Abse replied 'I am certainly not at all happy about this new move', while Lord Arran described the plans as 'an open flaunting of the new and legal freedom of outlet'.[15] Then, in 1968, the 19-year-old John Holland attempted to set up a social group in Wolverhampton called 'The Male and Female Homosexual Association of Great Britain' (MANDFHAB). The membership form listed MANDFHAB as 'a social organisation for homosexuals, the minimum age limit being sixteen years'.[16] Antony Grey lamented that Holland 'earnestly lectured' him about the organisation, and '[w]hen I endeavoured to explain that things were really not so simple as that, he gazed at us with pitying condescension and departed'.[17] Holland also claimed that Wolverhampton already 'had the best social club for homosexuals in Europe'.[18] The club was subsequently raided by police and charges of 'obscene and indecent acts committed on the premises' were brought against the owners; 'MANDFHAD sank without a trace.'[19] These events conspired with a lack of funding and other organisational problems to ensure that Esquire Clubs Ltd never saw the light of day.

Instead, CHE concentrated on setting up social organisations across the country that might operate informally and without the threat of legal sanction. They borrowed ideas from the Dutch COC, which also operated social groups and bars throughout the Netherlands, and was often visited by British men looking for a more tolerant approach to homosexuality. By November 1970 it had already set up 15 local groups, with a total membership of 500.[20] Over the following decade the organisation would regularly co-opt new groups into their network, and by 1979 CHE was 'the largest gay organisation in the country, with over 4,500 members and around 100 local groups'.[21] Despite their insistence that CHE was a campaigning organisation, with the President, Allan Horsfall, stating in the 1976 Annual Report: 'I make no apology for the fact that my work in CHE has been mainly concerned with law reform', the majority of people continued to join for the social opportunities on offer.[22] Indeed, the 1975 Annual Report recognised this, making the point: '[o]ur major achievement has been to change the attitude of gays towards themselves and to raise expectations about our rightful place in society.'[23] Moreover, this statement reflected the changes taking place in Britain. Despite, or perhaps because of, the fall of the GLF, older organisations like CHE were happy to begin to use the terms 'gay' and 'lesbian' to describe sexual categories in a way not previously possible.

For the members of CHE, typically older than the GLFers, and brought up in pre-law reform Britain, these social groups were the only way to combat the isolation they faced. Indeed, the Albany Trust noted their 'concern for the many lonely older people who seek their advice – all too often in a despairing or even suicidal mood'.[24] Many thus saw CHE as a lifeline. Elisa Beckett, in her early 30s at the time, recalled the first meeting she attended:

> When I went I found it very friendly and welcoming. I had this wonderful feeling coming into this room full of gay people and I really felt, 'At last I've come home. This is really what I've been waiting for without knowing it.' Suddenly coming into a whole room where everybody was gay.[25]

John Alcock, in his mid-40s at the time, described how:

> It was one lovely sunny afternoon on Hampstead Heath that I noticed a boy reading *Gay News,* and I didn't know that there was such a newspaper and I started to read [...] [it] and they were advertising a jumble sale or something like that that was going on. The fair, they called it, the Campaign for Homosexual Equality fair. And I went along to it and then of course I got hooked.[26]

One member summed it up simply that '[j]oining the CHE became one of the finest things I've ever done in my life.'[27] These group meetings were typically held in private, and despite describing themselves as a largest homosexual organisation in the country, they could easily remain invisible to local populations where they met, including other homosexual men and women.

While the organisation certainly improved the social life for many men and women struggling with their sexuality during this period, their work at normalising homosexuality in the eyes of the public was a slower process. In 1972 CHE decided to arrange what would become an annual conference to discuss policy and serve as an opportunity for members from across England to meet. Ten resort towns were contacted to see if they could provide conference space and accommodation:

> Of the ten, four replied that they were fully booked; two did not reply [...] and a letter was received from one explaining that the director of publicity concerned had been instructed to ignore CHE's approach. Two resorts asked for further information about CHE. After receiving this information, one of them voted to refuse facilities and one offered facilities[28]

Finally Morecambe was chosen, after the council wrote a letter to CHE that said 'I am sure we can be helpful to you to make your conference a success as we have the necessary facilities.'[29] Morecambe council then reneged on its decision, claiming both that there was no room for the conference, and that the pier, which had been the proposed site, would not be safe. Not only did these excuses turn out to be false, but CHE only discovered this after 'a member chanced to see a press report on the 13th September'.[30] CHE eventually held their first annual conference in Morecambe in 1974, but only after circumventing the council and going to the owners of the premises directly, at a greater cost. This episode revealed that despite the work of gay organisations which were providing a social scene that only ten years earlier would have been impossible, homophobia remained prevalent in the United Kingdom, with CHE claiming 'the only real reason [for the council's actions] is political prejudice against CHE'.[31] Unlike the GLF, however, they were still attempting to work with, rather than against, the wider public in a non-confrontational way, principally because CHE was an organisation of older people who were used to hiding their sexuality and were generally not part of the youth-based counter culture.

CHE went into steady decline after 1979 and their leaflet 'A change for the future' recognised the transformed nature of life in Britain:

> For many years, CHE provided good, and often the only, meeting places, help-lines and discos for gay people in over 100 towns and cities in England and Wales. Things have changed: alternative and commercial venues have grown enormously.[32]

Indeed the 1980s would be characterised by the exponential growth of the commercial gay scene, which would continue to define and evolve what it meant to be gay in Britain. In doing so it would expand the work of the GLF and CHE in the 1970s. By ensuring the continued public presence of homosexuality they helped build the facilities that made life easier for gay men and lesbians, and crucially, were seen to be doing so. Moreover, CHE reflected what was happening across Britain, even without the structure they offered. Groups, networks, organisations and friendships were emerging across the country, developing the 'community' structure that would prove to be so vital in the following decade.

However, CHE was always a male-dominated organisation, and despite repeated campaigns, it failed to attract significant numbers of women, in part due to its origins as an organisation campaigning for legal change as it affected homosexual men. Built on this foundation, CHE found attitudes towards women difficult to change. Barry, as a CHE member claimed, for example,

> even out and out lesbians resent it if a man does not make a pass, or at any rate does not treat them as a female woman. Although it was a great relief at Nottingham last year [1978] when the women withdrew. In my opinion, they're far more aggressive than we are. [. . .] when *Gay News* said that men wept when the women withdrew, I thought, what balls, really. Almost all the men there, if you got them quietly aside, they would have agreed that it was a good thing.[33]

Indeed, CHE's own discussion paper 'Women and men in CHE', published in advance of the 1973 conference, argued,

> [p]reviously a lot of people – heterosexual as well as homosexual – believed that because someone was gay then they have no need or wish to mix with people of the opposite sex.

> This assumption rests on the belief that the only worthwhile relationships are those that are (potentially or actually) sexual. It also confirms the mistaken belief that homo*sex*uality is just about sex and nothing else.[34]

Despite attempts to change this behaviour, many men continued to hold sexist opinions, and many more used CHE primarily for meeting other men for sex.[35] Its steady decline, rather than the sudden implosion of the GLF, belies their success, however. It provided a safe space for thousands of homosexuals, and further presented homosexuality as normal, visible, and a permanent feature in British life. For the heterosexual majority, if they were aware of homosexuality at all, this initial image, while even too much for Abse and Arran, nevertheless continued the legacy of the Wolfenden compromise. These organisations were quiet, often middle-class, and respectable.

In contrast, the Gay Liberation Front included far more women, and did not owe its origins to the Sexual Offences Act, although it undoubtedly made their activities much less restricted. 'Gay pride' was the principle philosophy of the GLF since their first meeting in London in 1970, and reflected the mantra of the Stonewall bar protests one year earlier. In addition to their political aims, the organisation was also attempting to achieve substantial social change. Their manifesto stated:

> The starting point of our liberation must be to rid ourselves of the oppression which lies in the head of every one of us. This means freeing our heads from self-oppression and male chauvinism, and no longer organising our lives according to the patterns with which we are indoctrinated by straight society. It means that we must root out the idea that homosexuality is bad, sick or immoral, and develop a gay pride.[36]

In order to do this, the GLF began organising social events two months after their initial meeting. The first disco was held at the London School of Economics on 4 December 1970, in which '[w]omen and men [...] were encouraged to touch, kiss and dance with each other, breaking the unspoken taboo (and legal threats) which had prevented this before'.[37] Then on 20 December they held their first public dance at Kensington Town Hall, which proved so successful that 750 people attended, while another 500 were left outside.[38] Indeed, throughout its existence, the GLF's London group remained the largest, and most visible. Weeks maintains that only by repeatedly holding these dances did they become accepted by the public.[39] Bernard Dobson, who was in his early 40 at the time, described how:

> [T]here was this great hall and there were all these men dancing with each other like at an ordinary dance. I was a bit self-

conscious about it, but I noticed that so many of the men younger than me weren't. They didn't care – bugger anybody who didn't like them. It really went to my head. It was like drinking champagne.[40]

While for many this was not a new experience – bars and clubs had been operating throughout the first half of the twentieth century – for others it represented a radical lifestyle change. The GLF were also unique in holding public dances, which did reflect a change from the hidden bars of the past.

When the GLF moved its meetings and discos to the Middle Earth nightclub in a basement in Kings Street, Covent Garden, this atmosphere prevailed:

You went downstairs and there seemed to be room after room with large pillars supporting the ceiling, it was all underground with no natural light. [...] The feeling was amazing – we were meeting in something like a catacomb, using coded language and symbols, we were anti-authority and had to cope with police interference. It really was like early Christians.[41]

Indeed the early days of the GLF were characterised by the excitement of feeling that they were operating on the edge of society, and where licensing and indecency laws were concerned, on the edge of the law. For many, an optimism for the future and the sense of excitement proved to be their main recollections of the period.[42]

The GLF's social revolution was fuelled by a generation coming of age in a period when counter cultural ideas had gained influence from the 1960s, and it was well aware that it needed to be more than an organisation that ran discos. Indeed, Arthur Marwick postulates a 'long sixties' which runs from 1958 to 1974.[43] During this period, he argues, a 'cultural revolution' took place, in which '[a]ll sections of society (workers, blacks, women, provincials) hitherto ignored became visible.'[44] For homosexuality, 'Gay Liberation shared one of the most salient characteristics of all the protest movements of the sixties: an insistence that it was a genuinely revolutionary movement.'[45] Indeed Sandbrook argues that 'many of the things we associate with the 1960s only gathered momentum in the first half of the following decade'.[46]

Writing in 1969, Roszak claimed that the 'rivalry between young and adult in Western society [...] is uniquely critical':

> For better or for worse, most of what is presently happening that is new, provocative, and engaging in political, education, the arts, social relations (love, courtship, family, community), is the creation either of youth who are profoundly, even fanatically, alienated from the parental generation, or of those who address themselves to the young.[47]

Highlighting the writings of Herbert Marcuse and Norman O. Brown, Allen Ginsberg and Paul Goodman, Roszak recognised the emergence of what he termed a 'counter culture' centred on 'an ambitious agenda for the reappraisal of culture values', in which '[e]verything was called into question: family, work, education, success, urbanism, science, technology, progress'.[48] The gay liberation movement emerged as part of this culture, which combined a desire for social and political change that was taking place throughout the Western world, with a specific challenge to British social norms. The rise of the feminist movement had also provided the opportunity for women to begin to develop social roles for themselves outside of the control of men at the same time, as had been the case with the subscription restrictions of *Arena Three*. With their links to the Black rights movement in America, and later the Irish 'Troops Out' campaign, the GLF became part of a wider youth-led protest movement.[49] For these new lesbians, the feminist movement was a crucial catalyst in their own social development, which would ultimately lead to women leaving the GLF in 1973.[50] But before that, the GLF had often close links to feminist campaigns, with *Time Out*, for example, recording in July 1971 how '[l]ast Friday night more than 150 Women's Lib supporters including members of the Gay Liberation Front staged their tenth, and, to date, most successful sit-in and picket of Wimpy Houses.'[51] Furthermore, the London GLF women's group were invited to, and attended, the National Women's Coordinating Committee in Skegness in October 1971, where they attacked the Maoist sections of the movement for trying to hijack it for their own political ends.[52]

The GLF was aware, however, that despite the emergence of liberalising social changes in Britain, its effects were not being seen uniformly. Aubrey Walter describes how:

> [T]he vast majority of gay men and lesbians hardly ever went to gay pubs, clubs or discos. [...] however inadequate the facilities for gays in London, in the rest of the country the situation was very much worse. Our target had to be the silent majority stuck in their lonely closets, too isolated, afraid, and intimidated to come out.[53]

The GLF philosophy was centred on this assumption that their desire to come out publicly and to live an alternative lifestyle – in contrast to earlier generations – was shared by everyone. There were, however, many men and women who were put off by the brash, public, and radical left-wing agenda of the GLF, and did not want to be associated with it. Moreover, many men and women were happy to stay 'in the closet', especially if 'coming-out' meant aligning themselves with a social and political organisation they had nothing in common with, in particular if they identified themselves as part of conservative Britain. Nevertheless, GLF regional groups were soon established across Britain in an effort to address this problem as they saw it, and were particularly associated with university towns – including Birmingham, Manchester, Bristol, Cardiff, Edinburgh, and Leeds – which contained their main youthful constituency.[54] They also concentrated on various 'consciousness-raising' activities that they hoped would change the way people thought about having a homosexual sexuality:

> During the summer of 1971 and 1972, GLF also organised some very beautiful Gay Days in parks throughout the London

area. There were often two or even three of these each weekend. People would get together, sit around talking, laughing and smiling, holding each other, touching, playing games of various kinds. Straight people would often gather round and watch these crazy gays, and many would themselves join in and have a good time. As with our dances, the political struggle to expand our space went hand in hand with creating a very different social scene for gay people.[55]

These were relaxed occasions, which reflected the GLF desire to provide a space for men and women who were unlikely to attend their dances, and to do so in a public setting. These 'gay days' provided the dual function of attempting to present a public image of homosexuality, as well as the opportunity for men and women to become more comfortable and open. They continued these efforts in the more private surroundings of GLF meetings during consciousness raising 'awareness groups', where GLFers would take drugs and discuss issues and experiences in order to attempt to root out and overcome ingrained prejudices.[56] These events became part of a broader agenda of the GLF to attempt to create a new social world, which would be free of prejudice and discrimination. These idealistic aims reflected the counter cultural and youth-based GLF, and also help to explain the limited support it had from the majority of homosexual men and women in Britain. Indeed, like those put off by this radical agenda, many older people felt similarly deterred by the GLF's youth-dominated constituency, which reflected a generational difference with older homosexual men and women who had lived through a period of greater repression.

Indeed, public visibility remained key to the creation of a gay social and group identity (and sexual identities more broadly), and, for the outside world, street theatre provided another light-hearted way for GLF to try to challenge public perceptions. Sue Winter describes one occasion:

> We all just got on the Central Line tube with some others who were in drag and pretended to be outraged housewives. We did

some same-sex kissing and then held up the placards while the 'housewives' complained about us to the other people on the tube and got them into conversation about us. Then when most people had got off or changed over, we'd repeat it again – round and round the Circle Line. It acted as recruitment, publicity and confrontation. We didn't call the press because it wasn't some publicity stunt, it was meant to reach people and get them into really serious one-to-one conversation, and it worked.[57]

This kind of stunt again reflected the idealistic nature of the GLF, who believed that through direct action they could eventually change the opinions of everyone in society. Nevertheless, since CHE often operated in secret, in members' own houses, any visibility influenced public ideas about homosexuality.

These events operated side-by-side with their own attempts to change the way they lived as part of the creation of a new social world, principally by setting up gay communes for some GLFers to live in.[58] In the article 'Fuck the Family' published in *Come Together*, the members of a commune described life there:

We intended to live closely of course, but as we all soon realised, this was not enough. After about a week we decided to share all our clothes; these were moved into one big cupboard. We pooled our money for food, tampax, toilet rolls and cat food. [...] Perhaps the two most rewarding things that have happened to us are firstly, that we have virtually done away with the concept of monogamy, and secondly, we now feel that we are living our politics.[59]

These communes were only ever home to the hard-core GLFers who believed that they were creating a new way of living, while the majority of others were more interested in the protest element of the organisation. For some, however, this new experiment in living was not as successful as they had hoped. Julie L, who lived at the Faraday Road commune, described how:

I remember I was talking to somebody once and they went 'Duck!' and a record hit the wall just above our heads and we carried on. Then somebody would say, 'Quickly, help, there's someone cut their wrist in the toilet!' and we'd say 'Oh dear, who is it this time?'[60]

Meanwhile, Michael James, of 42 Collville Terrace commune, recalled how '[w]e pooled all our money, it was put in a thirties teapot, but I've subsequently found out a lot of people took out far more than they ever put in'.[61] This petty crime reflected the tip of the iceberg of GLF's association with the law. GLFers had always had a fractious relationship with the police, but when in 1971 Angie Weir was arrested for alleged links between the GLF and the Angry Brigade, which had been responsible for bombings in the United Kingdom, this increased drastically. Carla Toney recalls how:

I left GLF because I was becoming in danger of being arrested for things I didn't do. [...] I was not involved in anything violent, but I was nervous of being accused of it so I disappeared for a while. Our phone was tapped for years after that. I used to pick it up sometimes and go straight through to a police station.[62]

For many GLFers, however, they were guilty of the crimes they were accused of. Power maintains 'that GLF flourished in an atmosphere when many in the counterculture and the left thought that some sort of social Armageddon really was just around the corner and acted accordingly'.[63] Post office and cheque fraud, drug taking and dealing, car theft, burglary, and organised prostitution were all associated with the GLF, in a potent mix of revolutionaries, counter cultural hippies, and gay rights protestors.[64]

It must be stressed that the GLF was always a marginal organisation, and despite its regional groups, remained London-centric. Furthermore, they often provoked negative reactions from other homosexual men and women, particularly older ones who had grown up in a period of stricter legal and social sanction:

What I wasn't so keen on was the Gay Liberation Front. You see, I am a deeply conservative person, with a small c, and I didn't like that kind of brashness and anger. As I say, I'd spent my life saying, 'No, no, no; we're just like everybody else' and here were all these terrible people making out that we were not. It was a completely different generation.[65]

Moreover, black and other ethnic minority men also felt excluded from the GLF, which, despite rebelling against the middle-class nature of homosexuality could still be inherently racist; similarly, women could often feel doubly excluded by their gender and their ethnicity. While the late 1970s and early 1980s would ensure anyone could identify, or be identified as gay, racist exclusions remained, both within the newly created commercial scene, and in the attitudes of individual white gay men and lesbians. Philip Baker remembers during the GLF period, for example, Black gay men would be invited to dinner parties because it became fashionable to invite us. You were patronized. It was quite vicious. [...] You were invited because you were Black and good-looking.[66]

But despite these problems, the legacy of the GLF prevailed. Weeks claims:

The difference the gay liberation movement represented was that an individual process of the construction of self now became a consciously collective process, a new form of agency through a social movement whose aims were radical.[67]

Indeed, while GLFers were partially responsible for the introduction of the word 'gay' in Britain, it was not the sexual category that a majority of the public would recognise today. 'Gay' reflected radicalism, and often left-wing activism. It was partially through their visibility that the term gained the prominence it did, although the willingness of the gay press to use the term (borrowing ideas from America) was equally as important. It gradually became not just a replacement for the term 'homosexuality' – to describe sexual behaviour – but also a label for sexual identity.

The GLF also established the foundations of new gay organisations in Britain, helping create this gay social world, and giving gay men and lesbians a greater sense of identity through them. Aubrey Walters and David Fernbach went on to found Gay Men's Press, which as well as providing a much-needed publishing arm for gay literature, would also have the distinction of publishing *Jenny Lives with Eric and Martin*, the book widely perceived to have instigated the introduction of section 28.[68] The London Lesbian and Gay Switchboard, which was founded in 1974 at the GLF office in Caledonian Road, and received 20,000 calls in its first year, still exists.[69] It continues to work to provide 'an information, support and referral service for lesbians, gay men, bisexual, trans people and anyone who needs to consider issues around their sexuality', and was credited with helping 13 per cent of London teenagers meet 'other homosexuals' in a 1984 survey. In 2007 it won the Queen's Award for Voluntary Service in recognition of its outstanding achievement.[70] GLFers also worked to found *Gay News* in 1972, which became an important link holding disparate elements of a self-identified 'gay community' together, selling 18,000–19,000 copies per issue.[71]

For women, leaving the GLF led them to a close association with the feminist movement in Britain. Juno Jones described the decision to leave as based on 'the attitude of the men, just because they were gay men didn't mean they weren't men and they were basically treating us like shit'.[72] Indeed, Sheila Jeffreys wrote how, Lesbians abandoned the position of little sisters they had occupied in homosexual organisations, separated deliberately from gay men to set up their own organisations, and started to create a specifically lesbian culture.[73]

Many went to the Women's Liberation Movement (WLM), and although initially treated with a degree of trepidation, eventually succeeded in having lesbian matters added to the WLM demands: 'The right to our own self-defined sexuality and to an end to discrimination against lesbians.'[74] Indeed, Jeffreys further claims that,

> Gay men's main concern may be to seek rights on the basis of a sexual identity, but lesbianism was always about more than this. Lesbians as women have to fight the power of men as a

class. Gay men are part of the class of men. The fight for lesbian liberation requires the dismantling of male supremacy and the self-assertive 'sexual identity' of gay men must be dismantled too if it reproduces the characteristic of ruling-class sexuality.[75]

Indeed, this dual oppression was at the heart of ideas surrounding lesbianism and a lesbian identity in this period. For women involved in the GLF, looking for genuinely revolutionary change, gender discrimination needed to be addressed head-on.

For some, this led to an interest in a more radical feminist agenda, initially focused on 'separatism' – living lives completely separate from men. Greenham Common became a case in point in the early 1980s, which Segal described as 'exemplif[ing] the feminist ideal of egalitarian collectivity': No hierarchies or leaders are recognised in Greenham's community of women. Decisions must be taken on a consensus basis and every woman is encouraged to participate. Actions must be non-violent.[76]

Greenham Common Women's Peace Camp emerged in response to the decision by the Ministry of Defence to allow the US army to place nuclear weapons at RAF Greenham Common. Initially a mixed-sex protest camp, it became a women's only protest where the philosophies of nuclear disarmament, feminism, and lesbianism became linked. For many homosexual women, the experience of Greenham (and the feminist movement more generally) was fundamental to their personal development:

> I think the most important thing for me was that I was actually surrounded by a lot of lesbians. [...] We didn't talk about being a lesbian, we talked about things to do with the fact that you were a lesbian.[77]

For others, it presented the opportunity to discover their sexuality:

> Without Greenham I wouldn't be where I am today. I wouldn't have come out as a lesbian at seventeen if I hadn't been to Greenham, and if I wasn't a lesbian I wouldn't be me.'[78]

Providing an image of lesbianism that was principally feminist, the (political) lesbian movement had much more in common with these feminist campaigns and their common experience of discrimination by men. Thus images of female homosexuality, when not associated with the GLF and other homosexual rights organisations, were instead linked to second-wave feminism. Indeed, as these political debates and movements played out, the concept of the 'political lesbian' developed: 'Our definition of a political lesbian is a woman-identified woman who does not fuck men. It does not mean compulsory sexual activity with women.'[79] Indeed, Segal commented that '[s]ome lesbian feminists, not surprisingly, were soon to object to such a desexualised, tactical definition in which their sexuality was seen to elect them as a type of moral vanguard'.[80] Debate over the 'political lesbian', especially from women whose sexual attraction to other women was central to their definition of lesbianism, led to new arguments (dubbed the 'sex wars') about the place of sex – including S & M, and butch/femme roles – in lesbianism. These debates resulted in 'a declining influence of a lesbian feminist perspective within the lesbian community'.[81] By the 1980s, 'the politics and culture of lesbians assimilated to a large extent into that of gay men with the cheerful connivance of some lesbians who saw gay male politics as a useful antidote to lesbian feminism'.[82] Indeed Jeffrey's bemoans this situation, describing lesbians as 'permanent underdogs'.[83]

The 1960s and 1970s represented some of the first emerging public sexual identities projected by homosexual men and women. Social groups were established that helped create new support structures, and as they grew these became more open, and thus more visible. But like the political and media images being projected at the same time, these were often in opposition to each other, and reflected the creation and recreation of identities that were being engaged in throughout the 1960s and 1970s. Initially dominated by older men and women who wanted to project a discreet and respectable image, they were replaced in the public conscience by gay men and women who openly challenged society and projected a youth-based counter cultural identity. Indeed, the success of GLF's visibility can be seen through organisations like the CHE, which

'OSTENTATIOUS BEHAVIOUR AND PUBLIC FLAUNTING'

began using the word 'gay' and becoming more public. As these social changes progressed, institutions and networks developed to support gay men and lesbians, which increasingly gave homosexuality a public face. This public image depended on an individual's interaction with these groups, however, which was more likely in large urban areas where they were more prevalent. While not perfect, in particular in the continued separation of men and women, they represented a huge change from just a decade earlier. But gay men and lesbians remained the victims of prejudice and discrimination, and this greater public visibility was not always welcomed. While it presented the public with a new image of homosexuality, it did not necessarily mean that old prejudices disappeared, but rather that there was now a face, and an identity, to attack. A growing conservative backlash was on the horizon, which would combine with a series of events to escalate a public homophobia that would come to characterise the 1980s.

SECTION 2
A VISIBLE SUBCULTURE

CHAPTER 4

POLITICAL BACKLASH

While many in the GLF, SLRS, and CHE had hoped that the Sexual Offences Act in 1967 marked the start of a permanent liberalising agenda towards homosexuality, it had instead created a growing hostility in law, and saw the failure of homosexual groups to affect any political change. While homosexuality continued to become more visible and part of everyday life from the late 1970s through to the early 1990s, its political image was turning negative. In part this can be explained by the growing hostility towards this more open and visible homosexual identity in Britain, but it also reflects an emerging social and political move to the right – the long 1960s cultural revolution had come to an end in 1974.[1] Where liberal change did occur it appeared to be grudgingly accepted by government rather than positively advocated. The various political images of a homosexual and gay identity – initially respectable, then radical and counter cultural – were being replaced with earlier hostile images of homosexuality, whose use had arguably only ever been suspended by politicians in Parliament to achieve a small measure of law reform. Proselytising, diseased, left-wing, and, once again, paedophile narratives were being created in Parliament and were regularly associated with homosexuality. When the HIV/AIDS epidemic developed within the gay community during the early 1980s, it only served to reinforce an association with disease, while offering new ways to attack homosexuals and homosexuality. With the election of Thatcher's Conservative Government in 1979, further liberalisation of the law appeared to be off the agenda, and instead homosexuality became the subject of calls in Parliament for increased restrictions, which for the first time directly affected lesbians as well. This had the cumulative effect of projecting worsening perceptions of homosexuality onto society, including those young gay men and lesbians growing up as the first post-1967 generation. Rather than ushering in a new period of increased acceptance, 1967 had instead paved the way for a new political hostility and backlash, which would be replicated in negative stereotypes played out with increased vitriol throughout the 1980s.

A decade after the introduction of the Sexual Offences Act, in 1977 Lord Arran attempted to lower the age of consent for male homosexual sex to 18, but was defeated in the Lords by a vote of 146 to 25. In a sign of how Parliament was hardening its attitude towards male homosexuality (lesbians still did not concern them at this stage), the House of Lords voted in favour of Lord Halsbury's amendment: [I]n view of the growth in activities of groups and individuals exploiting male prostitution and its attendant corruption of youth, debasement of morals and spread of venereal disease, this House declines to give the Bill a Second Reading.[2]

Arran had himself stated in his opening speech that 18 was the lowest age he would support: '[T]he buck stops here. I shall never be a party to condoning pederastic practices.'[3] Representing a new majority of conservative opinion in the Lords, Halsbury declared that groups such as the GLF, CHE, SMG, and the Union for Sexual Freedoms in Ireland (USFI) 'ceaselessly demand recognition of the false doctrine that homosexuality is a valid alternative to heterosexuality'.[4] In contrast, Baroness Gaitskell maintained that ' [h]omosexuals do not necessarily go more for young people than heterosexuals. It is exactly the same kind of bad conduct that both can indulge in.'[5] Despite this, the opposing view prevailed. This would prove to be the opening gambit for the emergence of an upper chamber dominated by conservative opinion, and led by Halsbury who would, in the following decade, succeed in his attempt to ban the 'promotion of homosexuality' by local authorities, further cementing the perception that homosexuality was inseparable from paedophilia.

Attempts to extend the provisions of the Sexual Offences Act to the rest of the United Kingdom were also being hampered. In October 1976, the Government had succeeded in passing the Sexual Offences (Scotland) Act, which aimed to 'consolidate certain enactments relating to sexual offences in Scotland'.[6] This reaffirmed the illegality of male homosexual sex, despite reassurances from the Lord Advocate that no prosecutions for homosexual acts between consenting adults over 21 would take place.[7] Conservative MP Malcolm Rifkind and Labour MP Robin Cook were defeated in the Commons in their attempt to have the sections criminalising male homosexual sex removed from the bill.[8] A year later, Lord Boothby – a close friend of Arran – introduced a bill to the Lords that attempted to replicate the provisions of the Sexual Offences Act to Scotland. Indeed, Boothby had been involved in earlier efforts to secure homosexual law reform, writing in his memoirs that '[t]o regard [...] [homosexuals] as wicked and "abnormal", and therefore as criminal and beyond the pale, is not only foolish but insane.'[9] The bill passed relatively quickly from its second reading on 10 May 1977 to its third reading on 7 July, despite opposition from Lord Ferrier who tabled an amendment to defeat the bill, describing it as a 'revolting subject' and asking '[i]s it fair to risk injuring normal people, as this Bill does, in order that the abnormal may be shielded?'[10] However, Robin Cook's attempts to get the bill read in the Commons were subjected to continual delays by Conservative backbenchers, who ensured that it lapsed at the end of the Parliamentary session.[11]

Meanwhile in Northern Ireland, the Standing Advisory Commission on Human Rights had published its 'Report on the law in Northern Ireland relating to divorce and homosexuality' in April 1977.[12] It recommended that 'the law of Northern Ireland should be brought into line with the 1967 Act':

> On the basis of the evidence we have received we feel confident that a majority of people (including those who are concerned

about the long term effect of liberalisation of sexual laws) would consider it appropriate to introduce legislation corresponding with the 1967 Act.[13]

In July, the Secretary of State for Northern Ireland, Roy Mason, confirmed in a memorandum to Cabinet colleagues that he would be accepting their recommendations:

> Traditionally legislation on sensitive issues such as homosexuality and divorce has often been enacted by Private Members Bills with the Government adopting an attitude of benevolent neutrality. In the present circumstances however I think that this would be impractical and I propose instead to introduce the legislation myself by means of Orders in Council.[14]

Since the abolition of the Northern Ireland Parliament in 1973, Orders in Council had been the principle means for introducing legislation only affecting the province. Despite Mason's commitment, it was a further year before the draft order was published in July 1978, and then only after the European Commission of Human Rights had agreed to consider a case by Jeff Dudgeon. Dudgeon had claimed that he was being unfairly discriminated against by the British Government through their failure to extend the provisions of the Sexual Offences Act to Northern Ireland.[15] In this interim period, Ian Paisley, the leader of the Democratic Unionist Party and Free Presbyterian Church, launched his 'Save Ulster from Sodomy Campaign', which gathered 70,000 signatures in opposition to the Government's proposal.[16] On 8 March 1979 the Leader of the Commons, Michael Foot, was unable to give a reason why the Government still had not introduced the order, with Leo Abse describing it as 'the victim of a squalid inter-party discussion'.[17] However, this small amount of momentum was quickly broken. In May the same year, Labour lost the general election and Margaret Thatcher became the new Prime Minister. On 2 July 1979 the new Government confirmed to the Commons that the law would not be changed.[18] Two months earlier, it had already signalled this, telling *The Guardian* that '[t]he subject is a particularly sensitive and controversial one. It is reasonable therefore for the law to be less liberal than in England.'[19]

However, external events would force the new Government's hand. In his submission to the European Court, Dudgeon argued that by criminalising male homosexual sex the Government was breaching Articles 8 and 14 of the European Convention on Human Rights, which provided a right to privacy, and protection from discrimination. In October 1981, in what would prove a landmark judgement for similar cases in Europe, the Court concluded that, the restriction imposed on Mr. Dudgeon under Northern Ireland law, by reason of its breadth and absolute character, is, quite apart from the severity of the possible penalties provided for, disproportionate to the aims sought to be achieved.[20]

They decided by 15 votes to 4 that the British Government breached Article 8, and by 14 votes to 5 that they breached Article 14. Consequently, the new Northern Ireland Secretary, James Prior, introduced an Order of Council in October 1982:

> The Government believe that they must stand by their international obligations and abide by the Court's judgement in this case. It was the will of Parliament that the United Kingdom should be a member of the Council of Europe; and our European connections, which Northern Ireland as a part of the United Kingdom shares, require us to comply with the rulings of the Court in Strasbourg, the authority of which we have freely accepted.[21]

He did not, however, make an argument in favour of the advancement of gay rights in the province, nor signal the development of further rights in the future. Instead, with a vote of 168 to 21, the Government appeared to be grudgingly accepting the authority of the Court.

In contrast, in December 1979, seven months after the Conservative election victory, the Criminal Justice (Scotland) Bill was introduced in the Lords. During the Common's committee stage in July the following year, Robin Cook again attempted to introduce the provisions of the 1967 Act to Scotland:

> We have tabled the clause because we firmly believe that what happens within the privacy of bedrooms is no concern of ours as Members of Parliament [...] It is oppressive and impractical of Parliament to say to that large body of citizens that they must choose between lifelong continence or committing a criminal offence.[22]

Unlike in 1976, this amendment commanded cross-party support, 'bear[ing] the name of hon. Members from all three major parties', although none of these parties had any specific commitments to homosexual equality.[23] Leo Abse also spoke in favour of the amendment, and now condemned the concessions he had had to make in 1967: '[e]ven this miserable new clause – it is a miserable clause – carries over all the compromises and blemishes which I had to put into the 1967 legislation to get it through.'[24] The amendment was passed with a vote of 203 in favour and 80 opposed, which included every Scottish Conservative MP.[25] Once returned to the Lords, the only subsequent amendment was proposed by Lord Fraser who ensured that the privacy constraints of the English and Welsh Act also applied to Scotland.[26] This was accepted by Boothby, who was leading the support in the Lords, to ensure that the bill passed. The apparent ease with which this bill progressed, in comparison to the 1967 Act and previous attempts at legal change in Scotland, suggested that, perhaps, the 1980s might witness the emergence of more liberal political attitudes towards homosexuality in Britain, which would, in turn, reinforce the growing public gay group identity.

Indeed, it appeared that homosexuality was increasingly receiving ambiguous treatment in the political arena, with the liberalising of the laws in Scotland and Northern Ireland going ahead despite Government rhetoric. Moreover, the Labour Party was increasingly finding itself the home of those who felt disenfranchised by the

Conservative Government, and was itself retreating to its core left-wing base.[27] By the 1980s it was clear that the gay rights battle was becoming a battle between Labour and the Conservative Party. Members from both parties were using it as a weapon to beat each other with, despite the presence of Labour members who opposed legal change, and Conservative members who supported it (including the Conservative Group for Homosexual Equality, formed in 1977).[28]

But homophobia was not limited to the two main parties. In 1982 Bob Mellish resigned as the Labour MP for Bermondsey, in an apparent final attack on the left-wing drift of the Labour Party. He had held the seat in its various incarnations since 1945, had a majority of 11,756, and was due to retire at the next general election.[29] The local Labour Party had selected Peter Tatchell as its candidate in 1981, which had unleashed a vicious personal attack against him, both for his radical views, and his sexuality. Tatchell recalls,

> [j]ust before the opening of the 1982 Labour party annual conference in September, Fleet Street stepped up its attacks with a vengeance. It was not coincidental that a barrage of outrageous smears took place at this time. These were designed to cause me and the party maximum embarrassment and sow discord in the ranks of my supporters.[30]

In an attempt to make his sexuality the deciding point of the election, *The Sun* claimed he had visited the San Francisco Gay Olympics, for (in their opinion) allegedly questionable reasons. Under the front page headline, 'Red Pete Went to the Gay Olympics', it claimed that 'the 30-year-old bachelor spent two weeks in the company of homosexuals at the bizarre sports event in San Francisco'.[31] When the by-election was called in 1983, the Liberal Party waded into the controversy in an attempt to pick up the votes of the moderate left and catapult themselves from their third-place position in 1979. While canvassing votes, Liberal party workers wore badges that read 'I've kissed Peter Tatchell', while their candidate,

Simon Hughes, was referred to as the 'straight' choice in election literature, in a veiled reference to sexuality (despite a later acknowledgement that he was bisexual).[32] Indeed, Hughes' decision to go along with this overt homophobia says a lot about what he and others considered acceptable for their politicians and public figures. Private behaviour, while not condoned, could at least be ignored, but those publicly displaying their homosexuality (along gay liberationist lines) could not. Indeed, the campaign's brand of homophobia seemed reserved only for those who were obviously gay.

Hughes subsequently won the by-election with a majority of 9,319, suggesting that many left-wing voters who had previously voted Labour were unhappy with Tatchell's selection, either because of his sexuality or his extreme leftist politics.[33] Although the Liberal Party had committed itself to a policy of homosexual law reform before the 1979 general election, the episode helped reinforce the perception that gay rights, and homosexuality, were associated with the far left in Britain, conjuring up recent memories of the radicalism of the GLF.[34] Tatchell's own radical agenda would come back again in the 1990s with the formation of 'Outrage!' and their various stunts, which suggested that at least some gay men and lesbians preferred the counter cultural politics and identity of the 1970s.

But prejudice was not always uniform in Britain in the early 1980s. In 1984, Chris Smith, the newly-elected Labour MP for Islington and Finsbury, and opposition spokesman on National Heritage, was invited to speak at a rally in Rugby. It had been called to protest against the Conservative council's decision to abandon its policy against discrimination on the grounds of sexuality. Getting up to speak, in a snap decision, Smith announced: '[M]y name is Chris Smith. I'm the Labour MP for Islington South and Finsbury, and I'm gay.'[35] He became the first MP ever to voluntarily come out, and was rewarded with a five-minute standing ovation from the crowd. He held the seat in the 1987 general election, with a slightly increased majority, and went on to serve as the UK's first openly gay Cabinet minister. Unlike Tatchell who was attacked on all sides for his radical left-wing politics, as well as his sexuality, Smith emerged relatively unscathed. This can, in part, be explained by Smith's 'respectable' background: in addition to having a PhD 'on solitude in the 18th century Romantic poetry of William Wordsworth and Samuel Taylor Coleridge', he also represented the moderate centre of Labour, and thus also the moderate gay man, in contrast to the more radical Tatchell.[36] The incident serves as evidence that the later tabloid attacks against homosexuality, which would result in the introduction of section 28, were, first and foremost, a political attack on the radical left of the Labour Party (and the 'unrespectable' gay men and lesbians who worked with them). The following year, in October 1985, the Labour Party conference approved a motion calling for full legal equality for gay men and lesbians by a majority of nearly 600,000. The previous month the Trades Union Congress (TUC) conference had also voted in favour of a gay rights motion.[37] Indeed, the 1983 Labour manifesto had already moved in this direction, claiming,

> [w]e are concerned that homosexuals are unfairly treated. We will take steps to ensure that they are not unfairly discriminated against – especially in employment and in the definition of privacy contained in the 1967 Act – along the lines set out in *Labour's Programme, 1982*.[38]

Labour's 'Programme 1982', had, however, committed the party to equal rights and to lowering the age of consent to 18, whereas this commitment instead simply offered protection from unfair discrimination.[39]

But for the public discourse on homosexuality in the 1980s, it proved to be HIV/AIDS that became one of its defining features. Politically, it provided the expediency with which to formulate rhetoric against homosexuality, develop policies that severely hurt gay men and lesbians, and prevent future liberalisation of the law. Despite the first deaths from AIDS in Britain occurring in 1981 (including Terrence Higgins, who would have the HIV/AIDS charity founded in his memory), it was not until November 1984 that the first written parliamentary question on the subject was tabled in the Commons, and a further four months, in February 1985, that an oral question was asked.[40] In the Lords, the first written question was tabled in February, before the first debate took place in March 1985 under a question put forward by Baroness Cox.[41] In introducing her question, she commented,

> [o]ne of the most regrettable aspects of the development of AIDS has been the tendency in some quarters for those who suffer from the disease to be treated as pariah figures. This may in part be due to ignorance and to fear of infection; it may also be related to the social stigma which many still attach to homosexuality.[42]

The debate proceeded without the homophobia that had accompanied the debates leading to the 1967 Act. Lord Glenarthur, speaking for the Government in reply, said,

> AIDS is a serious and often fatal condition. But I must stress, as others have done, that it is extremely rare; and it is not infectious in the way measles, chickenpox, hepatitis or flu are. [...] the Government believe that the steps we have taken, coupled with widespread international research, are sensible and practical means to control the spread of the disease and deserve the confidence of the public at large.[43]

While the language of Government on HIV/AIDS appeared moderate, the real test came from their actions. For those involved in the fight against AIDS, the Government's efforts were wholly inadequate. Peter Scott, formally of Terrence Higgins Trust, opined: 'The Government acted about four years too late, and many lives were lost, but what did you expect?'[44] Jeffrey Weeks contends that,

> [i]t was only when it seemed that HIV was likely to seep through into the heterosexual community that governments in

the USA and Britain displayed any urgency on the matter. The British government's launch into urgent action at the end of 1986 was precipitated by the US Surgeon-General's report on the danger of a heterosexual epidemic earlier that year. A tailing off in urgency followed in 1989 after reports circulated that rumours of a heterosexual threat were much exaggerated.[45]

Instead, the Government response was characterised by inaction, which, while not actively encouraging the impression that homosexuality was intrinsically associated with AIDS (which was already becoming a source of fear and disgust), nevertheless had the same affect. This left tabloid journalists, and often their broadsheet rivals, to offer their own interpretation of the epidemic. Auberon Waugh of *The Sunday Telegraph* had, for example, begun offering his own solution in January 1985: [N]obody has mentioned what might seem the most obvious way of cutting down this figure [of one million infections by 1990] – by repealing the Sexual Offences Act of 1967 and making sodomy a criminal offence once again.[46]

Since HIV/AIDS was being associated with the commercialised gay scene developing in Britain in the 1980s, the on-going argument between respectability versus unrespectability was again resurfacing. The discreet ideal of homosexuality that was embodied in the 1967 Act was not meant to be part of a growing subculture where an epidemic could spread so quickly. In response, it would prove to be the efforts of some journalists that would direct an increasingly negative public reaction in the vacuum created by Government inaction, and ultimately influence policy. This began with attacks on local Labour parties and their gay rights policies.

After two successive election defeats, which had increased the Conservative majority in the Commons from 43 in 1979 to 144 in 1983, local politics became the only way for Labour to realistically oppose the national Government. London became the centre of this battle, with Ken Livingstone, for example, as leader of the Greater London Council (GLC), publishing the country's unemployment figures on billboards on the roof of County Hall, opposite the Houses of Parliament. His battle with Thatcher, and the Conservatives, would ultimately be lost, when, in 1986, the GLC was abolished. But before that, he was determined to press ahead with a progressive gay rights agenda for London, setting up a Gay Working Party, which produced the document 'Changing the World: A London Charter for Lesbian and Gay Rights'. This was derided in the *Daily Express* in February 1985 in an editorial entitled 'Squander Mania', which accused the GLC and other councils of being 'these Labour-controlled money-shredding machines'.[47] Speaking later about Livingstone, Waheed Alli, who would spearhead gay rights in the House of Lords, said,

> you have to remember in 1996/97 when we started this agenda and this movement in terms of putting gay rights at the heart of the Labour movement, all those people that are there today at the Stonewall dinner, they weren't there. He was.[48]

It appeared that, although committed to gay law reform, Livingstone was keen to use the issue to further attack the Conservative Party, and vice versa. Indeed, this reflected Labour's move to the far left, with the arrival of gay rights campaigners who recognised the opportunity to get involved in the Labour Party at a grass roots level.[49]

At the same time, Labour-controlled borough councils in London were also pursuing a gay rights agenda. In the 1986 local elections, Haringey Labour Party produced a manifesto that had been written by a series of working parties that, due to a change in membership rules allowing the inclusion of ordinary party members, included many sympathetic to the lesbian and gay cause. A key plank of its equality agenda included the commitment to,

> encourage [equal opportunities practice] by establishing a fund for curriculum projects from nursery through to further education, which are specifically designed to be anti-racist, anti-sexist, and to promote positive images of gay men and lesbians, and people with disabilities.[50]

Indeed, in her anthropological study of local conflict in Haringey, Susan Reinhold has suggested that '"new urban left" activists in

London shifted their efforts to the borough councils', which helps explain the inclusion of this commitment in the manifesto.[51] Davina Cooper has highlighted 'the defiance of central government, and the prefiguration of a national socialist administration' as the two key objectives that helped advance a gay rights agenda in some Labour-controlled councils:

> In furtherance of these goals, policies clustered around a range of projects that included decentralization, anti-poverty strategies, solidarity gestures, environmental work and equal opportunity policies (EOPS). Initially, EOPs focused on race and gender. However, the discourse of anti-discrimination was such that its boundaries could never be conclusively sutured. In the 1980s, people with disabilities, the young, and lesbians and gay men slowly began to gain access.[52]

She stressed, however, that these changes were implemented in different ways, and to different degrees depending on the local circumstances of those councils.

Despite a vitriolic campaign against Labour, the party in Haringey won a majority of the seats on the council, and the manifesto was voted in. In order to pursue the policy, the Haringey Lesbian and Gay Unit was created, and opened on 1 April 1986, the day after the GLC was abolished. The unit wrote to all the head teachers in the borough introducing themselves and offering their assistance in implementing the 'positive images' policy, but without consulting the education department of the council. When the letters were received some were handed over to local Conservative parties and the press.[53]

The story then broke, at first locally, and then nationally when it was picked up by the tabloids. The council was branded the 'looney left', and on 7 July *The Sun* published an article entitled 'Bernie kids get lessons in gay love', in reference to the council leader Bernie Grant.[54] Two days later, a *Daily Mail* column described the positive images campaign as a 'left-wing conspiracy to brainwash children into the subversive belief that homosexuality is just as good, natural and desirable as heterosexual activity'.⁵⁵ Facing this tabloid attack, 'the Council leadership froze' and nine months passed before the Council Publicity Coordinating Committee published a leaflet on the policy to clarify the council's position.⁵⁶

Previously in May, a week before the local elections, another popular press attack on Labour-controlled local authorities was brewing. The *Islington Gazette* had broken a story that the Labour-controlled Inner London Education Authority (ILEA) had made available gay-themed books in the classroom.⁵⁷ *Jenny Lives with Eric and Martin* came to define the reason for the introduction of section 28, but with scant reference to the facts. The ILEA had in fact recommended the picture book about a girl living with her father and his male lover (with the consent of her mother), as an aid for teachers, and it had never been seen by a student in London. As with the 'positive images' policy in Haringey, the story was picked up by the national tabloids, happy to use it as an attack on both homosexuality and the Labour Party. *The Sun* ran the story under the front-page headline 'vile book in school' while *Today's* headline 'scandal of gay porn book read in schools' was published three days later.⁵⁸ When the debate reached Parliament the list of books increased to include *The playbook for kids about sex*, and *The Milkman's on his way*, the latter of which had been available in a public library in Haringey, and told the (often graphic) story of a 15-year-old boy engaging in sex with a man who turned out to be a school teacher. These events once again reflected the work of visible gay men and lesbians who were not conforming to the intentions of those who had supported law reform in 1967.

The bill's original intention had been to introduce a new governing structure in schools, but the inclusion of this clause appeared to be precipitated by events taking place in London. Two months later the Department of Education and Science issued a circular that stated that 'there is no place in any school in any circumstances for teaching which advocates homosexual behaviour, which presents it as the "norm", or which encourages homosexual experimentation by pupils'.⁵⁹ Both the Islington and the Haringey stories were used by the media, and the Conservative Party, to reignite the proselytising arguments from debates in the 1960s, which had ultimately led to the age of consent being set at 21. Initially these arguments had been centred on individual homosexuals grooming younger, impressionable men, as parliamentary debates and the Wolfenden Report had reported. During the 1980s, however, the arguments moved on to include an alleged political agenda to encourage children in school to be gay, with, for example, the Conservative Party printing leaflets in Tottenham stating 'you do not want your child educated to be a homosexual or lesbian'.[60] Gay men, and now for the first time lesbians, were being associated with paedophilia, an association that would frustrate future attempts to lower the age of consent in the 1990s and early 2000s, and which would only end in politics after the repeal of section 28.

Four months later in December, Lord Halsbury, the independent hereditary peer who had already made a name for himself in opposition to the liberalising of homosexuality in 1977, introduced a Private Members Bill entitled 'An act to refrain local authorities from promoting homosexuality'.[61] It amended section 2 of the Local Government Act 1986, which dealt with the neutrality of local authorities regarding political publicity:

(1) A local authority shall not –
(2) Promote homosexuality or publish material for the promotion of homosexuality;
(a) Promote the teaching in any maintained school of the acceptability of homosexuality as a pretended family relationship by the publication of such material or otherwise;
(b) Give financial or other assistance to any person for either of the purposes referred to in paragraphs (a) and (b) above.[62]

Claiming that he had 'been warned that the loony Left is hardening up the lesbian camp and that they are becoming increasingly aggressive', Halsbury signalled a return to the homophobia that had been mostly absent from previous debates on AIDS, Scotland, and Northern Ireland.[63] Indeed, in referencing women, who had been absent from political debate in this period – and almost entirely absent from political debate in the past – he signalled his intention to categorise lesbians in what had become traditionally negative male homosexual terms: as dangerous proselytisers, and, by association, paedophiles. Notwithstanding the restrictions imposed on them by virtue of their gender, this would prove to be the first time lesbians would be restricted by law, albeit in 'promotion' and not in personal relations. For many women, this marked the point at which they became politically involved at a personal level. For sexual identity more broadly, it signalled that, while in the past lesbianism had been ignored by the law, Parliament was now prepared to present its own unique image of the militant lesbian working to turn otherwise heterosexual children gay.

Debate proceeded along the tone Halsbury had set. Lord Longford who had, 30 years previously, introduced a motion in favour of the Wolfenden Report, claimed 'homosexuals, in my submission, are handicapped people', while Viscount Ingleby stated that 'homosexuality clearly is not what God intended for human beings'.[64] It appeared that while many politicians had been in favour of some measure of law reform (including Thatcher who had voted in favour of the Sexual Offences Act) in an effort to stop criminalising homosexual men, they did not condone homosexual acts or behaviour. Apparently unwilling to support their local Labour Party councillors in London, only one Labour peer spoke against the bill, pressing the need for 'a greater understanding of the sexual orientation of everyone who lives in our society'.[65]

The bill passed in the Lords and was sent to the Commons where it was championed by the right-wing Conservative MP Jill Knight, who had previously called for the death penalty for terrorists, and made several unsuccessful attempts to limit the time period during which an abortion could be performed.[66] It ultimately failed, however, due to a lack of parliamentary time when Thatcher called the 1987 general election. Knight's involvement set the stage for the issue to become part of the Government's larger moral agenda. Despite the Government's official position opposing the bill, believing it to be unnecessary, Thatcher exploited the furore against

Labour to further her rhetorical attacks on the party at the Conservative Party Conference in 1987, claiming 'children who need to be taught to respect traditional moral values are being taught that they have an inalienable right to be gay'.[67] Likewise the 1987 Conservative Party manifesto, while making no direct reference to either homosexuality or sex education in schools, attacked the controversy surrounding positive images:

> [T]he abuses of left-wing Labour councils have shocked the nation. The Labour Party leadership pretends that this is a problem in only a few London boroughs. The truth is that the far Left control town halls in many of our cities.[68]

In contrast, the Labour manifesto made a brief mention of homosexuality, claiming,

> [w]e believe that positive steps are needed to help women and ethnic minorities get a fair deal, and to attain more democracy in the workplace. In addition, we will take steps to ensure that homosexuals are not discriminated against.[69]

Any further mention of homosexuality in the manifesto might have served to galvanise even more criticism – both from the Conservative Party and the tabloid media – but did little to advance the cause of gay rights, which had been so key to some local Labour Party manifestos.

After the general election, and a third consecutive win for the Conservatives, with a slightly reduced majority of 102, a newly elected MP, David Wilshire, reintroduced Halsbury's original bill as an amendment to the Local Government Bill 1988 during the committee stage. The amendment passed in committee without a vote, since Labour appeared reluctant to defend the councils involved, and at this stage worried about the political cost of supporting gay rights and opposing section 28. The committee also included Labour MP Allan Roberts and the Conservative MP Michael Brown who would both later have their homosexuality exposed, and the Liberal

MP Simon Hughes.[70] Despite public protest, including the largest gay rights marches ever seen in the United Kingdom, it passed relatively quickly through its remaining stages of both Houses, and became law in May 1988.

For many observers, section 28 represented a worrying development in the evolution of a gay social identity in Britain. Although it was claimed to be a law that prevented children from unnecessarily sexualisation, the act only applied to homosexuality, and not heterosexuality. Indeed, witnessing the opposition to the development of the gay movement since the 1970s, precipitated in the warnings of Lord Arran, section 28 was, perhaps, a logical response. Reflecting on what was perceived to be the settlement of 1967, section 28 represented 'a great halt sign: thus far, and no further'.[71] Yet despite calls to the contrary, there were never any attempts to recriminalise male homosexual sex, with even *Gay Times* reassuring its readers by running an article entitled 'Gay Sex will not be outlawed, says PM'; indeed, Thatcher had voted in favour of the Sexual Offences Act in 1967.[72] Instead, the law reaffirmed the Wolfenden strategy of partial decriminalisation and attempted to control what Halsbury, Wilshire, Knight, and others saw as the expansion of homosexuality through tolerance and legitimacy conferred through its greater visibility.

Moreover, this was intrinsically linked to the Conservative Party's own political agenda, when 'in the third term, from 1987 onwards, morality came to the fore'.[73] Their claim to stand for 'Victorian values' was meant to represent a new wave of family-orientated politics, which excluded homosexuality and intended to 'push back the wave of "permissiveness"'. This included changes to the laws on censorship, David Alton's attempt to limit abortion to the first 18 weeks of pregnancy, and section 28.[74] Indeed, this political philosophy extended throughout government, with Thatcher claiming in her memoirs that, all the evidence – statistical and anecdotal – pointed to the breakdown of families as the starting point for a range of social ills of which getting into trouble with the police was only one.[75]

Writing in *The Guardian* at the time, David Wilshire confirmed this link, claiming, 'homosexuality is being promoted at the ratepayers' expense, and the traditional family as we know it is under attack'.[76] But despite these links to the family, Reinhold has noted,

> [i]n parliamentary debate on the subjects of 'positive images' and the 'promotion' of homosexuality, that traversed two years, family was invoked a total of 230 times. It was only positively defined twice. During this period, family was, in effect, only defined in opposition to homosexuality, and so an easy polarity developed.[77]

Indeed, this appeared in part a response to the changing nature of the family more broadly. Divorce, remarriage, step children, and half-brothers and sisters became a more standard feature for many households, destabilising the traditional narrative of family life. The desire of homosexual couples to have families of their own played into this narrative, and provided a useful scapegoat for these changes. Weeks contends that,

> [t]he emergence of non-heterosexual families of choice has to be seen as part of the wider pluralisation of forms of family life that has been a central theme of this world we have made. If there are indeed so many types of family, why should same-sex families be ignored?[78]

In turn, these attacks on homosexuality for the benefit of the heterosexual family, not only intended to exclude gay relationships from the legitimacy conferred by the term (and in doing so tried to keep gay men and lesbians on the margins of society), but also reflected a growing hostility towards homosexuality in the United Kingdom. The British Social Attitudes survey had reported a peak in public homophobia in 1987. When asked about sexual relations between two adults of the same sex, 63.64 per cent of people responded that it was always wrong, up from 49.58 per cent in 1983 when the survey began.[79] Colin Spencer has quoted even higher figures in his study *Homosexuality: a history*, where disapproval of homosexual relationships stood at 74 per cent in 1987, while 86 per cent said lesbians should not be allowed to adopt children, rising to 93 per cent for gay men.[80] Matt Cook notes that homophobic attacks continued into the 1980s, including homophobic murders, for which just 55 per cent were solved, compared with 92 per cent for all murders.[81] Similarly the police seemed more willing than ever to target gay men under the constraints imposed in the Sexual Offences Act. In 1989 prosecutions for indecency, sodomy, soliciting, and procuring added up to 3,065, 'the highest ever number of arrests and prosecutions for consensual sexual activity between men since records began'.[82]

Despite the ultimate success of section 28, the amendment did not pass unopposed. Indeed, three days after the new clause was introduced in committee, the small, but vitally important gay media (which we will see was growing in confidence), issued a rallying call under the headline 'Challenge of the Century':

> The Government is introducing the most serious legal attack on our rights since male homosexuality was outlawed more than 100 years ago. [...] The move was started by a Tory backbencher and has been taken up by the Government with the personal backing of Mrs Thatcher – and even has the qualified support of Labour leaders.[83]

The article went on to encourage readers to take action and offered advice on how to lobby Parliament: '[P]eople are urged to write – now – to their MPs and telephone them at the House on Monday afternoon.'[84] In the following week's edition, the paper celebrated its initial success under the headline 'huge wave of protests against Clause 27': An unprecedented response has come from the lesbian and gay community as an endless stream of lobbies, meetings, petitions and demonstrations are organised to oppose the Bill which threatens to remove many of our rights.[85]

Then, in January 1988, *Gay Times* announced that the Organisation for Lesbian and Gay Action (OLGA) was coordinating a campaign against the clause and asking for donations.[86]

CHE had continued its decline throughout the 1980s, with a remaining '120 campaigners' and '210 loyal supporters' by 1987.[87] Instead, newer, smaller organisations, often grown from the GLF tradition, with single issue membership (for example Gays Against the Nazis and Gay Rights at Work in London), and gay groups within political parties and trade unions, became the only serious gay rights groups in the United Kingdom.[88] In October 1986, the Legislation for Lesbian and Gay Rights Campaign (LLGRC) had been launched to unite all gay organisations in the United Kingdom to produce a gay rights bill. Unlike the CHE's draft Homosexual Law Reform Bill of July 1975, which was thwarted by the Government's decision to set up the Criminal Law Revision Committee, this group failed on its own when its conference on 23 May 1987 'degenerated into chaos and acrimony'.[89] Out of this fractious event, however, OLGA was formed.[90] This group would go on to organise the 'stop the clause campaign', the centrepiece of which was a series of protests and rallies across the country in early 1988, including a march in London attended by 10,000 people, and another in Manchester, which attracted 15,000.[91] It culminated with two women abseiling into the House of Lords from the public gallery on 2 February 1988, the day after the committee stage. While these demonstrations helped mobilise a 'gay community', and its newly threatened lesbian contingent, they ultimately fought using the same tactics that had arguably led to the introduction of the bill: visibility and brashness in the face of a law that was attempting to keep homosexuality, if not hidden, at least more discreet and in line with Wolfenden expectations.

Meanwhile, the arts lobby began a separate campaign against the proposed new law. They feared that without defining what the 'promotion' of homosexuality meant, projects that had relied on the support of local authorities would be prevented from future funding if they were judged to have any gay content. The actor Ian McKellen later commented,

> [t]he Arts Lobby was formed in early 1988 to fight Section 28. [...] We introduced ourselves to the press on Monday,

25 January 1988. Two days later, during a debate on Radio 3, I introduced myself to the public as a gay man.[92]

Under the headline 'Peers may alter gay clause', *The Times* ran the story of the lobby group's formation:

> An attempt is expected to be made by Lord Willis, the playwright, to delete it [section 28] from the Bill entirely next Tuesday when the issue is debated. [...] Public opposition to the proposed ban gained momentum yesterday with a large rally of actors and writers.[93]

Their campaign, while presenting a more measured approach to protest, had little effect. But despite that, the group distinguished themselves from the 'stop the clause campaign', positioning themselves against those activist tactics, and towards a more professional lobbying and campaigning organisation.

Michael Cashman, an actor who had played the gay character Colin in EastEnders and had been involved with the 'stop the clause' movement, was one of the first to recognise the limitations of their campaign. Writing in the September 1998 issue of the Stonewall newsletter, he recalled how,

> one Sunday morning [in 1988] I thought it should not have to be like this. We shouldn't be on marches reacting – we should be using any influence that we have to be proactive, to try to prevent the likes of clause 28 ever happening again. I told Ian [McKellen] of my idea to form a lobby group.[94]

Indeed, McKellen recalls,

> [i]n 1988, 20 women and men, most of whom had been active in gay politics long before the campaign against Section 28, which had brought me into their world, felt that the campaign should continue and broaden its demands. They planned a professional lobby group.[95]

In describing the structure of the new organisation in 1990, their first annual report explained that,

> looking at where that campaign [against section 28] had failed, many lesbians and gay men from different groups (the arts lobby, activist groups, the media) came to similar conclusions. They identified the need for a professional lobbying organisation, unaligned to any particular political party, which could put the arguments for lesbian and gay legal equality and social justice in terms that Parliament could understand.[96]

Unlike the 1970s, which had witnessed the expansion of gay social groups, often at the expense of political ones, these people were convinced of the need to re-engage in the political sphere. To an extent replicating the HLRS, but with the crucial difference that this organisation was set up by gay men and lesbians with the goal of full legal equality, 'Stonewall' was founded in 1989 initially as a not-for-profit company, which 'consciously decided not to compete with other groups for memberships, nor to claim to represent some fictional homogenous community.'[97] Stonewall had highlighted an often unsaid truth, that the diversity of experience among gay men and women meant that it was at best unhelpful, and at worst misleading, to categorise these men and women as an homogenous whole, when their own individual needs could be vastly different. Instead, Stonewall sought legal change, which would affect all these people and, crucially, did so through a respectability that shunned common activist tactics. Stonewall marked the beginning of an emerging new idea surrounding a gay and lesbian social and group identity – an integrationist effort that wanted to be accepted by society, rather than radically alter it.

Indeed, Stonewall was different. It deliberately prevented the factionalism that had drawn apart the GLF by making the organisation a structured company, and avoided any overt social role other than in pursuit of legal reform, which had seriously limited the political wing of the CHE. However, forming only two years after a third election win for the Conservative Party, which through its actions appeared hostile to any future liberalisation of the law, its ability to enact any serious legal change was severely restricted. Despite this, it set out to forge links in Parliament in order to build the network necessary for future legal change:

> We have nurtured an excellent relationship with the Labour Party, including two meetings with its General Secretary and one with its Deputy Leader during 1990. Their policy commitments were reaffirmed at the Annual Conference in October. [...] We are taking a careful and cautious approach to work with the Conservatives, concentrating on developing a good reputation among MPs and on press coverage in relevant media. [...] We also enjoy a friendly relationship with the Conservative Group for Homosexual Equality.[98]

By 1994 the group had secured changes to the Criminal Justice Act 1991, to remove 'discriminatory provisions which would undoubtedly have led to increases in sentences for various victimless, consenting gay sex offences'.[99] It had also secured law reform in Jersey and the Isle of Man, decriminalising male homosexuality, and achieved an '[a]mendment of Paragraph 16 of the draft guidelines to the 1989 Children Act which originally prohibited lesbians and gay men from fostering and adopting'.[100] For many, section 28 had provided the real impetus to work for political change, and replicated the HLRS's desire for middle-class respectability. Moreover, both Ian McKellen and Waheed Alli attributed their own political involvement to section 28, which Alli described as his 'political awakening'.[101] Weeks has suggested that 'by the early 1990s, there were signs that the lesbian and gay community had emerged strengthened rather than weakened by its trials by fire in the 1980s'.[102] Indeed, this forced political engagement encouraged many gay men and lesbians to feel they had a stake in society, which had previously been denied them. It meant that a political gay sexual identity was no longer necessarily predicated on the previously dominant negative stereotypes, which had rarely taken into account the actual lived experience of homosexual men and women who either considered themselves part of the respectable establishment, or else did not identify with the public images of homosexuality. But despite these successes, the big prizes of anti-discrimination legislation, partnership rights, an equal age of consent, and the repeal of section 28, remained long-term objectives, which, despite Ian McKellen's widely published meeting with the new Prime Minister, John Major, in September 1991, were unlikely to be secured under a Conservative Government.

At the same time Cashman, McKellen and others were setting up Stonewall, another gay rights organisation was being formed. Despite OLGA's success in organising the largest gay rights protests ever seen in the United Kingdom, their ultimate failure to prevent section 28 also coincided with a financial crisis for the organisation.[103] When *Capital Gay* reported this, it also reported that a new organisation, OutRage!, had been set up to launch the kind of direct-action stunts that had diminished with the end of the GLF. One of its organisers complained how,

> [w]e get bombarded with homophobia in the press, in the streets, in our everyday lives, and we want to focus the anger people feel about that into positive, direct action. It's a matter of gay rights being human rights, and our demanding we get them.[104]

In the transitory nature of protest politics, OutRage! took over the mantel from OLGA, and continued their activist tactics, which as well as involving abseiling lesbians, had also included the 'invasion' of a BBC news studio the day before section 28 received royal assent. In what was still a relatively socially conservative Britain, the harking back to the 1970s and the GLF tactics reflected the anger and frustration felt by many gay men and lesbians in the wake of section 28. OutRage! wanted to replicate the deliberate visibility and counter cultural nature of the GLF protests in a political climate that had increasingly marginalised gay men and lesbians, and seen little political reform since the early 1970s.

Describing themselves as 'a broad based group of queers committed to radical, non-violent direct action and civil disobedience', they appeared to reject the gay label that the GLF had championed just two decades earlier.[105] Instead, they rebelled against the whole concept of sexual identities, describing themselves as 'queer', to include all non-heterosexual and non-heteronormative lifestyles. They now described themselves as having rejected 'the assimilationist and conformist politics of the mainstream lesbian and gay rights movement', while at the same time fighting for the rights of self-identified gay men and lesbians.[106] As well as protests, with a visible presence at gay pride marches across the country, OutRage! positioned itself in opposition to the establishment, but also Stonewall, which sought to work within it. While Stonewall was taking possession of the image of the 'respectable' homosexual, traditionally deployed by heterosexuals opposing further legal reform, OutRage! was proudly becoming unrespectable in order to challenge a society they wanted to fundamentally change. Indeed, they cultivated a growing hostility towards the lobbying group, and in 1994 OutRage!'s leading light, Peter Tatchell, accused them of 'creeping complacency':

> [D]irect action can achieve things that lobbying can't. Media coverage is vital to make queer issues visible and create pressure for reform. Lobbying MPs and writing letters, although worthwhile, are rarely newsworthy. To get media attention necessitates being provocative. The shock tactics of direct action are more likely to grab the headlines.[107]

These shock tactics included their most famous campaign of 'outing' public figures that they deemed hypocrites for publicly condemning homosexuality, while at the same time privately practising it. On 30 November 1994 they protested outside the Church of England Synod with ten demonstrators each holding up a placard with the name of a bishop they claimed was gay.[108] Despite engaging in such tactics themselves, the tabloids widely condemned the move, but also reprinted the allegations and ensured their exposure and OutRage!'s desired publicity. Two days earlier

OutRage! had released 55 helium-filled condoms during a service at Westminster Cathedral, in protest at the Catholic Church's opposition to contraceptives.[109] In a press release on the 'outing' of the bishops, Peter Tatchell claimed '[t]he Church cannot possible sack so many Bishops. Once they are open about their homosexuality, the Church's ban on gay clergy will be effectively destroyed.'[110] They also wrote to David Hope, the then Bishop of London, and future Archbishop of York, claiming,

> [a]lthough OutRage! has been passed a lot of detailed information about your personal life, which would have enabled us to confidently name you at Synod on 30 November, we chose not to do so.

> The reason is this: we believe that you are, or can be, a person of honesty and courage. You have the potential to play a very special role, both morally and historically. It is our sincere hope that you will find the inner strength and conviction to realize the importance of voluntarily coming out as gay and of speaking out in defence of lesbian and gay human rights.[111]

Hope, at a hastily arranged press conference, interpreted this letter as a threat and in response to a question, described his sexuality as 'a grey area', although he did not resign.[112]

OutRage! justified their tactics as an essential part of their battle for change. According to Peter Tatchell,

> [n]o movement for social equality has ever succeeded without rocking the boat and disrupting the status quo. The direct action tactics of the Chartists, Suffragettes and the Black civil rights movement were all condemned in their time as being 'extremist', and 'alienating'. Yet their confrontational methods were vital to raise public awareness, provoke debate, and pressure the authorities for social reform. They would never have won justice if they had confined themselves to lobbying parliament and writing letters to MPs. It was precisely their

noisy, rebellious and troublesome direct action which forced society to sit up and take notice.[113]

Interestingly, he failed to mention the GLF in this list of direct-action groups, perhaps because they were still remembered as being too confrontational, and without any tangible political success. In an article in *Capital Gay* on 9 December, OutRage!'s Fernando Guasch simply claimed '[w]e retain the right to do this if someone is fucking with our community'.[114]

OutRage! is evidence that despite a move towards greater integration, with Stonewall encouraging a tolerant political climate for homosexuality, there was still a significant group of people who did not want to integrate, but rather wanted to change society to accommodate them. OutRage! is now, according to the organisation, the 'longest surviving queer rights action group' in the world.[115] It is a reminder that despite the changes that took place in relation to homosexuality in Britain, the idea of a homogenous community, or indeed identity, fails to take these differences into account. Their seeming rejection of the labels 'gay' and 'lesbian', and their re-appropriation of 'queer', is evidence that, for them, like the GLF, the campaign is not over until the need for sexual labels has disappeared.

The political situation that emerged after the gay liberation period in Britain reflected a backlash against homosexuality and the rise of a negative gay identity in the political and legal world. The political arena traded stereotypes of a gay identity predicated on unnatural sex, radical left-wing ideology, disease, predatory and proselytising behaviour, and, most damagingly, a paedophile agenda. But despite this, gay men and lesbians survived this peak in hostility in British society, and emerged in a stronger position than ever before to campaign for their political rights. In attempting to silence the growing visibility of gay men and lesbians, section 28 had instead encouraged them to pursue a modernised rights agenda, which helped to further integrate homosexuality into ordinary British life, and in doing so challenge what it meant to be a gay man or lesbian living in the United Kingdom. For the first time they would be the principle actors in the development of their political identity, and in doing so shape a legal framework that reflected that a gay political identity was, essentially, the same as a heterosexual one – based on equal and not greater rights, the family, and mainstream acceptance. This was not, however, and indeed never could be, the accepted identity of all non-heterosexual people in Britain, as OutRage! was only too keen to point out.

CHAPTER 5

CONFLICTING PUBLIC IMAGES

The emergence of a visible subculture in the United Kingdom from the late 1970s onwards produced contrasting images of homosexuality in the media. While gay publications continued to grow, becoming ever more confident in exactly what it meant to be gay or lesbian in Britain – even in the face of the HIV/AIDS epidemic – the press turned increasingly negative. Damaging stereotypes, particularly in response to HIV/AIDS (but also the growing visibility of homosexuality), became the norm, while emotive language and condemnation went hand-in-hand with news reporting. In contrast, film and television representations of homosexuality were moving away from earlier, guilt and depressed-ridden clichés of the gay liberation period and were beginning to explore a more diverse gay life, although not always without controversy. Thus gay publications, the mainstream media, and television and film reflected what was happening in 1980s Britain – where the concept of a gay social and group identity, commercialised scene, and community networks continued to grow, despite the increasing homophobia in society.

From the early 1970s through to the end of the 1980s, gay publications in Britain appeared preoccupied with creating, building, and reflecting a growing gay and lesbian subculture. The United Kingdom was still a relatively isolated place for the majority of gay men and lesbians not living in metropolitan areas. Gay publications became concerned with assessing the condition of an increasingly visible subculture – predicated on commercialism – that replaced an earlier gay liberation period predicated on the desire for political, cultural, and social change. While a gay social identity was worn more openly, it inevitably became focused on the urban social scene – and subsequently HIV/AIDS – while ignoring both self-identified gay men and lesbians living more isolated lives, and other homosexual men and women who could not or would not adopt a gay social identity.

Gay News was the first of this new generation of newspapers and magazines, marking a turning point in the history of gay publications in Britain. Published fortnightly, it became 'the world's largest circulation newspaper for homosexuals', and although initially run as a collective – like *Come Together* before it – claiming to have 'no editor, art director, sales manager or whatever', it quickly became a more professional newspaper reporting on news that directly affected gay men and lesbians.[1] In its first issue editorial, *Gay News* explained what it hoped to achieve:

> We feel that, despite legal reform and a certain relaxation in people's attitudes to sexuality, that nothing much has really changed. It is clear that many gay people are still extremely isolated, many still live restricted lives. We feel that a medium which could help us all to know what we were all doing, which could put us in contact, and be open evidence of our existence and our rights for the rest of the people to see, could help start the beginning of the end of the present situation.[2]

While *Arena Three*, *Come Together*, and others included articles examining the nature of a gay identity, *Gay News* differed in that it also focused on presenting news and articles about gay life in a deliberately news-focused way. While always taking a political line – that gay men and lesbians needed to be treated with respect and deserved equality under the law – it gradually moved away from the style of earlier editions that had had more in common with *Come Together* in, for example, attacking the 'rad fems' as 'oppressive chauvinist men'.[3]

Indeed, the paper served as a voice for gay men and lesbians, offering a mixture of news stories about the state of the law concerning homosexuality, stories about the social scene across the country, interviews with well-known public figures, and a personal advertisement section entitled 'Love Knoweth No Laws'. Reflecting the changes taking place in relation to homosexuality in the United Kingdom at the time, the magazine appeared keen to report on issues of visibility and progressive changes taking place, as well as negative stories that often dominated. In further evidence of the adoption of clearly understood sexual identities in Britain, for example, it reported on the BBC's decision to 'drop queer words':

> A top-level decision has been taken at Broadcasting House to forbid the use of words such as 'queer, poof, pansy and dyke' to describe gay people. The ruling applies to current affairs and talk programmes, where staff have instructions to use the words 'gay' and 'homosexual' in future.[4]

Likewise, it charted the emergence of a gay social scene, commenting on the opening of *Heaven* nightclub: 'A matter of £300,000 later, the old Global Village in Charing Cross just ain't the same. London's gay disco world has at last reached Heaven.'[5] But it would also report on issues that could have a negative effect on its readership. Under the title 'World Health Organisation', the paper noted with concern that,

> [i]n its most recent catalogue of illnesses, brought out last year, homosexuality is still included. The next review of this classification is not due out until about 1989. Over the next five or six years member countries will have to apply pressure on the WHO to delete homosexuality from its list.[6]

Its characteristic optimism, that change could be achieved, reflected its own discourse on homosexuality, focused on achieving greater visibility and not returning to its recent hidden past.

Written by men and women, the newspaper was careful to ensure too that lesbian issues were dealt with fairly – reflecting the growing interaction of lesbians and gay men in this emerging subculture. When writing about lesbians, *Gay News* invariably combined both the feminist and the gay rights campaigns in order to highlight the dual oppression that they believed women suffered. Thus many articles on female homosexuality often included reference to political campaigns, women's rights, and custody arrangements, among others, which affected women regardless of their sexuality. In contrast, articles on male homosexuality often centred on further legal reform, as well as the social scene for gay men and lesbians. In a section entitled 'the visible lesbian', for example, the paper reported,

> [t]wo lesbian custody groups in London and Sheffield have organized a lesbian custody conference [...] on the weekend of January 29 and 30. [...] One of the reasons for calling the conference is that 'as lesbians with children we may be in constant danger of having our children taken away by men and heterosexual institutions that see it as too threatening to have children growing up outside their control'.[7]

Gay News charted and contributed to the rise of a visible subculture of gay men and lesbians in Britain from its inception. While this was not universal, it was growing, and it made a gay identity much clearer in the minds of its readers based all over the United Kingdom – predicated on a commonality of problems, experiences, and desire for change. *Gay News* ran until 1983 when it ceased publication, was sold on and became *New Gay News*. By the time *New Gay News* was published, however, its readership had transferred to Alex McKenna's re-launched *Him* Monthly magazine, which was soon renamed *Gay Times*.[8]

The London-based *Capital Gay* followed in the tradition set by *Gay News* in reporting news stories as they affected gay men and lesbians. Initially operating as 'a weekly newspaper published by gay men' when it launched in 1982, it became a newspaper for both men and women, eventually amending the masthead to read 'for lesbians and gay men' in the 1990s. Maintaining a left-leaning political tradition, the paper notably challenged its readers to think beyond what they saw as the oppression in society in creating their own gay social identity:

> Most of us can learn to value ourselves in heterosexual terms; we're happy to work 45 hours a week helping our firm to sell more plastic cheese-graters, confident enough to complain to the gas board, happy to talk about and spend money on food, clothes, music, holidays. But when it comes to our gayness, we remain deeply self-oppressed. We don't value ourselves enough to take three hours off work to sort out a personal problem, don't trust our own feelings enough to take a decision, don't dare confront anyone's disapproval on our own. We need an 'expert' to give us permission to say what we want; we demand an expert who will wave a magic wand and make everything all right.[9]

Indeed, Eric Presland even encouraged gay men and lesbians to look beyond the emerging consumerist culture of gay life:

> All over London, little groups are having a good time, becoming friends, finding lovers, in scores of organised or informal groups. Gay vegetarians are cooking meals for each other, gay music lovers are playing for each other, outdoor types are going for walks or swims with each other, artists are sketching each other, gay smokers are getting stoned together, and so on.
>
> The most you'll ever see is a bald paragraph advertising an event, and mostly not even that; but together they add up to hundreds and hundreds of people who've found out that you can be gay without going to a disco.[10]

Witnessing the growth of the gay social scene around it (as we shall see), it tried to challenge the consumerism with which a gay group identity was becoming associated.

But it was perhaps its politics that defined *Capital Gay*. Handing over a section of the newspaper to CND cost-free, for example, it established the impression that being gay inevitably meant following an often radical left agenda:

> It's no good gays pretending that it's all just 'politics' happening somewhere out there. Nuclear weapons are starting to breed as fast as heterosexuals. If our planet is to survive, people must resist them wherever they happen to be – America, Russia, Israel, Pakistan or Britain. A mere electronic accident could now spell the end of the world as we know it. America's defence computer gives an average of two false alarms per week. Our gay community and everything and everyone we care about can be wiped out in a split-second flash of supernova intensity.[11]

As with the wider political scene, this inevitably had the dual effect of associating a gay group identity with leftist politics, while at the same time alienating other homosexual men and women who could not adopt an identity that included a political philosophy often the antithesis of their own.

The paper regularly reported on the growing homophobic backlash of the 1980s, which operated in tandem with the growing subculture. Under the title 'Four wasted years', for example, the paper lambasted the Government for its response to AIDS: 'It is time the Department of Health answered charges of gross negligence over its handling of Aids. But ministers still won't acknowledge, or maybe do not yet realise, the extent of their failure.'[12] Moreover, in what would later become part of a national campaign against section 28, *Capital Gay* became the first to challenge the local Conservative Party in Haringey for their attack on the 'positive images' policy of the council. Under a front-page headline 'Hands off Haringey', the paper described the Tottenham Conservative Association's claim that '[t]he Lesbian and Gay Unit in Haringey is more of a threat to family life than the bombs and guns of Nazi Germany', as an 'outrageous slur'.[13] Two years later, when the controversy had resulted in the introduction of section 28 in Parliament, the paper became the mouthpiece for the 'Stop the Clause' campaign, providing, for example, a cut-out petition for readers to canvas support against the section.[14]

Capital Gay ran until 1995, regularly challenging the Government over gay rights, maintaining its place as an integral part of the increasingly visible gay subculture in Britain. In contrast to earlier magazines and newspapers that had been part of an emerging discourse on gay identity, *Capital Gay* quickly became an established part of that subculture, encouraging a leftist political identity for gay men and lesbians, and ensuring that it remained visible throughout 1980s Britain.

In contrast to this move towards news, *HIM exclusive* had launched in October 1974, as 'a largely pictorial soft-porn publication for gay men'.[15] Indeed, the majority of the magazine was devoted to pictures of naked men, but could also include interviews, explicit fiction, features, classified and personal advertisements. The magazine represented a thriving market for soft-core porn among gay men, which also included other publications such as *Zipper*, *Mister*, and *Vulcan*. *HIM monthly* (from 1976 to 1982) gradually became less explicit, however, until nudes were the exception rather than the rule, being replaced with more articles on gay life. Then, in 1982, in response to obscenity trials against explicit publications, *HIM* launched a new format, which once again centred on news articles as well as features. As *HIM*, the magazine became gradually more interested in reflecting gay culture, although it would have remained a footnote in the history of gay publications in Britain if it were not for its further relaunch as *Gay Times*, coming as it did when *Gay News* ceased publication.

Gay Times attempted to combine all the earlier threads that had defined gay journalism. With a basis on news, but also an exploration of a social life as it affected gay men, and the challenges of defining a person as gay, it ran articles that included the negative effects of the emerging gay social scene:

> Since 1967, England's capital has evolved a thriving, ever-expanding male gay subculture. So what's the problem? Well, I live roughly 25 miles away in a largish new town called

Basildon. Here, it's virtually as if 1967 and Gay Liberation never happened. The town has no gay pub, no gay group, no gay life at all that I can discover. [...] We are now creating bigger and bigger ghettoes, and the London gay scene is becoming the biggest of them all. [...] But this creates a vacuum behind it. Instead of building up a small, but supportive, local community, smaller towns become gay deserts where the central cottage supplies the only oasis.[16]

Indeed, the fragility of the gay commercial scene outside of these 'ghettos' was an important feature of life in 1980s Britain. Recognising this, *Gay Times* tried to expand its readership beyond metropolitan areas by addressing this problem, while also highlighting the issue in the hope of affecting change.

Like *Capital Gay* – although less explicitly left-wing – *Gay Times* realised the role it could play in challenging the Government over policies as they affected gay men. As HIV/AIDS became more prevalent, *Gay Times* began openly criticising the inaction of Government and its reluctance to engage in a frank debate about sex:

These [Government] campaigns emphasise what you can't do rather than what you can do. They too confuse public morality with public health, though, as Tony Whitehead [former chair of the Terrence Higgins Trust] wrote, from a health point of view it makes not a scrap of difference whether you take a vow of celibacy or sit in a circle on a butt plug and wank with your friends. The government adverts still look like an Annual Report from the City Pages, or a notice from the DHSS about a Benefit which they don't want you to claim.[17]

Gay Times became a vital voice in the fight against HIV/AIDS for gay men, although this inevitably reinforced the association between gay men and HIV throughout the 1980s, in particular among men just becoming aware of their own sexuality. Indeed, gay newspapers and magazines were the first publications in Britain to report on the HIV/AIDS crisis from America, recognising the danger it posed, and continuing a tradition of reporting on all aspects of gay life, including internationally, which could then be used to inform ideas about homosexuality in the United Kingdom.

Moreover, after taking a similar position as *Capital Gay* in opposing the introduction of section 28, John Marshall, writing under the headline 'Flaunting it – the challenge of the 1990s in *Gay Times*, offered his own interpretation of the 1980s backlash against the increasingly visible gay subculture and individual gay men and lesbians:

> The recent backlash against homosexuality – which has clearly been gathering strength in the last few years – has involved an attempt to re-assert the basic legal principles of 1967. Most centrally, it has involved an attempt to re-assert the crucial distinction between public morality (which is still anti-gay) and private morality (which is still willing to permit homosexuality but only within strictly defined limits).
>
> Legislators and moralists have become deeply disturbed that gay men and lesbians have tried to blur this public/private distinction. [...] What recent events seem to demonstrate is that little real progress can be made unless we confront the thorny old problem of gay law reform. We need a campaign which concentrates not merely on Clause 28 but on the whole gamut of legal constraints in the '67 Act.[18]

He concluded by arguing for 'a political strategy in the 1990s which fully acknowledges the complex and fluid nature of human sexuality'.[19] This reflected the difficulty a gay magazine faced in attempting to create a product that appealed to a disparate group of readers with often only their sexuality in common. While on the surface it might appear that the magazine was only appealing to one gay demographic – principally city-dwellers with disposable incomes to spend in clubs and bars – it was also attempting to provide a voice for other elements of a disparate 'gay community', which would become more apparent throughout the 1990s and a greater move towards integrating into 'normal' British life. This emerging subculture period, where a gay group identity became more defined, and a social identity more openly worn, was clearly replicated in publications from this period. Though promoting a commercialised culture, they also sought to challenge ideas about identity, while at the same time protesting against society's own homophobia through political campaigns and a call for readers to resolve their own self-oppression.

In contrast to the gay media's attempts at tempering a growing hostility towards homosexuality in the United Kingdom in the 1980s, the press began what would became an almost universal attack on this growing subculture – initially through the outbreak of HIV/AIDS, but later through a tabloid campaign against the 'promotion' of homosexuality.

When HIV/AIDS began to be reported in the British press in the early 1980s, associations were almost immediately made with homosexuality – justified by its initial appearance in gay men. Under the title 'Mystery new killer disease', for example, *The Times* published a report on what was known so far:

> [C]onfronted with a disease which has now spread to 24 American states and eight other countries, doctors started to build up a profile of average patients. They are white, male homosexuals aged 25 to 44, regular users of an array of illicit drugs and highly active sexually with an extraordinary average of several hundred sex partners each, suggesting an involvement with male prostitution.[20]

By the following year, however, the epidemic had been renamed the 'gay plague' and articles became subjective, emotive, and condemning. *The Sun* initially justified this language by claiming journalistic objectivity: 'The disease – nicknamed the Gay Plague because it first appeared among homosexuals – breaks down the body's natural defence system and leaves it vulnerable to fatal infection.'[21] The following month, however, *The Sun* published the story 'Gay bug kills gran': 'A granny has died from the mystery blood plague, AIDS – which normally strikes gay men and drug addicts', beginning an association between homosexuality and other deviant acts.[22]

Throughout the following decade, HIV/AIDS became a staple of tabloid journalism. Derek Jameson – a former tabloid editor – maintained, in a Radio Four news programme in 1994, that 'the essential ingredients of a successful tabloid newspaper are the four S's: sex, sensation, scandal and sport'.[23] Since homosexuality had almost always been discussed in regard to sexual connotations, and tabloid journalism in the 1980s was inherently homophobic, the attack was entirely consistent with their agenda. Indeed, *The Sunday People* appeared to revel in reporting on the personal tragedies of the disease, with, for example, an article entitled 'What the gay plague did to handsome Kenny' writing, 'is this the wrath of God, asks Bible thumpers?'.[24] The *Daily Mirror*, meanwhile, carried the emotive story 'Boys' jail chaplain dies of AIDS': 'A prison chaplain who had 200 boys in his care has died of AIDS, the "gay plague"', suggesting, however casually, that the chaplain was homosexual, and that his contact with boys was inappropriate.[25] While tabloids (both left and right) were often the worst offenders, HIV/AIDS gave the more serious broadsheets an opportunity to replicate this homophobic agenda. Under the title 'AIDS: the price of promiscuity?' *The Daily Telegraph* 'sympathetically quoted the view that AIDS might be "a supernatural gesture by a disapproving almighty"'.[26] In an editorial in *The Times*, it was suggested that AIDS was a punishment:

> The infection's origins and means of propagation excites repugnance, moral and physical, at promiscuous male homosexuality. [...] Many members of the public are tempted to see in AIDS some sort of retribution for a questionable style of life.[27]

Interestingly, *The Times* seemed unwilling to make this their own definitive statement, and instead attributed it to public opinion. There are countless other examples; indeed, Terry Sanderson, in his study of the media, condemned the British press and their reporting of HIV/AIDS, describing their negative reporting as 'a conscious choice to sensationalize – and thereby trivialize – an enormous tragedy'.[28] Indeed, these stories were hugely influential. According to Richard Dyer,

> [h]ow a group is represented, presented over again in cultural forms, how an image of a member of a group is taken as representative of that group, how that group is represented in the sense of spoken for and on behalf of (whether they represent, speak for themselves or not), these all have to do with how members of groups see themselves and other like themselves, how they see their place in society. [...] Equally re-presentation, representativeness, representing have to do also with how others see members of a group and their place and rights, other who have the power to affect that place and those rights. How we are seen determines in part how we are treated; how we treat others is based on how we see them; such seeing comes from representation.[29]

For the newspaper industry in 1980s Britain, this representation was deliberately negative, and established as fact, for many, the association between homosexuality and this 'killer disease'. That gay men were considered responsible for the development and spread of the disease – according to these newspapers – only reinforced negative ideas such as blame and punishment for crimes against nature. Indeed, Derek Jameson, in the mid-1990s stated:

> Fleet Street takes the view that homosexuality is abnormal, unnatural, a bit evil because it's wrong. [...] The editors are not going to come out and say 'Be gay, it's wonderful and isn't it great?' They are going to say that gays are not normal, natural people.[30]

Frank Pearce has highlighted how these newspaper articles encouraged readers to make a morality judgement on homosexuality, and in the process demonise gay men and lesbians.[31] This served to reinforce a negative image of gay men and lesbians – associating them with death, disease, and promiscuity. Moreover, James Dearing has suggested that,

> [s]uccessful media advocacy essentially puts a specific problem, framed in a certain way, on the media agenda. Exposure through the mass media allows a social problem to be transformed into a public issue.[32]

By making homosexuality a social problem and a public issue, newspapers gave licence for old prejudices to resurface, and for a new wave of homophobia to develop.

For the press, then, homosexuality in 1980s Britain became intricately linked to HIV/AIDS. This association lasted throughout the 1990s, and even endures today. Newspaper reporting of the epidemic was crucial to the development of this association, and their decision to include judgement claims – religious or otherwise – condemned a permissive homosexual lifestyle that was not necessarily part of the majority of homosexual men or women's lives. Furthermore, by referencing homosexuality with the creation of a disease, these articles re-established a link with the medicalisation of homosexuality and reinforced the unnaturalness of same-sex sexuality. These articles were deliberately negative and thus fostered a negative attitude towards, and about, homosexuality – for the heterosexual majority, and for the homosexual, whether or not they chose to define themselves by their sexuality. While this was primarily an association with male homosexuality, women were also included in this identity, which would be further demonised through the reporting of the teaching of homosexuality in schools.

In contrast to the HIV/AIDS epidemic – where newspapers merely reported on the events, albeit in a negative and inflammatory way – the perceived threat of the teaching of homosexuality in schools, and the subsequent section 28, was born out of a direct campaign of tabloid pressure. As we have seen, these newspapers began their interest in homosexuality and education when they repeated the story that gay-themed books (in particular *Jenny Lives with Eric and Martin*) had been made available for use in the classroom.[33] *The Sun*'s front-page headline 'vile book in school', and *Today's* 'scandal of gay porn book read in schools' set the standard for the morality judgement that ensued.[34] Indeed, two months later when *The Sun* and the *Daily Mail* 'exposed' Haringey's positive images policy variously as 'Bernie kids get lessons in gay love', and a 'left-wing conspiracy to brainwash', they began a media frenzy that would involve the use of these articles as quasi-official fact by MPs in Parliament.[35]

Indeed, in his opening speech in the Lords in December 1986, introducing his bill, Halsbury claimed to have 'been warned that the loony Left is hardening up the lesbian camp'.[36] This language was taken directly from *The Sun*'s article. Following him, Lord Alloway described some of policies concerning gay men and lesbians:

> As your Lordships know from the papers, the Association of London Authorities, some ten London local authorities and three elsewhere, all in densely-populated area, in fact implement these policies.[37]

Lady Saltoun went on to claim 'the third leader in today's issue of *The Times* puts it [her argument] in a nutshell',[38] while Lord Bellwin commented:

> I too will desist from a whole series of quotations from the many publications I have seen. The list is long indeed. But I should like to refer to just two which I think are very apposite. One comes from the London *Evening Standard* of 10th December.[39]

He went on to reference an article on a Catholic priest who had vowed to go on hunger strike until Haringey Council reversed its positive images policy (something he later gave up). Furthermore, his comment that he would try not to quote from a series of publications highlights just how prevalent it was during this debate.

These articles were repeatedly quoted as fact without regard to the motives of the writers, editors, or the newspapers themselves. The articles, moreover, appeared to be the driving force behind these speakers. When the bill arrived in the Commons, the process continued. The Minister for Local Government, Rhodes Boyson, himself a former teacher, quoted a letter in *The Daily Telegraph* as representative of public opinion:

> I draw the following to the attention of hon. Members. The letter in the *Daily Telegraph* says: 'The book [an ILEA publication distributed to schools dealing with equality of opportunity] notes with approval the removal of a section on romance from a school library'. There is no romance in these sad days, according to how some people would like us to live. ILEA replaced the section on romance 'with a section on "relationships" – "encompassing lesbian and gay relationships, heterosexual relationships and family relationships." Organisations listed for schools to contact include a "Gay Teachers Group".'[40]

This was to be a formula repeated in subsequent debates on the introduction of section 28 as the self-perpetuating nature of the 'facts' these newspapers provided gained ever-greater legitimacy.[41] Moreover, since these articles invariably portrayed a devious and predatory group of gay men and lesbians, the identities mentioned in Parliament often replicated them.

When Wilshire reintroduced the wording of the original bill as part of the Local Government Bill in 1987, it again provided a forum in both Houses of Parliament for members to either quote or reference tabloid newspapers as legitimate sources of information. Thus in detailing his reasons for introducing the clause in committee, Wilshire said: '[I]f we believe what the newspapers say, we realise that millions of pounds are involved.' He did, however, point out that he had 'deliberately not introduced newspaper cuttings' into the dossier he had prepared, in order, perhaps, to give his claims legitimacy, in contrast to Halsbury, who had relied almost exclusively on newspaper articles.[42]

Ken Livingstone (now an outspoken MP after Thatcher abolished the Greater London Council, of which he was leader) was one of many opposition MPs to accuse supporters of the clause of basing their decisions on tabloid reports:

> Conservative members are responding to a wave of hysteria and bigotry that has been whipped up by the popular press. It has been absolutely disgraceful. Some people have the misfortune to believe what they read in the *Daily Express, the Daily Mail* and *The Sun*. They have come to accept that in some areas children are being taught how to be lesbians. [...] [T]hat pernicious lie has bitten deep into the popular conscience.[43]

Despite the criticism of several MPs and Lords on the legitimacy of these facts, they continued to be quoted throughout the debate. Livingstone went on to say:

> I am tired of debating with Conservative Members in radio and television studios and public meetings. When I ask them for examples of promotion, they always say that they have left them in the pile at home, or that they saw them in the paper. That is not an adequate basis for legislation. One does not legislate on the basis of gossip such as that.[44]

Indeed, the most famous of these, which became synonymous with positive images and section 28, was *The Sun*'s front-page article 'vile book in school'.[45] The story concerned *Jenny Lives with Eric and Martin*, and (most importantly for a newspaper title always reliant on imagery) that it was a picture book with photos of the family together. The nature of how this story was reported resulted in complaints to the Press Council. In their review, the council upheld the complaints they had received:

> According to the evidence before the Press Council the book was held by ILEA at a teachers centre, not in a school and was not available to pupils. The authority has said it should only be used with older pupils in particular and exceptional circumstances after their parents had been consulted. Under the

main headline: 'Vile book in schools' *The Sun* said it was being made available to junior schools by education officials and in another headline reported 'Pupils see picture of gay lovers'. The paper itself chose to reproduce across four columns a picture captioned 'Perverted [...] a page from the book showing Jenny in bed with her gay dad and his naked lover', thereby giving the picture and its caption far wider dissemination than otherwise it might have had. [...] the misleading but clear implications of the headlines was that the book was then in schools and had been seen by children there. The complaint against *The Sun* is upheld.[46]

The relative unaccountability of tabloid journalism, however, meant that the original story entered the public arena, by which time the Press Council's review was too late. In particular, the stories had already directly influenced Parliament, and set the agenda for the introduction of section 28.

In contrast to the earlier period of newspaper reporting, the 1980s witnessed the emergence of a media agenda that deliberately targeted homosexuality – and gay men and lesbians specifically – in a morality campaign. Indeed, it appeared that the media and the political arena remained intimately linked. The earlier newspaper articles urging the Government to decriminalise male homosexual sex had in part been responsible for the subsequent legal change. Similarly, the moral agenda in the media was being replicated in Parliament, feeding off each other in their attacks on homosexuality. Initially centred on HIV/AIDS, this morality campaign came to incorporate the teaching of homosexuality in schools, and its categorical unacceptability. The subtext to this was that gay men and lesbians were guilty of proselytising children, or even grooming them for sex, so again, homosexuality was being associated with paedophilia. The power of the media – culminating in its ability to influence the introduction of a new law – clearly extended to influence public opinions, and what it meant to define oneself as gay or lesbian in 1980s Britain. Sick, immoral, dangerous, promiscuous, predatory, diseased, and a threat to children – by either 'turning' them gay, or by raping them – were the messages sent out by tabloid newspapers at various points throughout the 1980s. While their broadsheet rivals had – with the exception of *The Daily Telegraph* – kept out of the teaching debate, the same could not be said of their reaction to HIV/AIDS. This period was thus hugely influential in the creation and recreation of gay and lesbian identities in affirming and creating stereotypes. It would prove to be another decade at least before the negative stereotypes, introduced in the 1980s, would finally be assigned to the past.

But in contrast, film and programme makers were beginning to challenge earlier representations of homosexuality. Nowhere was this more apparent than in the comedy-drama film *My Beautiful Laundrette*, written by Hanif Kureishi and released in 1985.[47] It tells the story of Omar – a second generation British Pakistani who lives with his alcoholic father Ali, a once famous journalist and left-wing intellectual. In contrast, Ali's brother Nasser is a successful businessman working with his brother-in-law Salim – reflecting the divisions in Thatcherite Britain. Nasser offers Omar a job in the business, which he accepts and excels at. When driving Salim and his wife home from a party one evening, the car gets attacked by a gang of skinheads. Omar realises one of the gang is an old school friend Johnny, and he gets out and to greet him. They then agree to call each other and meet up. Nasser subsequently offers Omar the chance to run a laundrette, which Omar accepts and brings in Johnny to help; they refurbish the laundrette using money raised from selling drugs belonging to Salim. Throughout this time they appear confident and happy together, kissing and hugging, with a soundtrack that suggests they are falling in love. After a few twists, including stealing to raise the money to pay Salim back, almost getting caught making love in the back office of the laundrette, and Johnny turning his back on his skinhead friends to defend Salim (and being badly beaten in the process), the story has a happy ending, with Omar and Johnny together.

The film's success lay in presenting a homosexual love affair without making the plot revolve around sexuality or identity; the word 'gay' was never used, and the film was equally about race and poverty in 1980s Britain. Indeed, the normalising of homosexuality on screen was recognised by the director, Stephen Frears, who said,

> I remember we ran *My Beautiful Laundrette* in Brixton and there was a lovely black gay man who came up to me and thanked me for showing gay people in a perfectly natural way and not as psychopaths or murderers.[48]

Moreover, Kenneth MacKinnon has claimed that the film,

> takes a recognisably queer attitude to its central themes by handling the same-sex love affair between a Pakistani and ex-National Front white Brit in a highly unusual way. This unusualness could be boiled down to a refusal to foreground the categories of homo/hetero any more than those of Pakistani and white-British 'identities'.[49]

The *Times Educational Supplement* was full of praise. Under the title 'Queues at last', Robin Buss described it as 'an excellent British film, a wry look at the society we live in, unencumbered by preconceptions, or nostalgia'. As far as sexuality was concerned, he wrote: '[L]ove triumphs – and, by a nice irony, the fact that it is homosexual is the least of its problems.'[50]

But while the British film industry appeared willing to push the boundaries of gay representation, the BBC was finding it harder to achieve the same on television. The two-part drama *Two of Us* was filmed in 1986, just as the section 28 controversy was beginning.[51] Telling the story of the homosexual relationship between two 17-year-old school boys, and designed to form part of a BBC schools programme that teachers could record and play in class, it seemed to represent everything that the sponsors of section 28 had being trying to prevent. As a result it was shelved for two years, edited to change the ending and remove a kiss between the two boys, and moved to 11.30pm, rather than the daytime slot it had been intended for.[52]

The programme told the story of Matthew – handsome, athletic, and openly gay – who has left school because of bullying, and his only friend Phil, who, while dating Sharon, secretly has feelings for him. Phil gradually realises this, and in a scene at the swimming pool when they are showering together, Matthew strokes Phil on the face and chest and tells him it will be alright. Phil replies: 'You do like me, don't you? It's important', as though he needs confirmation of his feelings before he can act on them. He later tells his girlfriend that he is bisexual, and after Matthew's father confronts him with gay porn magazines his mother found under his bed, they decide to run away together. In the second episode they are at a seaside resort together where they meet another runaway, Susie, with whom Matthew explains his relationship with Phil:

> Phil and me are lovers. We do it; we sleep together. We kiss, we hold hands, we touch. It's not a laugh; it's not even a bit of a giggle. We've dumped the other lot. But we're ordinary; same needs. It's like girls and boys trying it on at discos in dark corners. Same needs. We're not a summer holiday; we're not just mates.[53]

But unbeknown to Mathew, Phil is still unsure about his feelings, and calls his girlfriend Sharon to come and meet him. In the original version Phil realises his mistake and stays with Matthew, but in this revised ending Phil leaves with Sharon and Matthew is left alone, resolved that he is gay and cannot change. The drama raised a number of issues for the viewer – in particular, the age of consent, their status as outcasts, the ordinariness of the boys, and, in contrast to Phil and Sharon, the denial of gay children a sexuality.

Because it was aimed at a young audience, and despite the editing, it still received sharp criticism from some tabloids – this was particularly the case when it was rebroadcast during the daytime two years later. Under the title 'Boy meets boy love triangle', Geoffrey Levy, writing in the *Daily Mail* claimed,

> [i]t fails to warn against anything more serious than taunts (and stones) from fellow humans; it permits Phil to experiment without any kind of 'government health warning'.

> Where were the reminders about Aids [sic], for example? And why no mature criticism and warnings of the dangers of the promiscuity so prevalent in the gay community?
>
> This is a film which says to an uncertain boy that it is not unreasonable for him to see what it is like being homosexual. The strong message should have been to avoid experimentation, lest it overwhelms. After all some children of 17 – and most of us at 17 are still relatively childlike – are by no means sure of their sexuality.[54]

An editorial in *The Sun* maintained, '[i]t is wholly irresponsible for the BBC to screen this play', while the *Daily Express* wrote: 'There is nothing wrong with a play which deals sympathetically with homosexuality [...] [but] plays about homosexuality are not suitable for school children.'[55] Yet not all responses were negative. *Gay Times* used an image from the drama for its cover in May 1998, noting 'the cheerful simplicity of Phil's bisexuality [...] – without invalidating Matthew's gayness – blurs the boundaries on which laws like Section 28 depend'.[56] Jaci Stephen, writing in the *London Evening Standard*, called it 'a tender and moving evocation of the complexities involved in trying to understand one's sexuality'.[57] And Melanie McFadyean of *The Guardian* maintained that,

> [o]ne of the strengths of the film is its accent on love rather than sex. And far from reproducing stereotypes, it shows the complexity and confusion of young sexuality. There are moments of tenderness and subtlety in tv films about teenagers in love.[58]

Indeed, while it aimed to present more positive images of homosexuality, that neither relied on stereotypes, nor condemned homosexuality, it nevertheless presented life as a gay man as hard – with Matthew being abandoned by friends, family, and, ultimately, Phil.

In contrast, the magazine series, *Out on Tuesday,* beginning broadcast on Channel 4 in February 1989, attempted to present a grown-up, intelligent, and objective series for gay men and lesbians.[59] Presented by Paul Gambaccini, it was the first magazine series in the United Kingdom made for a gay audience. Its first episode included a tongue-in-cheek look at the promotion of homosexuality (in response to section 28), a more serious article on gay men and the use of condoms, and an exploration of actors who had taken on gay roles. The 'promotion of homosexuality' piece was particularly effective, and involved the programme makers employing the services of the advertisers Saatchi and Saatchi to 'promote' homosexuality. The article followed their progress, while interspersing various guests (balanced between men and women) discussing whether sexuality was innate or created. Of particular note was the psychotherapist Marie-Laure Davenport, who said: 'What is not possible is to make someone a homosexual, who doesn't have a desire for it. [...] It is possible to make it easier for people to lead a homosexual life.' The Haringey Labour councillor, Vince Gillespie, involved in the positive images controversy of 1986, was also interviewed: 'I'm not saying "it's great, everyone should be homosexual", that's nonsense. What I'm saying is: "be true to yourself, be what you are, what you want to be."' But the programme makers appeared keen to present a balanced report, and overall there were an equal number of people who believed sexuality was created, in particular a lesbian who claimed she became gay after meeting other lesbians, as well as comments from the MP David Wilshire.

In contrast to the controversy surrounding *Two of Us,* the response to this programme was generally positive. Indeed, in a slightly dismissive article by Richard Last in *The Daily Telegraph*, he concluded by writing,

> [i]t seems to me that the most sensible thing for the series to do is to get on with what it feels [is] relevant to its cause and pretend, for one hour a week, that the rest of us don't exist. If any of us choose to tune in and don't like what we see, that's our problem.[60]

Jaci Stephen was more positive, claiming '[t]he great success of the series has been its ability to have made the relevance of those issues known to a wider audience':

If the series can be said to have promoted homosexuality, that can only have been to the benefit of its audience. The discussion – both serious and witty – the entertainment and fun, the imaginative production have all been of a quality rarely witnessed in what we might call 'mainstream' television. It's a great pity that society dictates the late hour of broadcast.[61]

Kevin Jackson, writing in *The Independent*, described it as part of 'an honourable tradition of public service broadcasting', while *The Times*, in a listings guide two years later commented: 'The lesbian and gay series returns again raising the question of whether it is trying seek converts [sic] or mainly preaching to the converted.'[62]

Indeed, the series did help 'promote' a positive image of homosexuality, while addressing complicated issues that many gay men and lesbians were still contending with. For a heterosexual and homosexual audience, it was an opportunity to hear a more balanced approach to homosexuality, while presenting gay men and lesbians as ordinary members of society, albeit with niche interests that the programme addressed. Indeed, Diane Hamer and Penny Ashbrook (one of the programme's producers), claimed that *'Out on Tuesday* [...] had an enormous impact on lesbian and gay visibility and culture, and on mainstream television itself. The series set a trend and, in Britain at least, the rest of television is now following in its wake.'[63]

In contrast to this contemporary representation of homosexuality in a magazine series, *Oranges Are Not the Only Fruit*, first broadcast in 1990, represented a fictional account of lesbianism.[64] Following the life of Jess, the adopted daughter of a strict Evangelist mother, it explored her struggle growing up trying to balance her faith with her lesbianism. Broadcast in three hour-long episodes, the drama follows Jess, first as a child indoctrinated into the cult-like world of her mother's church, then as a young woman realising her sexuality. In the first lesbian sex scene on British television, Jess asks her lover, Melanie, 'This can't be unnatural passions, can it?'[65] Later, when her church discovers the relationship, they accuse her of being possessed by the devil and tie her up in a violent exorcism, framed for the viewer to resemble rape. As the pastor (a zealous man who sees the work of God and the devil almost everywhere) stands over her, he says: 'She's so pretty. Sometimes the devil scars you as he comes free. You might be scarred Jess. You might not be pretty anymore.'[66] Although Jess claims to have repented, she goes to see Melanie – also a member of the church – who says they will not be able to see each other anymore. While the scene goes back to images of the exorcism, the voice-over is of Jess and Melanie's earlier conversation:

Jess:	Will you write to me?
Melanie:	I can't. We've got to forget.
Jess:	I won't forget.
Melanie:	I'll miss you.
Jess:	You don't have to miss me. You could love me.
Melanie:	It's not simple anymore.
Jess:	I love you.[67]

The third episode shows Jess gradually becoming more confident in her sexuality, having left the church and her family. At the end of the programme Jess discovers she has been accepted to Oxford and goes home to make peace with her mother. While at the house she meets members of the church, who tell her she should give up the devil and come home. Jess smiles, wishes them a Merry Christmas, and leaves. The series ends on a positive note that life will get better for the ever-optimistic Jess.

Hilary Hinds has written how, uniquely, *Oranges Are Not the Only Fruit* was almost universally popular with the press: '[It] retained, and increased, its lesbian audience and its subcultural consumption, and has also been praised by a tabloid press usually hostile to lesbian and gay issues.'[68] Christopher Dunkley of the *Financial Times* described it as '[r]omantic, innocent and beautiful', while *The Observer* called it 'a wonderfully witty, bitter-sweet celebration of the miracle that more children do not murder their parents'.[69] Cheryl Smyth, writing in *Spare Rib* was particularly interested in the sex scene:

> Although a little pre-Raphaelite in style, the scene is uncomplicated and unapologetic. Their refreshing lack of embarrassment and shame is a breakthrough for a mainstream

TV drama slot. Is BBC2 stealing the radical remit from Channel 4? Jess is too knowing and sure of her desire for the scene to collapse into pre-pubescent coyness and 'innocent' caressing.[70]

The series went on to win BAFTAs for Best Drama Series/Serial, Best Actress for Geraldine McEwan (playing Jess's mother), and Best Film Sound. Although portraying a negative experience of coming out in such a small community, the drama was equally about Jess's relationship with her mother, the reaction of a cult-like religion, and, indeed, Jess's own determination to succeed. While it may have continued the tradition that films and television programmes on the subject of homosexuality often tell unhappy stories, the ultimately positive outcome for Jess, as well as the decision to portray lesbianism in such an open, and high-brow way (the series was based on Jeanette Winterson's 1985 Whitebread Award winning novel) helped legitimise homosexual content on television. Indeed, in contrast to earlier films and television programmes, the villain was portrayed by Jess's mother and her religious opposition to homosexuality, rather than any other lesbian character intimidating or manipulating the young Jess. Moreover, the innocence of Jess and Melanie's relationship (if ultimately unsuccessful) presented a more normalised image of lesbian relationships in the media.

For the media, then, this was a period of contradictory images. The gay media, becoming increasingly professional and assertive, played a vital part in the creation and maintenance of subcultural identities, becoming even more involved in political campaigns as section 28 progressed through Parliament. They faced the difficult task of trying to balance an often left-wing politics and commercialised gay scene with a desire to challenge stereotypes and reflect the real diversity of gay life. While for many this ensured that gay men and lesbians could not be forced back to the margins of society, for others, this image was not something they wanted to be associated with. The press, however, confronted with both the HIV/AIDS epidemic and the perceived 'promotion of homosexuality' became increasingly reactionary and homophobic, challenging the visibility and existence of a subculture that was still in its infancy. This contributed to a climax in public homophobia – with the introduction of section 28 a direct result of press actions – and confirmed for many the association between homosexuality, disease, and paedophilia. Finally, television and film appeared determined to create more nuanced portrayals of homosexuality, which, for the first time, included stories with happy endings, and unapologetic magazine series on gay life. While the image of the unhappy homosexual endured, it was being challenged. This period was, then, one of conflicting public images. While some were incredibly damaging with a legacy that survives today, others helped maintain and develop a positive gay social and group identity in 1980s Britain, which, like the politics of the period, would emerge stronger as a result.

CHAPTER 6

GAY SPACE

Despite the increasingly negative images played out in the political and press environment, the late 1970s and 1980s witnessed the emergence of a visible social subculture surrounding homosexuality, which would increasingly help define a gay identity in Britain. In contrast to the calls for greater restrictions on homosexuality in the political arena, gay men and lesbians were becoming an ever more visible feature of British life. The increasingly commercial gay social scene quickly established a particular image of homosexuality – predicated on clubs, drugs, and sex – which for many heterosexual and homosexual men and women represented the first clear image of what defining a person as gay meant. While for many the freedom the commercial scene brought was the 'prize' of the earlier gay liberation period, for many more this reflected only one type of gay identity, which many invisible or 'closeted' homosexual men and women did not or could not identify with. The exclusions of this hegemonic identity inevitably prevented many people from defining themselves as gay or lesbian, despite the continuing expansion of visible examples of homosexuality – marking a clearly understood binary sexual identity system. For the first time gay and straight became established and clearly understood sexual identities, despite those obvious exclusions. The traumatic effects of HIV/AIDS, however, allowed a renewed attack on this hedonistic gay lifestyle, creating an almost permanent association between a gay group identity and disease.

Gay bars have never been illegal in the United Kingdom. Rather, their perceived illegality has its origins in sporadic police raids on clubs and bars frequented by homosexual men, most notably in the first half of the twentieth century, 'using generic licensing and regulatory powers', or more rarely, 'statutory charges of "keeping a disorderly house" and "aiding and abetting"'.[1] Despite the Sexual Offences Act making such behaviour legal, raids still occurred. In 1968, for example, after writing in the *Wolverhampton Express and Star* that 'Wolverhampton had the best social club for homosexuals in Europe', the 19-year-old founder of MANDFHAB found the same club raided two months later and the owners charged with permitting 'obscene and indecent acts' on the premises.[2] When the GLF began organising one-off dances in London from 1970 they made it harder for the police to shut them down, while CHE's own social events represented a more moderate aspect of the emerging 'gay scene', which often attracted local support. Cook notes, for example, that the CHE group in Sheffield and Rotherham held discos in the city hall and assembly room with the support of 'the local press, vicar and MP'.[3] However, for most of the twentieth century, right up until the 1980s, the attitudes of individual police forces largely determined the local response to gay bars across the United Kingdom.

The first large-scale gay club night was launched in 1976 at the Astoria in London, by Jerry Collins. Attracting crowds of 1,000 every Monday night, as well as celebrities including Rod Stewart, Rock Hudson and David Bowie, 'Bang' showed that there was a market for American-style clubs, principally among gay men.[4] Three years later, in 1979, Jeremy Norman launched 'Heaven', the first gay club open every night, under the arches of Charing Cross railway station:

> At this time, gay clubs in London were discrete cellar bars holding a couple of hundred people apologetically hidden from public view. There was a brave 'one nighter' at the Astoria called 'Bang' which was drawing a crowd of about 1,000 every Monday – traditionally the hardest night to fill. That gave me confidence that the right gay product would achieve capacity at the weekends.[5]

'Heaven' initially operated a '"men only" door policy', beginning an association between gay men and the emerging club scene. Its sale to Richard Branson's Virgin Group in the early 1980s helped cement its position as a financial and cultural success. Norman claims that clubbing in the 1980s became an integral part of a gay social identity for many men:

> [T]he dance floor was truly a place of liberation: a place where we could feel free to express our sexuality and the unity of our tribe. The dance club was, in a sense, our cathedral; the music our liturgy and Disco our religion – a truly ecstatic and visionary experience. Gay guys have told me how their first visit to Heaven liberated them, making them realise that they were neither alone nor a freak, but one with thousands of other like-minded souls who were handsome, fun-loving, well-adjusted and happy.[6]

Indeed, gay bars and clubs were fast becoming the easiest way for gay men and lesbians to meet. In 1984, a survey of gay teenagers in London confirmed that 25 per cent had their first contact with 'other homosexuals' in a pub or club (18 per cent through the London Gay Teenage Group; 13 per cent through the London Lesbian and Gay Switchboard).[7] Eduardo Pereira, a Brazilian man living in London, described this commercial scene as 'very important', but recognised that the HIV/AIDS crisis had changed attitudes:

> Before AIDS, it was part of gay culture to pick people up [in bars]. Now you have to be so careful, sometimes it's simply not worth it. A shame, because I had always wanted to be a total sexual being, according to the Gay Liberation ideology.[8]

Indeed, many men believed that this new commercial gay scene, with its overt references to sex, was the prize of gay liberation, and part of a new gay identity and culture. It would prove to be this association that would increasingly became one of the most recognisable forms of a public gay identity, and one that would grow as the impact of HIV/ AIDS became more apparent.

The 1980s also witnessed the emergence of what have become known as 'gay villages', principally in Manchester and London, which were less dominated by gay men. While Soho had been associated with sex and homosexuality since before World War II, Frank Mort claims that the opening of Bang and Heaven helped bring 'a mainstream gay market to Soho':

> It was the appearance of these major projects which provided commercial anchor points for the return of homosexuality to Soho in the 1980s. Their visible success began to encourage smaller, more locally based businesses to target goods and services to gay customers. 1986 was a significant year for this process of commercial expansion. In June London's first explicitly gay café, appropriately called First Out, opened in St Giles High Street, on Soho's eastern fringes.[9]

Mort further claims that this commercialised gay culture 'crystallised a new homosexual type':

> The clone was an international phenomenon whose personality celebrated both the growth of urban gay culture and an optimistic, pre-AIDS sexual philosophy. Sporting an exaggerated masculine wardrobe – short hair, moustache, check flannel shirt, Levi's jeans and bumpers or workboots – he was a gay everyman, whose identity was assembled out of the signifiers of mainstream fashion.[10]

While earlier images of homosexual men were often associated with effeminacy, the emergence of the masculine-looking gay man (whose origins were American) suggested that homosexuality and masculinity were not mutually exclusive, blurring traditional identities. Indeed, as with the GLF, this international dimension in the origins of representations reflects the changes in identity that were taking place across the Western world.

In Manchester, the area surrounding Canal Street developed along similar lines to Soho. The district had been well-known as a cruising ground owing to its run-down, former industrial nature, while The Rembrandt, widely recognised as Manchester's oldest gay pub, is located on the corner of Sackville Street and Canal Street. When commercial gay venues began to open in Manchester in the 1980s, they developed in this geographic area. Stephen Whittle claims the 1984 municipal elections, which saw the re-election of Labour and the radical left, were integral to this development:

> Since 1984, initiatives taken by Manchester City Council, combined with the setting up of a Gay Business Association, and the increasing politicisation of the gay community in the city – through AIDS awareness and the battle against Clause 28 have led to a substantial growth in the number of trades and venues catering for lesbians and gay men in what has become known as the Gay Village.[11]

Whittle asserts that 'people who use the facilities of Manchester's Gay scene, who are not lesbian or gay and yet who are not straight, are placed in some form of unity by outsiders'.[12] Thus while visitors might not identify themselves as gay, their presence in recognisably gay commercial locations often meant that they were – and are – given that identity nonetheless. These bars, clubs, cafés and other services also became the home to other sexual 'outsiders', including transvestites, transsexuals, bisexuals, swingers, and fetishists including S & M. While they are not necessarily homosexual, they contributed to the evolving identity of gay men and lesbians in the public discourse, which recognised non-heterosexual sexual behaviour and the blurring of gender identities as distinctly gay.

Weeks has argued that '[t]hrough the creation of a gay mass market, lesbians and gays were being tied by cords of silk into the pleasures of consumerism, ending the isolation and ghettoization of gay life. The ghetto was coming out.'[13] Indeed, around the commercialised gay scene there was also an emerging concept of a gay community based on this visibility:

[T]he 'community' exists as an idea, embodied in a series of activities (such as gay pride parades, festivals, candlelit vigils for people with AIDS, as well as more intimate and personal involvements) that constantly evoke, recreate and sustain a common belonging, whatever the class, racial, ethnic and gender differences that nevertheless exist and continue to flourish.[14]

Since a public discourse recognised this commonality in the 'gay community', it existed as a way of categorising what a gay group identity meant in 1980s Britain, and helped reaffirm the construction of identity within this group. According to Weeks, this community created a 'common belonging', which did not necessarily exist before 1980s Britain.

The gay social scene continued its expansion in the 1990s, becoming ever-more commercialised and incorporating an increasing number of pride marches and festivals. Manchester's Canal Street was pedestrianised and the lighting improved, leading to a concentration of gay bars and clubs within walking distance of each other.[15] Soho in London was also expanding, with the arrival of a number of bars representing its further commercialisation. Indeed, while the 1970s and 1980s had witnessed the creation of the first open bars and clubs for gay men and lesbians, it was during the 1990s that these areas expanded into the villages and zones that we would recognise today. For Frank Mort, this was intimately connected with capitalism and the commercialisation of the gay social scene. Observing Soho's 'Queer Valentine Carnival' organised by OutRage! and held in February 1993, for example, he wrote,

> Soho's carnival involved something more than an exercise in sexual politics. It was also testament to the growing commercialisation of homosexuality. Every time the Valentine parade stopped on its way through the area, it drew attention to the diverse network of consumer culture which was now established. Bars and clubs, cafés and shops held out the promise of a homosexual life, shaped by the market. In

these spaces the carnival promised a 'mixed' utopia – a commingling of lesbians, gay men and their friends. However, it was one particular constituency – young homosexual men – who laid particular claim to the streets of Soho.[16]

Indeed, while this scene remained male-dominated, it nevertheless reflected the power of the market to provide a relatively safe social space for gay men and lesbians (as CHE had realised a decade earlier). While the nebulous concept of the 'pink pound' is often used to describe the relative financial freedom enjoyed by gay men and lesbians, it would perhaps be more useful to see the growth of the commercialised gay social scene as a response instead to the relative absence of an open social space in a society becoming gradually more tolerant of homosexuality.

But the generalisation of all gay men and lesbians based on the visibility of a small subculture is problematic. Lesbians living in the 1980s were often in the position of being associated with the narrative of a hedonistic – and predominately male – gay commercial scene, while in fact often being excluded from it.[17] Many women were instead part of a much smaller scene that often involved a clear demarcation between 'butch' and 'femme' lesbians:

> I used to go to the Crown in Blackfriars Road mostly [from the late-1970s]. The butches and femmes would go there several nights a week. It was a world of extremes and the acting out of frustrations. The butches had these hideous suits that you get off the peg at C&A's [sic] and most of the femmes dressed like ultra stereotyped females. I found it a very violent, alcohol-ridden environment.[18]

While these bars were characteristic of pre-GLF attitudes to sexual, and gender, freedom, they were beginning to change. Jennings notes that '[w]omen were less likely to socialise exclusively in one venue and frequently visited both mixed and women-only spaces [from the 1970s onwards]'.[19] The most visible and popular clubs remained male-dominated, however, and continued to project common ideas of what it meant to be gay on both men and women, with Jeffreys noting how,

> In the gay culture of the twentieth century male influence and money have ensured that gay men have hegemony. The articulation of a separate lesbian consciousness has been difficult and lesbians have been routinely submerged. Since gay men were the only 'homosexuals' of interest to sexologists, the media and other men generally, homosexuality has come to mean male homosexuality.[20]

Moreover, the lived experiences of many individuals were often overlooked when 1980s Britain began constructing ideas about what it meant to be gay. While some were excluded from this identity, either through dominant images in the public discourse or by gay people themselves, others felt they could not identify as gay when it did not represent their own life. For men and women with a homosexual sexual orientation this proved a complicated dynamic. Society increasingly saw them as part of a gay group identity, particularly through the commercialised gay scene, but within this 'community' prejudice could often exclude them, leaving them on the margins of both homosexual and heterosexual life. Kursad Kahramanoglu, a Turkish immigrant recalled how,

> When I first came to this country [in 1977] and started to get involved in politics I was welcomed by political middle-class lesbians and gay men. Here I was as a sort of Black person welcome to all these political meetings and I got lots of encouragement. Then the problems started. When I started to become equals with these people in the sense that I started to develop my own political ideas and initiatives and started to articulate these ideas, the same 'right on' people who welcomed me like an exotic flower started to resent me. [...] [Y]ou're all right as long as you're a decoration so that these political queens and femocrats can have the credibility of being part of a mixed Black and white organisation.[21]

As the commercial scene expanded, this overt racism moved to the entry policies of bars. Topher Campbell remembered that while he was reluctantly let into bars and clubs in London, outside of the capital he 'was point blank refused entry or faced crude stereotyping'.[22] Zahid Dar, from Kenya, described a confrontation between gay skinheads at a disco run by Icebreakers when one of them was overheard saying 'I don't like coloured', and which despite his protests, the organisers refused to challenge:

> [T]he core of the debate was that Icebreakers could not impose a ban on 'members of the gay community' because of their dress, whereas the LGBG [Lesbian and Gay Black Group] – myself in particular – felt that the ban was against gay racists and fascists.[23]

These events in turn led to many people questioning whether being gay was more important than being Black. Dar claims,

> being Black was probably a larger part of our identity than being gay. [...] [P]olitically, we should try working within the Black community, strengthening our ties politically with Black activists and raising issues of sexuality within those circles, rather than the issue of racism within gay politics.[24]

For others, however, it was not the already prevalent racism in the United Kingdom that affected them, but the relatively new ideas of masculine beauty, personified by the 1980s clone culture. For Glenn McKee, born with Morquio's Syndrome – a condition that causes abnormal skeletal development and dwarfism – dealing with the assumption that 'if you're disabled you don't have any sex drive', proved painful:[25]

> I can remember years ago walking into the Salisbury on my own and being looked over by all the men. You could see rejection on everyone's face. You have to be able to take that and it's not easy if you're a little nervous, a bit screwed up about the

way you look. I know my coming out as gay also involved coming to terms with my body and what it was like, what it could do and what it couldn't do.[26]

Groups such as Gemma – an organisation for lesbians and gay men with disabilities, the Lesbian and Gay Black Group, and the Long Yang Club – for south east Asians, proved crucial in building an alternative gay identity that was often not recognised in the more mainstream aspect of the gay commercial scene of the 1980s. Indeed, even with the increased diversification of commercial venues – to include leather, S&M, dance, and alternative bars – the image of the hedonistic male prevailed. This was despite a parallel growth in regional clubs and bars catering for smaller communities, with often very little in common with the bigger clubs and bars of the capital. For many gay men and lesbians, this would have been their only interaction with the gay scene, and would have been very different from a night out at Heaven in London.

But despite these contradictions, a certain commonly understood gay group identity prevailed, predicated on this social scene, which the tabloids and other commentators would increasingly refer to when the HIV/AIDS epidemic developed in the United Kingdom. This can, in part, be explained by a London-centric bias of the press, and the increased visibility of gay men and lesbians (both by virtue of numbers and ability to live openly) in the capital. It was in the middle of this emerging commercialised social scene that HIV/AIDS arrived. First diagnosed in gay men in the United States in 1981, it moved quickly to the United Kingdom, despite initial views that it was an American disease:[27]

> I remember the posters going up about AIDS and condoms and poppers, but nobody paid much attention. The risk did not seem great at that stage, and we still didn't know of any English people who'd actually come down with it.[28]

However, on 4 July 1982 Terrence Higgins became one of the first recorded deaths from AIDS in the United Kingdom, dying in

St Thomas' Hospital, London.[29] At this stage little was known about the disease, although through its initial diagnosis in gay men it was originally known as GRID, or Gay Related Immune Deficiency Syndrome, and was already being associated with sexuality, rather than sexual acts.[30] For gay men themselves, 'there was little solidarity at that stage':

> Anyone infected kept it hidden, and it was just a matter of great shame. [...] The impression you got was that it was somehow connected with promiscuity, and the people who got it defined themselves as being sluts. I just remember so many instances of people who kind of died fairly quickly and refused to admit it to anybody. One of them was part of the glamorous model crowd, an actor, at Joe Allen every night. He clearly died as much of shame as anything. He was one of those 'pneumonia' death certificates which were pretty common at that time. Doctors conspired in this, responding to the signals that we were all giving out.[31]

Weeks claims that HIV/AIDS 'emerged in the midst of [...] an "unfinished revolution" in attitudes towards, and in the regulation of, sexuality, and especially homosexuality'.[32] In this 'unfinished revolution' public perceptions of gay men and lesbians were chiefly associated with the visibility of the emerging commercial scene, and for many – including gay men themselves – AIDS was something to be ashamed of, as the result of individual promiscuity. For others, this new disease – seemingly only affecting gay men – was evidence of the unnaturalness of their sexuality. James Anderton, the Chief Police Constable of Greater Manchester, famously commented: I see increasing evidence of people swirling about in a human cesspit of their own making. [...] We must ask why homosexuals freely engage in sodomy and other obnoxious practices, knowing the dangers involved.[33]

Meanwhile, Princess Anne described the AIDS pandemic as 'a classic own-goal scored by the human race against itself'.[34]

Moreover, the lack of information about the disease inevitably led to fears of infection. As a doctor at Middlesex Hospital recalled,

> one night I was sitting in a patient's room, and this hand came round the door with food on it and just dumped it. I laughed with the patient, who said 'it happens all the time'. Within five minutes a bunch of flowers flew across the room – whoosh! That time I didn't even see the hand.[35]

A former patient remembered a period in a rehabilitation centre, recovering from brain surgery: 'I had to have my own knife and fork, my own basin and everything. I remember cutting my finger one day while I was peeling the spuds, and they threw them all away!'[36]

For gay men, and also lesbians, this fear manifested itself in a virulent homophobia. Nettie Pollard worked in a co-operative restaurant that had received funding from a gay organisation. She remembers that when the other community organisations that worked out of the same building – including disability and racial equality groups – heard about the funding, the 'reaction was absolute horror and panic':

> There was an enormous boycott of people who apparently thought they were going to get AIDS. Considering the one man who was working with us had left at that point, so it was entirely lesbians and straight women that were doing it, how they thought they were going to get AIDS is beyond me.[37]

Another witness claimed the homophobia was so intense that he 'really believed that they were going to round up all the gays and put them in concentration camps'.[38]

Faced with this increasing public homophobia, which was initially compounded by the inaction of government, gay men and lesbians were forced to organise their own response to the disease. After the initial fear and judgement among gay men and lesbians, networks emerged to offer safer-sex campaigns, coordinate volunteering, and begin fund-raising.[39] Indeed, after the death of one gay man,

Terrence Higgins, it was suggested to his boyfriend, Rupert Whittaker, that a charity be set up in his memory to raise money for research. The first event was held at Heaven nightclub, and the money raised was donated to St Mary's Hospital, Paddington, where HIV/AIDS research was being carried out.[40] Tony Whitehead, who held Terrence Higgins Trust (THT) meetings in his flat between 1983 and 1984 recalls,

> [t]here was a real sense of digging in, of being besieged. We were getting no help from the government, and there was a very real concern that they wouldn't deal with AIDS through education, but just by proscription, by controlling those people who were thought to be infected. It is hard to stress how deeply entrenched anti-gay prejudice was, and still is. There was all this prejudice, and a feeling that no one outside the community cared about our well-being. It was a war situation, but it was a war only recognized by those that were actually being shot at.[41]

Their first leaflet, published in 1983 – some four years before the Government's own campaign – cautiously advised gay men to '[h]ave as much sex as you want, but with fewer people and with HEALTHY PEOPLE'.[42] But even this was controversial. Whitehead remembers 'being accused at gay student meetings and elsewhere of trying to further some secret agenda of putting gay men back in the closet'.[43]

Jennings maintains that during this period many of the women who had left the gay movement for feminist campaigns came back to support HIV positive men.[44] Indeed, one woman remembers,

> I thought, now I've got to do something about these boys because we're not suffering – look at all these women laughing their heads off and look at you boys, you need help. What can I do? I'll do anything, scrub floors, make beds, go to the laundrette, make food.[45]

Later, on 1 April 1987 Caroline Guinness organised the first AIDS fundraising concert:

It was not until a month or so before the concert, at Wembley Arena, that bands agreed to perform. Artists committed following the securing of the world TV rights. We had so many acts that we ended up doing a week of concerts all around the UK. We called it 'The Party' wishing to dispel the 'doom and gloom' that surrounded the subject. It was a huge success and I was very proud to be a part of it.[46]

Thus while most lesbians were not HIV positive themselves, they became intimately involved in the campaigns to raise awareness, and to support HIV positive men. For many this epidemic represented the coming together of gay men and lesbians after the fractiousness of the 1970s, reinforcing the gay social scene and creating new community-based groups that soon became an integral part of the gay social world.[47]

Meanwhile, nationally, efforts were under way to ensure that the public understood this was not simply a gay disease. The 'AIDS: Don't Die of Ignorance' campaign by the Department of Health and Social Security had seen television advertisements, posters, and a leaflet sent to every household in the United Kingdom. Princess Diana's visits to an AIDS centre in 1989 proved particularly symbolic, holding hands with HIV positive people at a time when most were scared to be in the same room as them. In addition to helping change attitudes towards HIV/AIDS, she also helped lift the mood of individual patients:

She opened our new premises in Islington and I remember her strict instructions that her aides should wait outside, she just wanted to talk to the women. She stayed for ages, not just chatting about HIV, but anything.[48]

In his address to 'The Diana, Princess of Wales Lecture on AIDS', Bill Clinton credited her with changing public opinion:

In 1987, when so many still believed that AIDS could be contracted through casual contact, Princess Diana sat on the sickbed of a man with AIDS and held his hand. If the Princess of Wales could hold the hand of a man with AIDS, who could claim to be above it? She showed the world that people with AIDS deserved not isolation, but compassion. It helped change world opinion, helped give hope to people with AIDS, and helped save lives of people at risk.[49]

World AIDS Day was observed on 1 December 1988, becoming an annual event, while in 1991 Jeremy Irons famously wore the now synonymous red ribbon to the Tony Awards, created by the Visual AIDS caucus in Manhattan that year.[50]

For many, however, while these actions helped normalise HIV/AIDS and lessened its association with homosexuality, it did so at the cost of diverting funds towards heterosexual campaigns, when the evidence still suggested that it remained a predominately gay male disease:

> The whole UK debate about AIDS continues to be dominated by a phantom – a heterosexual epidemic running out of control – which is summoned up whenever anyone questions the accepted wisdom. It dominates the debate to such an extent that epidemiologists find it impossible to acknowledge the importance of targeting gay men except as a means of preventing the heterosexual epidemic.[51]

In January 1989 this led to the formation of groups such as GMFA (Gay Men Fighting AIDS), and Act-Up (AIDS Coalition to Unleash Power). Act-Up harked back to earlier GLF tactics with activists floating helium-filled condoms carrying safe-sex leaflets into Pentonville Prison, in defiance of Home Office Minister Douglas Hogg who had refused to fund research into drug-taking and homosexuality in prisons.[52]

The late 1970s and 1980s witnessed the emergence of clearly defined and binary sexual identities, as 'gay' went from a minority identity to a universally recognised one. It achieved its prominence through the exponential growth of the gay social scene, which came to represent a hedonistic and overtly youth and beauty-orientated culture – personified in the British version of the American 'clone'. While the outbreak of HIV/AIDS increased public hostility towards gay men and lesbians – with many associations made between a gay group identity and the disease – it nevertheless ensured that a series of networks developed, which provided the medical care and advice necessary to tackle its spread, years before the Government's own efforts. By the end of the decade, HIV/AIDS was no longer solely associated with homosexuality, and from 1996 no longer represented a necessarily fatal condition. Instead, the response to HIV/AIDS – including the cooperation of gay men and lesbians, as well as support structures including The Terrence Higgins Trust – left a legacy of support in the gay social scene and community-based groups. But with this greater-defined identity came exclusions. 1980s Britain still contained strong elements of racism, and many Black and Asian homosexual men and women felt that a gay identity remained a White identity, and something they were not welcome to become a part of. For women, the social scene remained male-dominated, although this was gradually changing, and for men who did not fit the stereotype of 'youth and beauty', this identity continued to exclude them. While a gay social identity was now clearly understood in Britain, the illogicality of defining all men and women based on the public visibility of a minority remained a problem. While the late 1980s and 1990s would witness the increased visibility of those who did not fit the stereotype, including many men and women who were more interested in an integrationist agenda, 1980s Britain had not yet recognised them.

SECTION 3

JOINING THE MAINSTREAM

CHAPTER 7

'AN END TO UNJUSTIFIABLE DISCRIMINATION'

In 1997 the Labour Party won a landslide election victory, with a manifesto commitment 'to seek to end unjustifiable discrimination wherever it exists'. The party used this commitment as justification to press for a lower male homosexual age of consent and the repeal of section 28 in England, Wales, and Northern Ireland, representing part of a new rights agenda – typified by the introduction of the Human Rights Act.[1] But this process of legal change had an earlier genesis. 1994 had marked the setting in motion of a political discourse that began a new relationship between homosexuality and the law. Aside from the extension of the provisions of the Sexual Offences Act to Scotland, Northern Ireland, and later, to the Isle of Man and the Channel Islands, there had been no liberal legislative changes in relation to homosexuality since 1967. Indeed, for England, the only successes had been Stonewall's prevention of laws that would have exacerbated the situation for gay men and lesbians. This changed in 1994 when the Conservative MP Edwina Currie tabled an amendment to the Criminal Justice and Public Order Bill, seeking to lower the age of consent. This set in motion a series of legislative changes that culminated in the introduction of the Civil Partnership Act (passed in 2004, becoming law in 2005), legitimating those same relationships section 28 had sought to disqualify.[a]

The Criminal Justice and Public Order Bill had, like similar bills in the past, been introduced 'to make further provision in relation to criminal justice' and while it did not deal specifically with sexual offences, it did intend to amend the Sexual Offences Act in relation to the armed forces and the merchant navy.[2] Since it dealt with criminal law, and the Sexual Offences Act, it provided a useful opportunity for proponents of homosexual law reform to try to gain a tangible legislative achievement. The Conservative Party had won the 1992 general election with a reduced majority of 21 (down from 102 in 1987), but with a record 14 million votes – higher than any other party in British electoral history.[3] There had been hope that the new Prime Minister would offer a fresh relationship between the Government and gay rights groups, after Ian McKellen, representing Stonewall, had been invited to Downing Street in 1991 to meet John Major and discuss gay rights. Stonewall's annual report claimed,

> [t]he most memorable event of the years was Sir Ian McKellen's meeting with Prime Minister John Major, the first time a British premier has ever agreed to meet a lesbian and gay campaigner. Mr Major listened as Sir Ian catalogued Stonewall's proposals for change and the discrimination that we face [...]. Mr Major now has another term of government. Stonewall will campaign to ensure that he continues to listen and inspires his Government to act.[4]

The signal that, perhaps, the Conservative Government was preparing to relax its traditional hostility towards gay rights, which had been characterised by procrastination or open hostility, was a welcome shift for some within the party who had long been anxious about the direction in which the Conservatives were heading. Currie, a former junior health minister for two years under Thatcher, had a traditional conservative political philosophy about the intervention of the state:

> I took the view that gays were citizens like everyone else, and as long as they paid their taxes they were entitled to the same

treatment as their neighbours. It was not the police's business who adults slept with; their job was to catch real criminals, not hang around public toilets.[5]

This liberal conservativism (in contrast to a conservativism rooted in morality or the family) was particularly useful for Stonewall that could again claim to be representing the respectable homosexual who sought equality with heterosexuals, and not a radical review of sex laws – and, crucially, were prepared to work for gradual change. Currie remembers how '[a]fter the introduction of clause 28, a number of Tory MPs met to support TORCHE - the Tory Campaign for Homosexual Equality. As a former Minister under Margaret Thatcher, I was one of the leading lights.'[6] After the further visibility of gay men and lesbians in society, and a gradual lessening in the fear of an HIV/AIDS pandemic (especially after the development of combination therapies from 1996), negative attitudes towards homosexuality were receding from their 1980s peak.

Working closely with Stonewall, Currie and TORCHE decided to concentrate on the age of consent, which in her view was 'far bigger than clause 28, and it would be easier to persuade Tories to leave personal matters to personal choice'.[7] While Stonewall had been discretely lobbying Parliament since its formation in 1989, circumstances offered a unique opportunity. The opening included a new Prime Minister, a group within the Conservative Party offering to introduce an amendment, and a bill that was already going to amend the Sexual Offences Act along Government lines. Stonewall's pamphlet, *The Case for Change*, published the previous year, had labelled the unequal age of consent a 'historical compromise' and 'the price of reform'.[8] It challenged the arguments used against advancing gay rights, comparing the United Kingdom with other continental countries, which showed that the age of consent was the highest in Europe. The pamphlet offered advice on lobbying MPs, and reflected similar documents Stonewall would later produce specifically for Parliament as their lobbying campaign continued after 1997.[9] Anya Palmer, of Stonewall, noted later how,

[s]ome MPs received huge postbags but no two of the letters they read were the same. Each letter would include personal arguments – heartfelt reasons why the author wanted a change in the law. Few lobbying organisations can rely on so many supporters with such a stake in the outcome.[10]

Currie's amendment was introduced during the committee stage of the bill on 21 February 1994; it was seconded by the former leader of the Labour Party, Neil Kinnock. In introducing the amendment she noted,

[i]t is the first time in over a quarter of a century that the age of consent for homosexuals has been discussed by the House of Commons. The taboo of silence that has denied the sexuality of young gay men has been decisively broken. Tonight's free vote establishes the question as a matter of conscience – as it should be – and the huge number of hon. Members who will support the new clause will demonstrate that it is not an issue for gay men alone, and no longer a minority issue, but one of human rights, which touches us all.[11]

The arguments that proceeded in favour of a lower age of consent centred on equality, the rights of young men not to be made into criminals, and compassion for difference. Currie gave the example of three young men who intended to take their case to the European Court:

Two of them – Hugo and Will, who are lovers – spoke openly on television. I understand that they were promptly reported to the police by a self-appointed guardian of public morality, Mr. Stephen Green. [...] The young men found themselves in Rochester Row police station for several hours, and they were subjected to the most intimate and intrusive personal questioning. Eventually, they were released, and no prosecution has been brought. Had such an episode occurred to a heterosexual couple, we should all have been appalled.

We ought to be just as disgusted that in 1994 this can still happen to gay men.[12]

The lower age of consent was also supported by the British Medical Association (who had published a report on the subject in January), Barnardos, the Health Education Authority, and Project Sigma – a study funded jointly by the Department of Health and the Medical Research Council, which 'proffered strong evidence that homosexual orientation was fixed and well understood by homosexuals by their mid-teens.'[13] Unlike in 1967 when legislation was catching up with public opinion, Kinnock acknowledged that,

> [e]veryone who has been elected to the House knows that, in some cases, we follow public opinion. But in others, it is our duty to step slightly ahead, although not so far as to make ourselves invisible to the public.[14]

Indeed, while attitudes were changing, in 1993, according to one survey 50.36 per cent of the population still thought homosexual relations were always wrong (although this was less than the peak of 63.64 per cent in 1987).[15]

The Home Secretary, Michael Howard, confirmed the issue would be dealt with by a free vote, but that he thought 18, rather than 16, 'strikes the right balance'.[16] Currie later claimed,

> [m]ost Tory MPs were indifferent; some were scared (because they were gay) a few hostile (sometimes because of childhood abuse in public schools etc), a few supportive (including some gay). Had the leadership been keen, the indifferents would have voted with us. The party outside parliament was largely hostile (and much of it still is).[17]

Indeed, despite sympathetic voices within the Conservatives, the party still had no official policy in favour of gay rights. The future Labour leader and Prime Minister, Tony Blair, however, who was at the time Shadow Home Secretary, signalled his own personal commitment to gay rights:

> Let us be clear about the issue before us tonight. It is not at what age we wish young people to have sex. It is whether the criminal law should discriminate between heterosexual and homosexual sex. It is therefore an issue not of age, but of equality. [...] At present, the law discriminates.[18]

He went on to argue in committee that,

> people are entitled to think that homosexuality is wrong, but they are not entitled to use the criminal law to force that view upon others. [...] Some change is indeed progress. Let us recognise it when it happens. After all, 100 years ago there was no universal suffrage for men, and no votes for women. Fifty years ago there were no laws against racial intolerance. Each change was fought for, but resisted by prejudice wrapped in a coat of reason.[19]

But there was still a strong group within Parliament, including in the Labour Party, who did not support homosexual equality. The Conservative MP, Sir Nicholas Fairbairn, for example, had interrupted Blair to announce, 'I hope that the Committee will not be misled by the fact that heterosexual activity is normal and homosexual activity, putting your penis into another man's arsehole, is a perverse' – at which point he was stopped by the first deputy chairman.[20] For some MPs like Fairbairn, the physical act of anal sex was how they principally understood homosexuality. Furthermore, some MPs still believed that homosexuality could be learnt through contact with older gay men. Michael Alison claimed that if the age of consent was reduced to 16, then gay clubs and bars would lower their membership age to reflect the law and thus,

> [t]hey will draw into that particular vortex exactly those whose sexual orientation is not properly determined and is open to

alteration and redirection in the context of a highly organised, self-conscious community. If it does introduce young men to safer sex of a homosexual kind, it will have the effect of predetermining them perhaps to lose precisely that option of family life and normal parenthood which is what they should have held open for them.[21]

The sexuality of adolescents was still regarded as fluid, and these politicians still considered it the role of the law to protect them from the proselytising efforts of older gay men (as they had from the 1950s with an age of consent set at 21). Although the language used was not as explicit as in the debates in 1987, the inference remained: older gay men were a risk to children, who should be protected from becoming gay themselves – a continuous theme in parliamentary debates on the age of consent.

The final vote reflected this hostility. Currie's amendment for an equal age of consent of 16 failed with a vote of 280 in favour, and 307 opposed, but was followed by another to reduce the age of consent to 18, which passed with a large majority. The bill also extended the scope of the Sexual Offences Act to the armed forces and the merchant navy. This prevented homosexuality from being a criminal offence, punishable by prison, but instead replaced the law with a provision making it grounds for dismissal under various army disciplinary acts.[22] This was a Government-led initiative, which, in a written answer by the Secretary of State for Defence in November 1993, had been confirmed would take place 'as soon as the legislative programme allows'.[23] After further amendments, the bill finally became law on 3 November 1994.

The reaction to this change was mixed. 3,000 demonstrators had held a candle-lit vigil outside the House of Commons, organised by Stonewall, which spent £30,000 on the campaign.[24] The then head of the organisation, Angela Mason wrote,

[n]o one should doubt that a new political force drew breath on February 21 1994 which, sometimes slowly with a light touch, and sometimes fiercely with great force, will finally allow

lesbians and gay men to live freely in our society as equal
citizens under the law. Beyond our anger and disappointment,
we should see this larger political movement taking shape.
Nothing like this has ever happened before in Britain. Ours is
one of the very few causes where people are willing to put aside
party labels and work together for a common good.[25]

Indeed, Stonewall was prepared to present this as a victory of sorts, and evidence of their new position of strength. Their on-going poor relationship with OutRage! continued, however, with Peter Tatchell criticising them in *Gay Times* under the headline 'Up against the Stonewall':

The Stonewall Group's absence from the huge march against
the Criminal Justice Bill in July was symptomatic of its
creeping complacency. [...] Incredibly, there has not been a
squeak of criticism of the Bill from Stonewall — only silence
and inaction. [...] [L]obbying invariably imposes restraints and
compromises on the lobbyists. We see this in Stonewall's
dependence on the votes of Labour MPs to win law reform. As a
result, Stonewall rarely criticizes Labour when it fails our
community.[26]

For OutRage!, Stonewall's level of engagement with political parties represented a transgression that prevented them from truly representing homosexuals. For Stonewall, pragmatism remained the only viable option in achieving any measure of law reform, something that would not be achieved by marching against a law that had lowered the age of consent. The episode revealed an evolving picture of a gay identity from the prospective of Parliament and the law. On the one hand the cross-party coalition, which had also included charities and lobbyists, began to challenge the political/legal image of homosexuality that had been allowed to develop in the 1980s, and instead suggested that gay men and lesbians were no different from anyone else. On the other hand hardliners in Parliament (from all parties and with a mixture of motivations) were doing their best to maintain old stereotypes. The failure to achieve parity with heterosexual sex reflected this evolving picture and the remaining hostility in Parliament.

Three years later, in 1997, New Labour won a landslide election victory with a majority of 179, and a manifesto commitment to 'seek to end unjustifiable discrimination wherever it exists'.[27] Waheed Alli later interpreted Labour's win as a 'generational shift':

> [W]hen Tony Blair got elected in 1997 and we arrived in Downing Street the world had changed. [...] [H]e had three gay cabinet ministers. [...] Tony Blair was a young man. He didn't have any sense of why you would discriminate against someone because they were gay [...] we were his friends, this was the man who couldn't think 'why would I hold you back because you're gay'.[28]

Although this was Alli's personal view, it seemed to be reflected in changing public perceptions towards homosexuality. The Social Attitudes Survey was now reporting a further decline in public homophobia, with 38.52 per cent of respondents stating that homosexuality was always wrong in 1998 (the first survey after Labour's election victory). It was in this climate that the Labour MP Anne Keen introduced an amendment to the Crime and Disorder Bill in June 1998, to further lower the age of consent for homosexual men to 16.[29] Keen's interest in gay rights was personal, having being recently reunited with her gay son whom she had put up for adoption after a teenage pregnancy.[30] Framing the debate around equality and access to medical services, she claimed,

> [y]oung men are fearful of being open with their parents or those adults to whom they would normally look for information, help and support. Prejudice protects abuse; it does not prevent it. I do not want our children to grow up to live in a world that has laws that discriminate and offend the right for everyone to be himself or herself. Fearful of being branded criminals, many young gay men are unable to seek

health advice and sex education. [...] We compromise reputable agencies that cannot give practical support and advice, because to do so would condone sexual relations between young men that the law brands as criminals.[31]

Other supporters argued that by criminalising the younger partner in underage sex, the law was discriminatory, and prevented vulnerable men seeking medical or legal help. Despite some opposition, the amendment received support from both sides of the House and was adopted with a vote of 336 in favour and 129 opposed in a free vote.[32]

Once in the Lords, however, it was attacked as 'flawed' by Baroness Young – a former leader of the House, and the only woman ever appointed to the Cabinet by Thatcher.[33] This would prove to be the beginning of a concerted campaign on her behalf to defend what she saw as the erosion of family values. She claimed that legislation on the age of consent should not be rushed through Parliament, but instead should be dealt with after consultation in a Government working party. She successfully framed the issue around the protection of vulnerable groups from those in positions of trust, using the recently published Utting Report, which had examined residential child care:

> What I do find extraordinary is that the Government have accepted an amendment, passed by the House of Commons, to lower the age of consent to 16 and have at the same time immediately recognised that it is seriously flawed and that it is necessary to set up a working party to deal with those young people most at risk. I ask myself, as a simple person: how can they allow this provision to go forward on to the statute book in this unsatisfactory state?[34]

By doing this she claimed that a lower age of consent could not be accepted unless there were provisions to protect young men – provisions that did not exist for heterosexual 16-year-olds in a similar position. As a result, she ensured the spectre of paedophilia remained a key characteristic of gay men, and their main motivation for a lower age of consent – an image that had been in place since the publication of the Wolfenden Report over 40 years earlier.

She did, however, concede that she disapproved of the bill in principle:

> I believe that this is the thin end of the wedge. I know that many homosexual organisations say that they are not in favour of lowering the age of consent to 14, but some are. It will lead to a demand for gay and lesbian marriages and for the right for such couples to adopt children.[35]

Despite the vitriol of her comments, where gay marriage and adoption rights were concerned, history has proven her right. The reaction from other members of the Lords, while mixed, tended to reinforce her views, with Lord Jakobovits, the Chief Rabbi of Britain, for example, questioning whether 'we have already conceded too much under pressure from the gay lobby'.[36] This can in part be attributed to the growing professionalism of Stonewall, which after 1997 had increased their lobbying efforts, and the election of a Government committed to gay rights. As a result of this opposition, the clause was rejected with a vote of 290 to 122.

Faced with this defeat, the Government was unable to use the Parliament Act to force through the legislation since the Crime and Disorder Bill had originated in the Lords and not the Commons. Instead, the Government introduced a new bill to the Commons in 1999, aiming to equalise the age of consent at 16, but including measures to protect children from abuse of trust. Introducing the bill, the Home Secretary, Jack Straw, explained the inclusion of child protection measures:

> We are dealing with the matter in this Bill because of the very strong views about the vulnerability of 16 and 17-year-olds of both sexes expressed during debates on equalising the age of consent held in the House and another place last summer.[37a]

Once again under a free vote, the Commons approved the bill at third reading by 281 to 82. And as with the previous bill, Stonewall launched its own lobbying campaign. An on-going pragmatism was central to their work, with the later head of Stonewall, Ben Summerskill, noting 'if you've got to get something through the House of Lords the only people that matter are the people who are voting'.[38] They published briefings for wavering peers, countering the arguments over abuse of trust, and listed the support of a number of organisations, including the NSPCC, Save the Children, and the British Medical Association.[39] This complemented the words of Lord Williams, who, in introducing the bill to the Lords, attempted to address the arguments Young had used in the previous debate:

> The noble Baroness, Lady Young, raised, I think, two objections [...] the first of which was that the proposals on the last occasion were rushed and did not give proper time for consideration. Secondly, she thought that the Government should introduce their own Bill to deal with the age of consent. Dealing with those matters the noble Baroness further made the point that we had the constitutional right to ask the other place to think again. We have done so and it is a commonplace that the House of Commons has discussed the matter at some length and overwhelming majorities have been achieved on every occasion.[40]

Again, however, Young accused the Government of ignoring public opinion, and urged the House to support her amendment to reject the bill. In an impassioned speech from Lord Alli, he presented himself as the champion of gay reform in the Lords, and acknowledged that, unlike in the past, the upper chamber had become more conservative in its approach to homosexuality, and was the main obstacle to law reform:

> My Lords, many of your Lordships will know that I am openly gay. I am 34. I was gay when I was 24, when I was 21, when I was 20, when I was 19, when I was 18, when I was 17 and even

when I was 16. I have never been confused about my sexuality. I have been confused about the way I am treated as a result of it. The only confusion lies in the prejudice shown, some of it tonight, and much of it enshrined in the law.[41]

Despite this, the final vote in favour of Young's amendment was 222 to 146, and the bill was rejected. The age of consent debate had ensured that the link between homosexuality and paedophilia was again sustained. In addition, those opposed to law reform had tried to maintain the stereotype of a predatory gay identity that could potentially see adolescent homosexuals 'becoming' gay after an encounter with an older man. Lord Longford, for example, commented that,

> if I were the parent of a boy who had been seduced by some middle-aged gentleman, I should feel that his life had been taken a long way towards ultimate ruin. It would not be quite certain, but the chances are that if he was installed in life as a homosexual, he would never marry. He would probably in the end become promiscuous. A lonely old homosexual is one of the most pathetic sights that I know. In my humble way I will do anything in my power to protest against anything that threatens the young adolescent boys of our time.[42]

The success of these arguments helped prevent a new image of homosexuality being created in law, which would have centred on equality between heterosexual and homosexual adolescents. Instead, the message being presented to the public was clear — 16-year-olds were mature enough to engage in heterosexual, but not homosexual, sex, since they lacked the emotional maturity to understand the seemingly 'negative' choice they were making.

But the Government had anticipated this defeat by introducing the bill in the Commons where the Parliament Act would apply if the Lords rejected the bill again. Therefore, just over a year after the bill was first introduced, the Home Office Minister, Paul Boateng, reintroduced it exactly as it had been sent to the Lords previously, and confirmed there would be no committee stage.[43] Despite some opposition, including Teresa Gorman claiming the Commons were pursuing the issue because '[w]e have a much higher percentage of people of homosexual persuasion in the House than in the population at large', the bill passed and was sent to the Lords.[44] Once there, Young again attempted to derail it, while Baroness Blatch continued associating homosexuality with paedophilia by referencing the Waterhouse report 'Lost in Care' which detailed issues of abuse in care homes in Wales.[45] Rather than reject the bill completely, as she had done in 1999, Young instead tried to amend it, since she knew the Government was planning to use the Parliament Act. Building on the arguments in favour of equality that had been used by the proponents of the bill, she introduced an amendment which would decriminalise 'gross indecency' between men at 16, but retain the age of consent of 18 for sodomy:

> Amendments Nos. 1 and 2 have the effect of keeping the age for buggery at 18 for both boys and girls. But they allow homosexual acts, other than anal intercourse, to be committed at 16. That therefore gives an equal age both at 18 and at 16.[46]

This amendment would equalise an age of consent for anal sex at 18, and an age of consent of 16 for any non-penetrative sex. In describing it as 'a compromise', she hoped to gain the support of the Government and frame her argument not as homophobia, but rather as a health protection measure:

> By keeping the age of buggery at 18, we protect young 16 year-olds from the most dangerous of sexual practices; namely, anal sex. Others far better qualified than I will speak on this, but I have received a number of letters from doctors pointing out the great dangers to teenagers of this practice.[47]

The use of the word 'buggery', however, seems very deliberate, and suggests her own judgement of gay male sex was at the forefront of her decision to amend the bill, and not a health protection measure.

Despite Alli describing it as a 'wrecking amendment' it was passed with a vote of 205 to 144. The final bill was then passed by a vote of 139 to 124 and sent to the Commons. But there the Speaker, in line with the Government's commitment to use the Parliament Act, confirmed that the relevant procedures had been fulfilled, and the bill, in its original form (without Young's amendment), received royal assent the same day. The Government's use of the Parliament Act – for only the sixth time in its 91-year history – reflected Labour's long support for gay rights. In addition, since the Commons had passed this legislation twice, Labour could claim to have democracy on its side, in contrast to the unelected House of Lords, while its strategy of fulfilling the requirements of the Parliament Act in advance of any defeat was a clear indicator of how important it considered the legislation. Whether or not Young was homophobic, her opposition centred on the premise that homosexuality was a learnt condition, and that only adults should engage in anal sex, having made an informed decision. For the wider public interpreting these events, the on-going debates presented a confused and evolving image of gay men and lesbians. The Government appeared keen to present homosexuality as no different from heterosexuality, in the face of an oppositional political image that had dominated in the previous decade.

The same year, however, a Government-sponsored attempt to repeal section 28 in England, Wales, and Northern Ireland had failed in the Lords. The Local Government Bill 2000 had passed the Commons, despite Conservative opposition led by the then leader William Hague, and after the defection of Conservative MP Shaun Woodward to the Labour Party over the issue. But when in the Lords, Baroness Young had led a morality campaign that included an exhibition of homosexual literature, photographs, and a video she claimed was being used in schools.[48] Unlike her later conciliatory tone on the age of consent debates, she began her speech in February 2000 by declaring that she believed 'there was no moral equivalence between homosexual and heterosexual relationships'.[49] Since arguments over repeal had centred on the perceived inability of schools to deal with bullying, she successfully inserted an amendment to the original section, entitled 'prohibition on promotion of homosexuality: bullying', so section 28 would remain law, but with an extra commitment to prevent bullying.⁵⁰ Building on the legitimacy of the Lords, which had been reformed to remove almost all hereditary peers in March that year, she convinced the House to exert its will. Again, like the first attempt to lower the age of consent, the Local Government Bill had originated in the Lords, so the Parliament Act could not be used, and it was confirmed in the Commons that the Government this time would not be pursuing repeal.⁵¹ In Scotland, however, under the powers of the newly devolved Scottish government (led by a coalition of Labour and Liberal Democrats) the fight to repeal section 28 had succeeded. By a vote of 99 to 17 (with two abstentions), members of the Scottish Parliament abolished the law as part of the Ethical Standards in Public Life etc. (Scotland) Act 2000 on 21 June 2000. The previous year the Ministry of Defence had lifted the ban on gay men and lesbians serving in the armed forces, but not before a European Court of Human Rights ruling, suggesting that a gay rights agenda remained inconsistent and not always at the forefront of Government policy.⁵² The cautionary approach of Government and its defeat on section 28 in the British Parliament reflected how recently the 1980s backlash had occurred, and the slow process towards shifting ingrained political attitudes towards homosexuality. Furthermore, these mixed events showed that Labour was not pursuing a gay rights agenda at any expense, but remained concerned at the possible electoral repercussions from legal changes in the highly emotive arenas of education and the military.

When, in 2001, the Labour Party won its second general election, it set the record straight on its failed attempt to repeal section 28. The manifesto explicitly stated that,

> [t]he repeal of Section 28 of the 1988 Local Government Act was grossly misrepresented as an attempt to use teaching to promote particular lifestyles. We will ensure that such teaching continues to be prohibited, based on the provisions of the Learning and Skills Act, while removing discrimination on grounds of sexual orientation.⁵³

The commitment to 'ensure that such teaching continues to be prohibited' indicated that Labour politicians still thought it was possible to teach children to be gay, and that the law therefore had some merit. The description of the attempt at repeal, however, as 'grossly misrepresented', challenged the arguments of Young and other peers, and while it was its only manifesto reference to homosexuality after the resistance faced on the age of consent and section 28, it did commit the party to a second attempt at repeal. The more complicated concept of promoting 'particular lifestyles', however, is harder to explain. While on the surface it appeared to be a rejection that homosexuality can be learnt, it ignored the reconstruction of a gay sexual identity that was occurring as a result of other Government policies, and suggested a certain ambiguity in Labour's approach to gay law reform. It appeared to be deliberately trying to redefine homosexuality in law to 'normalise' the image of gay men and lesbians, while at the same time denying its actions, perhaps with the 1980s 'positive images' controversy in their minds.

Having addressed the most pressing of the legal restrictions on homosexuality by lowering the age of consent to 16, Labour and the Liberal Democrats began to challenge the public discourse on homosexuality as separate from family life and society. Notwithstanding Stonewall's success in changing the wording of the draft guidelines to the 1989 Children Act, sexuality had never been a bar to adoption. Despite this, the law did discriminate against unmarried couples, and thus homosexual couples. Gay men and lesbians could only legally adopt a child individually, which presented a manner of legal difficulties, not least over next of kin arrangements and discrimination in the adoption procedure when the agencies involved discovered that the child would be brought up as part of a same-sex relationship. When the Government introduced the Adoption and Children Bill in 2002, various backbench amendments from Liberal Democrat and Labour MPs were introduced to allow unmarried couples, and thus homosexual couples, the right to adopt. David Hinchliffe's amendment to leave out the word 'married' from the bill so it simply read 'couples' was accepted with a vote of 288 to 133, with the Government confirming they would 'undertake whatever consequential amendments are necessary'.[54] This ensured that where section 28 had tried to delegitimise same-sex families as a 'pretended family relationship', amendments to adoption law could begin to challenge that. This normalising of sexual difference, and the extension of the rights traditionally afforded to married couples, helped reconceptualise the public perception of homosexuality as a part of society, and not on the fringes of it. While in the past any attempts at creating a homosexual version of the family would have been met with references to paedophilia, the new respectability being created by Stonewall, Labour, and an increasingly integrated and visible gay group identity, presented gay men and lesbians' desire for a family as distinctly respectable. With this new legal right in place, homosexuality was becoming increasingly integrated into society, leading in turn to greater calls – both inside and outside Parliament – for the liberalisation of other discriminatory laws.

Indeed, Labour was increasingly empowered after 2001, having secured a second election victory, and in terms of gay rights, felt it was on the side of popular opinion. In a survey by Ipsos Mori in 1999, 76 per cent of respondents asked about what had changed for the better in Britain cited 'tolerance of homosexuality'.[55] Although this appears to be a questionnaire with a list of possible responses rather than an open-ended question, it nevertheless reflected a sizable majority supporting gay equality. With a strong majority in the Commons, the Lords now became the location of the battle for the repeal of section 28, something Blair later acknowledged in an interview with *Attitude* at the 2005 general election, describing the opposition to gay law reform there as 'the last bastion of prejudice of all kinds'.[56]

Baroness Young had died in 2002 but her mantle had been passed to her colleague Baroness Blatch.[57] This time, however, the Government had a manifesto commitment for repeal, which, under the Salisbury Convention, the House of Lords would traditionally not block. But Stonewall, working closely with Lord Alli, was not prepared to risk defeat again. As Alli later commented, 'every time we lost a vote, we made sure we didn't the second time round'.[58] Following the resignation of William Hague, the Conservative party, under Iain Duncan Smith, retained its opposition to repeal, but offered its MPs and Lords a free vote in the debate. Stonewall thus launched a campaign that focused on targeting individual peers, sending out lobbying papers entitled 'sensible de-regulation of redundant legislation', which challenged the arguments that had been used by the opposition. This included claims that section 28 still had 'some role in regulating sex education in schools', that repeal would lead to 'inappropriate materials being used' there, and that the recently amended section had helped to 'tackle homophobic bullying'.[59] It aimed to create as broad a coalition of supporters as possible to secure repeal:

> [W]e actually got a group of peers from all parties including a Conservative Lord Norton, a bishop, [...] [and] Shirley Williams, a well-known Roman Catholic, to write to [...] every peer, the day before the vote saying [...] we are looking incredibly old-fashioned and this issue is [...] undermining [...] the reputation of the House of Lords.[60]

Since Lords reform was still on the political agenda, arguments about looking old-fashioned carried weight, and, according to Summerskill, 'put pressure on members of the House of Lords'.[61] When it came to the vote, the Lords backed the bill, and rejected all amendments, meaning that the Government did not have to force through the legislation with the Parliament Act. Opposition did remain, with, for example, Blatch quoting the results of Brian Souter's referendum in Scotland, which had shown 86.8 per cent of people opposing repeal, although only 31 per cent of the public had responded.[62] Despite her claim that 'Section 28 was introduced for a reason', the momentum of the opposition campaign had dissipated, and only 25 peers voted against repeal.[63] For those who had been personally involved in the campaign, this marked a feeling of intense satisfaction: Alli recalled a 'moment when, literally, I was sat there staring at Margaret Thatcher, and she was staring at me, and I remember thinking "the world has changed, this is my time, yours is the past".'[64] The bill received royal assent on 18 September 2003;

three months later, the Employment Equality (Sexual Orientation) Regulations became law, making it illegal to discriminate against lesbians, gay men and bisexuals in the workplace. As well as representing a huge symbolic achievement, the repeal of section 28 showed that Parliament respected the rights of school children to learn about homosexuality, and for homosexual families not to have their status devalued as 'pretend'.

But perhaps the most significant legal change affecting homosexuals had an earlier genesis in the work of two parliamentarians. Two years earlier, in October 2001, Jane Griffiths had introduced her Relations (Civil Registration) Bill in the Commons under the ten minute rule, which allows backbench MPs to introduce bills with a restricted ten-minute speech. This began a process that would see the eventual introduction of civil partnerships in Britain. The bill passed with a vote of 179 to 59 in favour, and was presented for its second reading in November. There was not enough parliamentary time to hear it, however, despite being scheduled for a later date. Instead, the Government launched 'a major review of the policy and cost implications of a civil partnership registration scheme, supported by the Women and Equality Unit in the Department of Trade and Industry' from November.[65] Heading the review, Barbara Roche claimed there was a strong case for civil partnerships and that a consultation paper would be published in summer 2003.[66] In this paper, the Government claimed '[o]ur plans for civil partnership would provide: [a] [...] Culture change: a new legal status would, of itself, affect attitudes more widely and could make a real difference to the lives of same-sex partners.'[67] But as later debates would prove, the nature of a completely new registration scheme was complicated. The paper looked at areas including pensions, insurance, children, break-ups, ceremony, and cost, among others.

While this review was taking place, a second parliamentarian attempted to introduce a similar bill in the House of Lords. Reflecting a complicated interplay between alternately homophobic and strong liberal credentials, the peers approved a bill by Lord Lester to introduce civil partnerships in January 2002.[68] As later debates would prove, however, this was – for Conservative peers at least – much more a debate about inheritance tax than gay rights. Indeed, the Liberal Democrat was initially moved to introduce the bill to provide protection in law for unmarried heterosexual couples, who, unlike in other countries, were not afforded the legal right of common law marriage. He later said that Angela Mason, the then head of Stonewall, had convinced him to include gay couples as well.[69] He claimed, [t]he Bill seeks to achieve a law which gives full partnership rights and responsibilities to all mature adults, whether same sex or opposite sex, who wish to enter into a binding legal compact to organise their common life together.[70]

Lester's bill was thus framed around an issue of rights and responsibilities, which would help to further integrate gay men and lesbians into society. Despite some opposition, including Lord Acker claiming the bill 'will undermine existing marriages; it will devalue marriage. It will take away from marriage its status as a protected institution', it passed to a committee stage, but was not taken any further.[71] Lord Williams, speaking for the Government, stressed that it had 'a genuinely open mind' on the subject.[72]

It would prove to be another year, however, before a Government bill was introduced, based on the review carried out by Roche. Unlike the Local Government Act 2003, which was introduced in the Commons to satisfy the conditions of the Parliament Act, this bill was introduced in April 2004 in the House of Lords. In comparison to Lester's bill, however, this new Civil Partnership Bill only applied to same-sex couples, which Baroness Scotland explained was to ensure that it did not undermine traditional marriage – an argument that had been used in the previous debate.[73] The Conservatives, under Michael Howard, offered its support for the bill, but confirmed that it would be subject to a free vote. This represented a notable turn-around for Howard, who, as Minister for Local Government in the 1980s, had helped to pass section 28 into law. This was further reflected in an apology one year later in *Attitude* magazine for having supported the clause: 'I think I was wrong. Yes. I was wrong.'[74] Since the British Social Attitudes Survey was continuing to show a decline in homophobia and an increase in tolerance for homosexuality, this shift reflected a realisation that traditional hostility was looking increasingly outdated. While the personal attitude of individual politicians might not have changed, their public statements did. Yet it would be a further year, in the 2005 general election, before the Conservative Party would make any positive reference to homosexuality in its manifesto: 'A Conservative Government will govern in the interests of everyone in our society – black or white, young or old, straight or gay, rural or urban, rich or poor.'[75]

Despite Conservative support, some members of the Lords continued their traditional opposition. Lord Maginnis attempted to link homosexuality with child abuse, describing it as 'abnormal sexual activity', while Baroness O'Cathain successfully extended the scope of the bill to include opposite-sex couples and family members.[76] Indeed, in claiming '[a]n inheritance tax abolition Bill would be much more popular and benefit many more people than the Civil Partnership Bill, and would prevent hardship for many more people', she summed up the mood of many Conservative members.[77] Once in the Commons, the openly gay Alan Duncan, speaking for the Conservatives, attempted to garner their support, and present a modernised party, despite some insistence that the bill would 'undermine the uniqueness of marriage'.[78] Once in committee the bill was again restricted to same-sex couples, rejecting the Lords amendment.[79] The final bill received royal assent in November 2004, allowing for the first civil partnerships to take place in December 2005.

But the act was not marriage. Lord Lester later claimed that it would have been 'hopeless' to push for marriage, and that the compromise on civil partnerships was a 'political necessity'.[80] Summerskill continued the pragmatic position of Stonewall, commenting later:

> [W]hen dear old folk like Peter Tatchell were protesting against civil partnerships altogether, we were doing the hard work of getting a quarter of a billion pounds out of Gordon Brown to fund public sector pensions for gay people.[81]

Indeed, the only recognisable differences between marriage and civil partnerships proved to be the name, the absence of a legal requirement to repeat vows in front of witnesses, the ban on holding ceremonies in religious premises, the requirement of 'consummation as a criterion for legal validity', and their lack of international recognition.[82] The law, moreover, continued to integrate homosexuals into society and reflected the changes that had taken place among gay men and lesbians in the gay rights movement over the last four decades, from respectability, to radicalism, to respectability again. For Weeks, same-sex unions represent the 'queering of traditional institutions', while others, particular those opposed to the further integration of homosexuality into everyday life, have seen it as part of the heteronormalisation of gay social and group identity.[83] Depending on personal political philosophy, it can be either of these things. Without a desire to be accepted as part of the 'normal' majority, social and political integration would not have occurred, but what became accepted as 'normal' expanded to include these previously excluded terms.

Over the next few years the Government proceeded to introduce the Sexual Orientation Regulations 2006, which banned discrimination in the delivery of goods and services, and the Criminal Justice and Immigration Act 2008, which banned homophobic hatred. In 2004 the Sexual Offences Act had abolished the crimes of buggery and 'gross indecency', which had remained on the statute book despite the introduction of an equal age of consent; these were replaced with reformed sexual offences laws that did not make distinctions based on sexuality. In a speech to the Stonewall Equality Dinner in 2007, Blair would pay tribute to the organisation and the integral role it had played in the campaign for gay law reform:

> Stonewall, in my view, played a fundamental and often insufficiently recognised part in achieving this [gay law reform]. [...] What actually matters enormously is that the people from outside politics that you are trying to do it with have a sufficient intelligence and sensitivity, which I think has

really defined the Stonewall campaign. I define it as a polite determination.[84]

Although this praise would be expected from a Stonewall event, it reflected the integral role it had played. From the beginnings of legislative change in 1994, Stonewall was at the centre of attempts to push for reform. Despite it being only six years after the political backlash of section 28, a modernised gay rights organisation had emerged, which concentrated on political lobbying. While it was not successful in lowering the age of consent to 16, it did set in motion a softening of the laws surrounding homosexuality, which culminated in the Civil Partnership Act. This was a remarkable transformation, which reversed the political hostility towards gay men and lesbians, moving them from outsiders to equal members of a society still built on a foundation of the family.

For some, this integration was unwanted and reflected the opposite of what the GLF had campaigned for as 'gay' men and women in the 1970s. For others, however, political equality represented the further normalising of homosexuality, and the reinterpretation of the gay man and lesbian as another acceptable face of diversity in modern Britain. Law reform had met strong resistance, but attitudes had shifted, exemplified in the changing response of the House of Lords. This was the result of a small number of key individuals who had used the momentum of previous changes to press ahead for further legal reform. In the space of just ten years, gay men and lesbians became legal partners, parents, equal under the law, and protected from discrimination. But these changes were never inevitable, and reflected the dedication of all the individuals involved, in particular individual MPs and peers who often risked their political careers on achieving law reform.

CHAPTER 8

REAL LIVES IN THE MEDIA

As seen in the political/legal field, homosexuality was increasingly becoming an accepted feature of British life in 1990s/2000s Britain, with integration – on both sides – making the differences between homosexuality and heterosexuality harder to define. Nowhere were these changes more apparent than in media representations. Gay publications became ever more concerned with lifestyle (although still reporting news items), and increasingly tried to appeal to as a wide a group of people as possible – recognising the diversity of life experience among gay men and lesbians. Television and film became more daring in introducing gay characters to soap operas, producing films and popular dramas which told a positive story of gay life, and even appearing deliberately to provoke controversy. The popular press, were, however, still grappling with the issue of homosexuality. Preoccupied with the legal changes introduced by the Labour Government after 1997, the vitriol of the 1980s was still largely present in the British press, although this would subside as each legal change was won. Gradually, the more nuanced lives of people who happened to be gay became the focus of media representations of homosexuality, albeit with lingering stereotypes.

After the concentration on news and a narrowly constructed gay lifestyle that defined gay publications during the 1970s and 1980s, magazines began a shift towards a more diverse lifestyle focus in the 1990s and early 2000s. Through their attention on HIV/AIDS awareness and prevention, as well as their fight against section 28, the gay media had contributed to an increasingly understood gay social and group identity in Britain among homosexuals. With the institutions either in place or emerging (in particular THT and Stonewall) to tackle these problems, as well as a clearly established gay social scene and a commonly understood binary system of sexual identities, these magazines began to replicate their non-gay counterparts. *Attitude*, launched in 1994, arguably led this trend; an editorial marking its five-year anniversary in May 1999 explained its original philosophy:

> When *Attitude* launched five years ago, amongst a handful of rivals that have since come and gone, its aim was to shake up the ghetto-minded mentality of the pink press with a magazine that would cut across sexuality lines, dare to speak its mind on what was really great and what was frankly appalling about (the rather nebulous concept of) gay culture, and embrace the wider interests of gay men beyond poppers, pills and pop-trash. Inevitably it was treated with suspicion and cries of 'sell-out' in some quarters. People said you weren't ready for a magazine that would bring together some of the world's finest photographers and sexiest men with intelligent writing that would actually delve deeper than a layer of lycra. You proved them wrong.[1]

While it was inevitable that *Attitude* would historicise their past, they did appear keen to explore what sexual identity in 1990s Britain actually meant. Neil Tennant's coming-out article, for example, deliberately challenged the commercial scene that had emerged in the 1980s:

> I've never wanted to be a part of this separate gay world. I know a lot of people will not appreciate hearing me say that. But when people talk about the gay community in London, for instance, what do they really mean by that? There is a community of interests, particularly around the health issue, but beyond that what is there, really? There's nightclubs,

music, drugs, shopping, Pas by Bad Boys Inc. Well I'm sorry, but that really isn't how I define myself. I don't want to belong to some narrow group or ghetto. And I think, if they're really honest, a lot of gay people would say they felt like that as well.[2]

Reflecting the increasing diversity of 'gay life', however, the same edition also included the article 'shopping and the sex war':

Gay men have always treated the world like a vast supermarket, chucking sacred icons and sexual encounters into their shopping baskets along with their pop tarts and Kylie records. Previously, cultural critics have called this irreverent tendency camp subversion. Now they call it shopping.[3]

While obviously a satirical approach to consumerist culture, it nevertheless perpetuated a particular stereotype, although the article pursued a serious point:

Gary Henshaw, managing director of the UK's first gay business consultancy, argues: 'As the commercial aspect of the gay scene expands, it gives gay culture a good public image. It makes gay culture more accepted in the mainstream, which is what gay political activists have been trying to do for years.'[4]

Indeed, the magazine seemed aware that the expansion of a gay subculture in the United Kingdom from the 1970s onwards had helped to create a visible gay group identity, making it easier for a person to define themselves as gay, but also working to constrict that identity around consumerism. Nevertheless, as a commercial enterprise, *Attitude* was part of that very same commercialism, trying to balance the desire to expand restricted ideas about a gay group identity, while at same time relying on a visible (and to an extent stereotyped) gay scene in order to stay in business. The continued introspection of the gay media from the very first publications belied changes taking place, however. The magazine also contained the (usual) mixture of music, film, and television reviews, interviews with celebrities, features on the gay social scene, political reports, news articles, and even the history of homosexuality. These articles reflected the diversity of experience among gay men – ranging from the obviously camp to the increasingly respectable. Readers could take from the magazine what they wanted, embracing or ignoring articles as they saw fit.

Gay Times had also developed along the lines set out by *Attitude*, with, for example, the website *Gaydar* providing an opportunity for an article with an interesting mixture including a report on gay life, but also an analysis of what the website meant for a gay social and group identity more broadly:

> The website just reflects what goes on in the gay world. If you go to any gay bar, there's someone hoping to meet the love of their life, some are out talking to their friends, and some are just looking for a shag. [...] It's changed the way that gay men socialise, almost eradicated al fresco cruising. [...] For years, gay men relied on clubs and bars as a source of sex, solace and friendship. Young gay men are increasingly likely to have their first gay experience via the net. For those who live at home, without access to the bars, *Gaydar* offers a shame-free chance for contact[5]

Indeed, while keeping a lifestyle focus, it had maintained its distinctive news agenda. An editorial in 2000, recalling the political campaigns the magazine had been involved in, reflected on its evolution from the 1980s to the 1990s:

> The style and the format of the magazine were changing too – more colour, more photography, more emphasis on design. But, in the midst of the interviews and reviews from the world of pop, film, music, theatre and the scene, *Gay Times* remained, at its core 'a gay news magazine'.[6]

Notably, within this news format, the magazine was able to continue challenging definitions of sexuality and sexual identity. In one earlier article, in 1991, the magazine quoted Chris Woods of OutRage!:

The divide between 'homosexuals' and 'heterosexuals' is a modern idea, with a history of just over 100 years, he said. But these are transient categories and are subject to possible change.

Sexuality is defined (at present) on the single axis of the gender of the person you sleep with. But gender preference is just one of many axes, ranging from whether you seek S&M sex or public orgies. It includes drag queens and transsexuals, as well as foot-fetishists and those turned on – or off – by porn.[7]

When, in the early 1990s, 'queer' emerged as a more inclusive identity for sexual minorities who did not identify as heterosexual or heteronormative, it appeared to challenge the binary definitions of sexual identity in the United Kingdom. *Gay Times* seemed engaged in an almost philosophical exercise exploring the concept in its articles:

'Queer' was a reaction to assimilationism (the softly-softly approach to equality, emphasising our 'normality') and its use of political correctness to police lesbian and gay identity, 'defining who's in, and as a result who's out'. [...] Gay culture still tends towards homogeneity: house music, muscle-men and designer clothes dominate our clubs, bars and media, creating a lesbian and gay mainstream which feels exclusive to those who cannot or do not want to conform.[8]

Reporting on the changes taking place among gay men, these magazines gradually became more mainstream, while retaining their distinctive edge. They replicated non-gay publications like the magazine *FHM* with glossy covers and a content that tried to take into account the diversity among gay men. They also increasingly appealed to readers who no longer felt themselves isolated from society, but rather part of it. In contrast to earlier publications in the gay liberation period, they were keen to explore what it meant to be gay, not from the prospective of establishing an identity, but rather to challenge prevailing assumptions. While the publications of the 1970s and 1980s appeared preoccupied with reporting and shoring up this emerging gay social and group identity and subculture, the publications of the 1990s and 2000s appeared confident enough in it to challenge homosexuals to think of themselves as part of ordinary society.

At the same time that *Gay Times* and *Attitude* were challenging the homogeneity of a gay male group identity, *DIVA* emerged to attempt the same for lesbians. Indeed, writing in 2006, the editor, Jane Czyzselska, maintained,

> [a]t DIVA, we don't hold up one icon of perfect lesbian identity: what's helpful is to give people a really wide range of ideals or images and not rely on just one person to wave the Sapphic flag. [...] In DIVA we have featured hip lesbian rap stars, successful pop and sports personalities, powerful civil servants and a couple of enterprising lesbians who set up a chocolate shop in Rutland. All are important because they are all role models in their own field.[9]

Indeed, in their first year of publication in 1994, the magazine had deliberately challenged its readership's definitions of sexuality and sexual identity with an article on HIV/AIDS entitled 'sticky moments':

> Rates of new HIV infections are growing dramatically among women. Nearly all are acquiring HIV from the semen of the men they've fucked – others from blood in shared works. Some of these women are queer, lesbians, bisexuals, dykes. [...] Queer women have sex with men for lots of reasons: because we enjoy it, for work, to fulfil our fantasies, to pay the rent, out of curiosity, to get pregnant. That doesn't mean we stop being queer, or lesbian, or bisexuals, or however you define yourself.[10]

The deliberate use of the words queer, lesbian, dyke and bisexual – although rarely gay – reflected this desire to be appeal to all sections of the non-straight world. Rather than attempt to explain and define a specific identity, articles such as this instead attempted to acknowledge and record those diverse experiences. This was especially the case in the graphic article 'Beyond me' which chronicled the writer's experience of S&M, in particular 'playing with a piercer and her needles':

> The effervescence of my adrenaline and culminating endorphins made a heady cocktail that caused me to ride wave after wave of pure warm pleasure. [...] The feeling you get when you puncture somebody's flesh is a potent concoction of concentration and stimulation. [...] [I]t was beyond pain, beyond fear. I was alive and could feel my body's power.[11]

Although an extreme example, this also reflected *Diva*'s move towards a lifestyle focus, replicating other magazines, and marked a departure from *Arena Three* and its focus on self-definition, and *Gay News* and its focus on building and maintaining a subculture.

Diva also sought to challenge the increasing desire among lesbians towards homogeneity with heterosexual society:

> In the thirteen years we have been together, we have always resisted defining our relationship in terms of marriage. We would certainly like our partnership recognised and protected by law and by the Church, but we do not want to be associated with or incorporated into an institution laden with social expectations. [...] We need to be very cautious of buying into heterosexual ideals or unconsciously modelling our relationship on theirs in the mistaken belief that it is the 'natural' thing to do.[12]

Despite this, subsequent articles appeared to advocate the opposite, reflecting the move towards the mainstream – where lesbians and gay men appeared to want to replicate heterosexual institutions around them, rather than fight against them:

> Almost imperceptibly, it's happened. Over the last decade there's been a shift, so that now it's not just accepted that

lesbians – once seen as barren, lifeless, entirely unfruitful – can have children, it's become almost expected that we will, or at least that we will have thought seriously about it, especially when we're a part of a couple.[13]

Indeed, as a gay lifestyle became more integrated, lesbians and gay men appeared less keen to challenge societal institutions – as had been advocated by the GLF – and instead become a part of them. In a sense this replicated the earlier *Arena Three* readers' correspondence, but without the need to categorise and define that had preoccupied their work. The mainstream period reflected a greater move towards the blurring of those precise sexual identities that had been so vital to self-identity in the early gay liberation and emerging subculture periods. Instead, at least as far as these magazines were concerned, sexual identities became a lot more complicated than simply defining someone as gay or straight, and included a whole plethora of variety. At the same time, these identities became much more specifically sexuality-based, in contrast to the all-encompassing identities of the 1970s, 1980s, and indeed the 1990s.

In contrast to the lifestyle shift taking place in gay publications in the 1990s and 2000s, the press was instead concentrating on legal reforms being implemented by the Labour Government. While these campaigns became gradually less intense as time went on, with fewer newspapers engaging in the hostility seen during the HIV/AIDS crisis, they still traded in the stereotypes and the morality pieces that had served to demonise homosexuality in 1980s Britain.

The first of these debates was the age of consent. When, in June 1998, Labour MP Anne Keen introduced her amendment to lower the age of consent for male homosexual sex to 16 (the same as heterosexual sex), it provided the press with the opportunity to play on old stereotypes that associated male homosexuality with paedophilia. *The Sun* had pre-empted Keen's amendment a year earlier:

Parents do not want a politically-correct charter for homosexuals to prey on immature boys.

The argument that the age of consent should be the same for homosexuals and heterosexuals is wrong on one vital point:

Sex between two men is different from sex between a man and a woman.

Gay sex is not the norm, it is an unnatural, minority act.

That is why we need different laws for gay and straight sex.

If adult men want to sleep with each other, that is their business.

But there has to be a deterrent to persuade them to keep their hands off youngsters.[14]

Later, in 1998, when the bill had passed the House of Commons and was being debated in the Lords, the *Daily Mail* attacked 'militant gay campaigners':

[A] minority of homosexuals would like the freedom to induct into their world boys uncertain about their own, still-developing sexuality. And militant gay campaigners want society's acceptance of the notion that homosexuality is equated on every level with heterosexuality. [...] If the age of consent is reduced to 16, as surely as night follows day there will then be calls for it to be lowered to 14.[15]

As with the section 28 debates, this mirrored the comments of Baroness Young who had said the same thing in Parliament the day this article was published. The *Daily Star*, the following day, claimed that '[m]ost parents are horrified by moves that will encourage older men to corrupt young boys into a tawdry life of designer sex'.[16]

In contrast, the broadsheets (with the exception of *The Daily Telegraph*) argued strongly for the equalisation of the age of consent. Under the headline 'Vote yes for 16', *The Observer* claimed:

It is virtually certain that MPs will vote to equalise the age of consent. What is in more doubt is the size of the majority. There is no obligation on Mps [sic] to take part in a free vote. They can opt instead to take Monday off. We hope they don't. Let's see a large turn-out in the lobbies. A grudging shoulder-shrugging vote to equalise the age of consent would send a depressing message to gay men and women. The biggest possible majority would signal that equal rights belong to every citizen.[17]

Meanwhile, even *The Times* argued that 'this is a reform for which the British are now ready':

In 1994, weeks of passionate debate preceded Edwina Currie's attempt to lower the age of homosexual consent from 21 to 16. The temperature is cooler now. The discussion has taken on a much calmer tone. This suggests that the House of Commons was right to travel towards a single age of consent in stages. Individuals will always differ in their attitudes on this subject. But in a pluralist society, the statute book should not make such distinctions.[18]

After the vote in the Lords was lost, Miriam Stoppard wrote in the *Daily Mirror* that,

[i]f only we could see straight we would realise that lowering the age of consent to 16 would mean that many young people could openly seek advice and guidance from family, friends and doctors. We'd be protecting them rather than driving them underground, as the House of Lords action surely will. There's sound historical precedent for believing the majority is almost invariably wrong. In the House of Lords on Wednesday it was again.[19]

As well as signifying a shift in reporting, which saw some tabloids support gay rights, these articles served to show some of the changing attitudes in Britain, and the changing representation of homosexuality in the media, which in turn fed into more liberal attitudes in public. The continued resistance of some newspapers, however, served to present the British public with conflicting images of homosexuality, especially when those opposed to law reform were continuing to trade in old stereotypes such as paedophilia and inculcation. The result remained a mixed picture depending on which newspaper a person read, which was often itself linked to education and social position – often an indicator of a person's views on homosexuality.

In 2000, when the debate was repeated and the Government used the Parliament Act to equalise the age of consent, the same newspapers maintained their hostility. *The Sun* claimed the Labour Party had,

> legalised a perverts' charter. Anal sex is now lawful with boys and girls aged 16. They cannot vote. They cannot drive a car. They are not adults. But they can be buggered. [...] Nothing is allowed to stand in the way of Labour's crusade to lower the age of consent and appease the gay lobby.[20]

Its deliberate attempt still to equate homosexuality almost entirely with anal sex, as well as alluding once again to paedophilia and rape, while ignoring issues of equality, no doubt fed this still very present negative public perception of homosexuality in 1990s and 2000s Britain. But for others, however, the battle had been won and, gradually, the majority of the British press was coming out in favour of gay rights, and beginning to report homosexual law reform in a dispassionate way, avoiding the stereotypes that they had created, and traded in, decades earlier.

However, this paedophile narrative was repeated again in the build up to 2000 when the repeal of section 28 was voted down in the Lords. When Labour announced that it would repeal the law, *The Sun* remained consistent in accusing gay men of proselytising:

> School teachers will be allowed to promote homosexuality as a normal lifestyle under a dramatic law change planned by

Tony Blair. He is set to scrap the controversial Section 28 ruling which forbids town halls actively backing gay relationships. [...] It will anger millions of parents who fear pro-gay lessons in schools. The ruling was brought in by Margaret Thatcher to halt 'loony left' ideas.[21]

In January the following year the paper published an article written by Brian Souter, shortly after he had announced he would be funding a poll in Scotland on repeal, as part of the devolved responsibilities of the new Scottish executive. He claimed 'Section 28 is a gatekeeper to stop militant gay pressure groups who are determined to infiltrate the education process.'[22] Meanwhile the *Daily Mail* had published an article in 1999 that included pictures from the book *Jenny Lives with Eric and Martin* that had proved so damaging – and effective – a decade earlier:

Far from repealing the ban, we should be considering whether it should be extended, to cover health trusts and other bodies which have been used to get around the current legislation. [...] [F]or taxpayer-funded schools to teach our children that living with a girl or boy of the same sex is just another value-free selection from some social smorgasbord is another matter entirely. If Tony Blair is serious about promoting family values, he cannot countenance the repeal of Clause 28.[23]

When the Government lost the vote for the repeal of section 28 in the Lords in 2000 it signalled that it would not be pursuing repeal as part of the Local Government Act. Hilary Armstrong, speaking for the Government, stated that 'much of the concern about the repeal was whipped up by sections of the media, fed by the opponents of repeal on a diet of exaggeration, misinformation and sensationalism'.[24] Despite this, there were voices in favour. *The Guardian* had written in 1998 that '[b]ullying of pupils who are gay or believed to be gay is common in British schools, but most teachers feel unable to raise the issue because of the law [section 28]'.[25] *The Independent*, meanwhile, commenting on the use of the

Parliament Act to secure an equal age of consent, suggested Blair should seize the initiative:

> This modest Bill to remove one element of discrimination has provoked a furious reaction – which speaks volumes for the sexual obsessions of its opponents. [...] Mr Blair should take heart from doing the right thing yesterday, and press on with securing full equality for homosexual men and women.[26]

Thus while social and political changes were progressing in this period when the lives and identities of gay men and lesbians were becoming increasingly public – including in TV/film and gay media representations – the picture from newspapers was more complicated. Broadsheets – *The Daily Telegraph* notwithstanding – had begun advancing a liberal attitude towards homosexuality that went beyond the pity that newspapers had exhibited in the 1960s in favour of legal reform. Instead, readers were being told that homosexuals were entitled to equal rights under the law, and were increasingly being referred to in neutral, non-judgemental terms. This attitude was even extending to some tabloids – notably the *Daily Mirror*. While some newspapers continued their homophobic agenda – particularly *The Sun*, which sustained a continuing hostility towards, and negative image of, homosexuality – there was the sense that the fire had gone, and these attitudes were anachronistic in Britain in the new millennium.

Those same newspapers used the same arguments again, however, in 2003, when repeal of section 28 was once again on the political agenda. Unlike in 1999/2000, there was a sense of inevitability – not least because Baroness Young had died – but also because of a manifesto commitment, and the further liberalising of public opinions. The *Daily Express* had tried to keep opposition going, carrying a full-page obituary to Baroness Young in 2002. Describing her as a 'zealous champion of family values' it noted that 'as a politician she was living proof that integrity could still be powerful in Blair's Britain'.[27] But for the most part, those newspapers gave fewer column inches to the story and appeared resigned to their inevitable defeat. When the repeal was confirmed, *The Sun's* Richard Littlejohn remained defiant in his opposition and concluded:

> Having junked Section 28, it's full steam ahead for sex, sex and more sex in schools. [...] Children will be instructed in the art of anal sex, oral sex and every other kind of sex. [...] All this at a time when the Government is supposed to be cracking down on paedophilia. The sickos and perverts behind these lessons shouldn't be working in schools. They should be in prison.[28]

In 2001, the news that Ken Livingstone (as London mayor) was planning to introduce a London Partnership register for gay couples, albeit with no legal standing, showed that attitudes were continuing to change. Steve Doughty writing in the *Daily Mail* remained hostile, remarking,

> Mr Livingstone said the move was 'a step on the road to equality' for homosexuals. But it will outrage many traditionalists, including Christian and Moslem [sic] opponents of new rights for homosexuals.
>
> It will also be seen as an attempt to undermine the institution of marriage. One critic of the scheme called it 'an affront to married people'.[29]

But in the same paper, a few months later, the journalist Jo Willey soberly described how '[t]he happy couple beamed as they walked down the aisle. Then, watched by their friends, they exchanged loving glances, held hands and finally made public their commitment to one another.'[30] The *London Evening Standard*, meanwhile, called it 'a love story that could never happen in London until now'.[31]

When it became clear that Parliament was going to debate civil partnership legislation, the reporting became evermore dispassionate. While *The Independent* typically described them as 'a crucial step towards giving gay and lesbian couples equal legal rights', when they were first discussed in 2001, *The Times* suggested that the consultation paper, published in 2003, 'will be criticised for discriminating against unmarried heterosexual couples. Campaigners said the proposals should have been extended to provide legal recognition for all unmarried couples.'[32] Meanwhile, in 2000, the *Daily Mail* had commented on the decision of the Liberal Democrat leader, Charles Kennedy, to back civil partnerships as party policy:

> Liberal Democrat leader Charles Kennedy risked a backlash from voters last night by backing gay marriages.
>
> He declared his support for a new party policy of 'civil partnerships' which would give same-sex couples a raft of legal rights and duties similar to those held by married couples.
>
> But his comments, on the eve of the LibDem [sic] annual conference in Bournemouth, sparked fears that he may have gone a step too far in his new crusade to win over disillusioned Tories by attacking William Hagues' 'headcase' policies.[33]

Days before civil partnerships became law in 2005, *The Daily Telegraph* reported on the first three couples to register for them, ending on a quote from OutRage! that '[o]nly same-sex marriage is genuine equality'.[34] The *Daily Mirror*, seemingly unable to avoid a controversial story, wrote how 'a painting of bride and groom has been removed from a register office in case it offends gay couples tying the knot', but nevertheless went on to describe how, [f]rom December 21, gay weddings – officially called civil partnerships – will allow single sex couples to sign documents in front of a registrar and witnesses. Those in a partnership will have new pension and inheritance rights.[35]

These changes represented a broader transformation taking place in Britain, which was witnessing gradually more liberal attitudes towards homosexuality becoming the majority opinion. It also seemed that once the debates and the law reform that could be specifically linked to children were over, the British press became far less hostile to future reform. In a sense, therefore, the long association with paedophilia – primarily with men in age of consent debates, but also women with section 28 – had been laid to rest with the reform of these laws. Civil partnership legislation was, for many, about securing partnerships rights so that homosexuality would become even more integrated in society. As such the hostility that had characterised previous legal changes was notable by its absence. The result was a dispassionate press that no longer attacked homosexuality as some outside 'other' threatening society, but rather saw it as another part of British society.

With these attitudes in place, and the public no longer being fed intolerant homophobia on an almost daily basis, public attitudes towards homosexuality continued their shift towards greater tolerance, where gay men and lesbians were no longer characterised in previous emotive terms, but rather seen as 'ordinary' couples who wanted to live 'ordinary' lives. But the press had proved to be one of the principle instigators of homophobic attitudes in the United Kingdom throughout the second half of the twentieth century. While these actions had less political impact in the 1990s than they had in the 1980s, nevertheless they perpetuated stereotypes which in turn influenced public opinion. Although these newspapers eventually stopped producing those articles, the ingrained hostility they created endeared, but without constant repetition this began to fade. Yet, what it meant to be gay in Britain in 2004 continued to have associations with this previous hostility (which cannot be understated), but, for the most part was characterised by integration, similarity, and growing acceptance in the British media.

Meanwhile, in television and film, the move towards more fully-formed characters and mainstream representation was continuing, with soap operas becoming the next frontier for gay characters. BBC's *EastEnders* had already introduced its first gay man in 1986 with the arrival of Colin Russell, played by Michael Cashman, who would go on to have the first mouth-to-mouth gay kiss on the soap in 1989 (Russell had kissed his boyfriend Barry Clarke on the forehead in an earlier episode). Five years later, in 1994, Channel 4's *Brookside* repeated this 'first' with a lesbian storyline between Beth Jordache (played by Anna Friel) and Margaret Clemence (played by Nicola Stephenson). Culminating in the first lesbian kiss on a soap, the storyline centred on the women coming to terms with their feelings for each other. Unlike Colin in *EastEnders,* dealing with accusations that he suffered from AIDS, and arriving as a gay character (albeit hidden at first) at the height of public homophobia in 1980s Britain, the *Brookside* storyline centred on characters already present in the soap, with the kiss deliberately sold as a plot point. Indeed, Channel 4 had developed a reputation for boundary-pushing broadcasting, which made it the natural home of this kind of storyline.

In portraying the confused sexuality of two young women, it – perhaps inadvertently – presented lesbianism as more ordinary, without any stereotypical characters traits. Indeed, the first kiss occurred after Beth had spent the evening with Margaret, as they were saying goodbye, and showed the characters exploring their feelings for each other, while suggesting that lesbianism was not very different from Beth's own heterosexual past:

Margaret	I'm glad we talked. It's good we can be really honest with each other.
Beth	Well that's the way it should be.
Margaret	Why don't you stay here again tonight?
Beth	No, it just wouldn't be right.
Margaret	Why not?
Beth	Well if you want me to be totally honest I wouldn't feel content to stay in the spare room.
Margaret	What do you mean?

Beth	You know how I feel about you. It doesn't just end with me finding you attractive, liking your personality. I fancy you in the same way I fancied Peter Harrison. I wanna kiss you the way I kissed him. I'm sorry, I shouldn't have said that.
Margaret	It's okay.
Beth	No, it's not. I've said too much and I've spoiled everything. How could you possibly stay friends with me now?
Margaret	Cos I want to. Come here [they hug]. I hate it when you go all sad on me. Everything's gonna be alright you know.[36]

Beth then kisses Margaret briefly on the lips, before Margaret initiates a longer kiss; after Beth leaves, the scene cuts to an advertisement break. Not only was the inclusion of lesbian characters in a soap opera a milestone in attitudes towards homosexuality – and what was considered appropriate for pre-watershed British television – but also the decision to concentrate on the emotional aspect of a same-sex love affair reflected the changes that began with films such as *My Beautiful Laundrette* a decade earlier. These stories did not centre on homophobia, political change, stereotypical images, or unhappy lives, but instead concentrated on more positive portrayals of homosexuality.

Similarly, the 1996 film *Beautiful Thing* seemed more concerned with exploring the emotions of the characters rather than a labelled sexual identity (in a sense de-gaying a gay relationship).[37] Adapted for the screen by Jonathan Harvey – and based on his original play – it told the story of Jamie and his neighbour Ste, during a summer heat wave on the Thamesmead council estate in London. Jamie, who hates sports and is often bullied at school, has begun to realise that he is gay, while Ste, who is more popular and sporty, remains apparently unaware of his feelings. When Ste gets beaten up by his abusive drug-dealing brother, whom his alcoholic father often defends, Jamie's mother, Sandra, takes him home with her. Later, Ste gets beaten up again, and stays the night in Jamie's bed. After a montage showing Ste and Jamie topless and asleep in bed together, Ste wakes up the next morning, naked, with his arm around Jamie. The film follows them gradually falling in love, in particular going to their first gay bar together, then playing in the woods, chasing each other while Mama Cass's *Make Your Own Kind of Music* plays over the scene. The story ends with Ste and Jamie dancing together in the middle of the estate with everyone looking on, suggesting that they are happy, and, like a fairy-tale, will live happily ever after.

Indeed, Harvey addressed the way in which people interpreted the story as a fairy-tale in an article in *The Guardian*:

> If people want to think of it as a fantasy, that's all right by me. I think it's about time we started to put a smile on our faces and celebrate good things in life. When you have a life like this, you seize any beautiful thing that comes your way and you don't let it go. Tomorrow you might get a brick through your window.[38]

Moreover, it was its mixture of realism and fantasy that made the film so interesting. In a review in *Gay Times* it was described as 'romantic without being sickly, realistic without being depressing, fantastic while remaining down to earth':

> The story addresses difficult issues like coming out, education and physical abuse without being preachy or dealing with extremes. It treats realistically the milestones in the coming out process from buying your first gay magazine [...] to the first kiss, the first rejection, first visit to a gay bar and coming out to your mum. None of the main characters are stereotypical. They are human with flaws and complex personalities.[39]

While Ros Jennings, writing in *British Queer Cinema,* described the film as 'a kind of "throw-back" in that it explored "coming out" as its major motif', the story was actually about first love, with the coming-out story happening as a consequence of this.[40] Jennings concluded by wondering 'whether positive images have the power to change the hearts and minds of those who have so internalised dominant ideological notions of sexuality that anything but heterosexuality is an aberration'.[41] Describing the film as 'a kind of metaphorical "comfort food"', she suggested that what was most interesting was the film's representation of homosexuality. Indeed, with a happy ending, combined with a realism with which the viewer could identify, and a positive portrayal of the coming-out process, the film — written by a gay man — presented a story about love rather than a story about homosexuality. In doing so it became like countless other low-budget romantic films, but (despite Jennings view) also reflected a positive shift in presenting homosexuality on screen, both for a heterosexual viewer, and for a young gay man growing up in the United Kingdom at that time.

In contrast, other programmes were appearing that seemed defiantly to revel in presenting homosexuality as different and unique from heterosexual life. *Gaytime TV,* first broadcast in June 1995, was a late-night BBC2 magazine series presented by Rhona Cameron and Bert Tyler-Moore in the studio, and Amy Lamé on location.[42] Indeed, the relationship between gay men and lesbians in the articles and among the presenters served to show the interconnectedness of male and female homosexual lives and interests. With the tagline 'it's not daytime, it's gaytime', it was a deliberately camp and light-hearted production — the first lesbian and gay series on the BBC. Its opening sequence showed an extravagant beach scene with an attractive muscle-bound man apparently noticing an equally attractive woman. They run towards each other, and instead of embracing, pass to kiss their same-sex partners. Everyone on the beach starts to cheer and then kiss their own same-sex partner. It included light articles following a group of men travelling to London for their first Pride, and a piece on an American gay soap opera (*inside/outside the Beltway*). Cheap, colourful, and cheerful, it seemed to have more in common with drag shows than a topical magazine programme. Although even the *Daily Mail* praised it for 'lightness of touch that other minority interest magazines would do well to emulate', Mark Simpson of

The Guardian was less enthusiastic.[43] Under the title 'Grey-time TV' he wrote,

> Homosexuals used to be 'cured' of their condition by the application of electric shocks or the ingestion of emetics while being exposed to homosexual images. By associating pain, nausea and discomfort with desire for the same sex the doctors hoped to set up a 'normal' response in the patient.
>
> We've come a long way since then. Nowadays, this kind of inhumane treatment is permitted only when perpetrated by other homosexuals. On television.[44]

Despite this, it seemed to represent a turning point in positive gay representation on television, when homosexuality neither had to be grown-up and serious (in a magazine format) nor deliberately 'normal' (in actual images of individuals).

This was nowhere more apparent than in Russell T. Davies' *Queer as Folk*.[45] Broadcast on Channel 4, it told the story of a group of men living in Manchester, centring on friends Stuart and Vince, the unresolved tension of their relationship, and their nights out in Canal Street. The first episode included the controversial arrival of 15-year-old Nathan (at the time three years below the age of consent), who Stuart picks up one night. The series was full of outrageous behaviour, sex, drinking, drug-taking, and a generally hedonistic lifestyle. This was deliberate, with 'no HIV storyline [...], nor any heavy-handed discussion of safe sex [...] [and] relatively few weeping relatives shown struggling to come to terms with a gay member of the family'.[46] Indeed, Davies claimed that he was motivated to write an entertaining drama 'which touched on issues in his own life' and did not attempt to represent gay men for any political agenda:[47]

> They're always looking to see themselves be represented. Most people had a brilliant time. Most people are out buying a soundtrack and liking the gags and fancying the boys and seeing a bit of arse and were very happy.[48]

Despite this, the series nevertheless had the effect of presenting a hedonistic, unapologetic, sex-obsessed gay culture as typical of gay social and group identity. The inclusion of the main protagonist's repeated sexual encounters with the 15-year-old Nathan only served to reinforce old stereotypes about gay men and paedophilia. Indeed, this became one of the main reasons for the series to be attacked in the media. The *Daily Mail*, under the title 'Gay sex with boy of 15 – the latest offering on Four', wrote how, 'consistent with controller Michael Jackson's mission to flout the boundaries of taste and decency, it will feature a sex act with a boy of only 15'.[49] Gary Bushell, writing in *The Sun* under the headline 'Telly's gay mafia are out to lure our kids' argued that,

> we can't afford to ignore this charmless garbage. It has to be seen in the context of campaigns to 'normalise' homosexuality and reduce the age of consent – campaigns the culturati are winning *despite* public opinion.
>
> Telly's powerful gay mafia played a huge part in the battle to legalise gay sex at 16. The goalposts are still moving. The next target is 14.[50]

The *Daily Telegraph*'s Stephen Pile, meanwhile claimed that '[i]f this had been a 15-year-old school girl receiving the repeated, explicit and illegal attention of a self-centred 30-year-old man there would have been outrage'.[51]

That said, the series also served to present gay life on gay terms. It did not look for sympathy as other programmes had done, or to further any gay political movement. Instead, it offered an alternative, proud look at one (important) aspect of gay life. Indeed, writing in The *Independent,* Precious Williams described the characters as 'rather anti-climatically normal and predictable':

> [I]ts content proved that being young and openly gay was not fundamentally different from being young and openly heterosexual. The *Queer as Folk* characters are attractive and

socially active men who just happen to lust after other men rather than women. In swerving away from surreal and over-the-top media-friendly gay stereotypes like Julian Clary and Dale Winton, *Queer as Folk* succeeded in creating believable and unapologetic characters who were capable of striking a chord with a wide range of viewers.[52]

With hindsight, the British Film Institute has also seen the drama as playing an important role in the development of a gay group identity on television. Despite the type of identity it presented, what was more important was that it was bold and unapologetic:

> The depiction of promiscuity, drug use and underage sex predictably sparked complaints, many of them from the gay community, but these arguments missed the point. For the first time gay men took centre stage and were neither victims nor villains, seeking the approval of no one. Funny, sexy and confident, these guys presented new, exciting role models. A true landmark of British television.[53]

In contrast to the media images being projected in earlier periods, then, this 'becoming mainstream' period witnessed the gradual emergence of realistic portrayals of gay men and lesbians in all three formats. Gay publications became more lifestyle focused, increasingly trying to appeal to as wide an audience as possible – recognising the diversity of experiences among gay men and lesbians. The press, however, remained preoccupied with legal change, with, broadly, the tabloids opposing law reform (although not always). Seemingly out of step with the lived experiences of gay men and lesbians, these views nevertheless perpetuated negative stereotypes reminiscent of the peak in homophobia in the 1980s. Despite examples of Baroness Young seemingly repeating claims from those articles during parliamentary debates, newspapers were unable to affect legal change as they had in the 1980s. It was only by the end of this period, and the introduction of civil partnership legislation, that these images began to change, replaced with more dispassionate reporting. In television and film, however, there appeared to be two different agendas at play. The first was concerned with representing gay men and lesbians as indistinguishable from their heterosexual neighbours. Soaps and films concentrated on deliberately ordinary people coming to terms with their sexuality through loving relationships, rather than a clichéd coming-out story in the traditional sense. But the second agenda was more concerned with reflecting the more nuanced lives of gay men and lesbians – whether that be through a camp, light-hearted magazine series, or through a controversial drama. Either way, these representations were not concerned with negative stereotypes, but instead with reflecting a diversity of gay life.

CONCLUSION

It is often assumed that the labels 'gay' and 'straight' – and the identities they describe – have always existed. Modern Britain – and most of the modern Western world – has taken it for granted that there is such a thing as a gay man and a lesbian, and that homosexuality confers with it an identity society automatically understands. Indeed, sections of the public often discuss gay people in the past as though they are timeless, invariably ascribing them contemporary identities they never had. They define people, and trade in language, prejudice, and stereotypes without understanding their origins. They assume an unchanging and ever-present system of defining identity based on sexuality. This book has sought to dispel these public myths and present a new history of homosexuality spanning the past 40 years. It shows how recent historical events have created this sexual order. Between 1967 – when male homosexual sex was partially decriminalised – and 2004 – when civil partnership legislation became law – defining yourself and being defined by others as homosexual changed entirely in the United Kingdom. A hidden sexual act became a public identity, and, gradually, political reform gave it legitimacy, images in the media brought it to life, and social changes made it real.

Recalling life in pre-law reform Britain, interviewees in projects examining the history of homosexuality recalled a marked lack of knowledge in their understanding of what homosexuality was and what it meant for them. David recalled how '[a]t that time I didn't regard myself as homosexual, I never thought of this word, nobody knew such a word. It was just something that you did.'[1] Diana, on reading *The Well of Loneliness,* remembered feeling 'shattered': 'I thought, "This is me; this is what it's all about." I wept copiously; I went about in a daze.'[2] From the GLF, through to the 1980s commercial social scene, the devastation of HIV/AIDS, and the reform agenda of the 1990s and 2000s, homosexuality emerged as a visible feature of British life. This book is a study of those political, social, and media changes. It is an examination of the historical events that have shaped a discourse on homosexuality; it is an exploration of the compartmentalisation of sexuality into binary categories; it is an examination of the evolution of sexual identities; and it is a challenge to the homogenisation created through the concept of group identity.

Political, social, and cultural change in Britain has not been linear. Seemingly liberalising events (including the decision of newspaper editors to support law reform in the 1950s and 1960s, and the public visibility of Gay Liberation in the 1970s) have been met with regressive legal change, renewed and intensified homophobia in the press, and a devastating HIV/AIDS epidemic. But despite this, changes that improved the lives of gay men and lesbians from the 1990s onwards (including legal reform, an expanding social scene, and realistic portrayals of homosexuality in the media) were often the result of the very repression that sought with some success to attack homosexuality throughout the 1980s. As mentioned, it is too simplistic to suggest that the political has influenced the media, which have then together influenced the social, or any other permutations of the three. But there is evidence that a desire for law reform and acceptance in society framed the emergence of sexual identities in the United Kingdom. Indeed, before 1967 some men and women were already defining themselves by a specific sexual identity, but it was often hidden and discreet. There were also labels for men and women who engaged in homosexual behaviour, but they were not universally understood, nor publicly acknowledged. In contrast, this study has looked at

CONCLUSION

public images of homosexuality and how they have been created and recreated and turned into social and group identities.

Throughout this period, then, as a discourse on homosexuality developed through public representations, a binary system gradually emerged where people were labelled 'heterosexual' or 'homosexual', 'straight' or 'gay'. While arguably a gay identity was more important in defining a person – as it set them apart from an assumed heterosexuality – the rise of a system of sexual classification relied on an oppositional relationship between homosexuality and heterosexuality. This was still in its infancy when sexuality was hidden at the beginning of this period, was not as important a public signifier of identity, and the homosexual was only just publicly emerging. But Gay Liberation in the 1970s helped solidify this binary – in particular in building its identity in opposition to the family, and using its manifesto to attack 'straight society': '[W]e face the prejudice, hostility and violence of straight society, and the opportunities open to us in work and leisure are restricted, compared with those of straight people.'[3] By the 1980s this binary system emerged as universally understood categories in the United Kingdom, in association with a widely understood gay group identity. Curiously, a bisexual sexual identity has not similarly developed during this period, and instead society recognised these two labels and identities despite the obvious contradictions. While Britain in 2004 was more open in its attitude towards homosexuality, conversely making a gay sexual identity less important to social and group identity, the homo-hetero binary remained in most public discourse, despite the problems with labelling sexuality that way.

But sexual identities have not been static in this period. In 1960s Britain the HLRS and MRG, and films like *Victim*, characterised a homosexual identity through a middle-class respectability. In working for legal and social change – as well as exploring the nature of sexuality more broadly – these images reflected a very specific class of people. For men, they were, ironically, created by heterosexual law reformers who believed that the law persecuted a minority unfairly. The HLRS and MRG hoped to present an acceptable image of the homosexual man that British society would be happy to emancipate to ensure that they could lead private lives free from blackmail and imprisonment. For women, they were well educated, self-identified lesbians well-versed in the work of sexologists and keen to create a social network in a society with far greater restrictions on women than men. While these were the first public sexual identities in the United Kingdom, they were not universal, and it soon became obvious that they did not reflect the majority of homosexual men and women.

Gay liberation instead reflected the counter cultural aspirations of a generation of young men and women coming of age at a time when male homosexuality had been partially decriminalised, and when women were gaining greater control over their own futures. Like the respectable images that preceded it, GLF's depiction of a gay identity was never representative of the entire homosexual population of the United Kingdom. But they were the most visible. In contrast to the almost apologetic earlier homophile movements, they defiantly proclaimed their sexuality and sexual identity – which at this stage rested on breaking gender and societal norms through revolutionary fervour. In doing so they ensured that homosexuality became a visible and permanent feature of British life, even if ideas surrounding sexual identity were still developing and many people could not or would not be defined as a gay man or a lesbian when it involved a perceived allegiance to left-wing radicalism.

But Gay Liberation, and the Gay Liberation movement (as well as other organisations that had ensured the continued development of a gay social world) created the foundations for the future growth of a discourse on homosexuality in Britain – including the idea of a gay and lesbian identity. As the gay social scene expanded through commercial development, gay men and lesbians became an ever more visible and permanent feature of British life. However, this came at a cost. The growth of an open, sex-orientated social scene – often seen as the prize of gay liberation – provided the perfect conditions for the spread of HIV/AIDS among gay men. This, combined with the greater visibility that many in society saw as a threat to traditional standards, led to a public backlash against homosexuality. While this could have set in motion a decline in open and visible sexual identities, it instead served to reinforce these emerging identities through a community of networks and support structures. While for many the group identity remained exclusionary – whether through age, race, gender or physical appearance – the public had come to understand that defining someone as a gay man or a lesbian was as legitimate as defining them as Black or White, or male or female, in terms of a personal and public profile.

The 1990s and 2000s witnessed the continued expansion of public representations of homosexuality and a gay and lesbian group identity, as well as of people defining themselves as homosexual. Indeed, as it became more inclusive as a defining label for homosexual men and women of all ages, ethnicities, religions, and backgrounds, it also became less indistinguishable from heterosexual society. For many this was a welcome evolution in a system that had developed from a desire for social and legal equality, but for others represented a betrayal of the revolutionary aims of the Gay Liberation Movement which had coined the term in the 1970s. While a gay social and group identity remained a clear feature of British life at the end of this period, for many it was moving towards a simple label of sexuality. But, like other identities such as religious or political affiliation, it was increasingly worn in conjunction with other labels, and was no longer seen in the public discourse an all-encompassing and defining feature of a person's public and private identity. Instead, with a network of communities, a distinctive social scene, and a shared history, a gay identity (both social and group) was emerging – at the beginning of the new millennium – as one aspect of an increasingly multi-identity world.

But, crucially, it is the origin of these identities which is most important to this study. This book is premised on the central assertion that sexual identities did not emerge in a vacuum, but instead were created, shaped, and sustained by images in society. While other histories of homosexual identity in this period have concentrated on self-created social and group identities, this book argues that the majority gained their ideas of what homosexuality meant through engaging with a public discourse presented in the media, the law, and the social lives of gay men and lesbians (indeed these social lives have thus far been the focus of most historical enquiry). Weeks has written extensively on the social role of self-adopted labels, and how they represented 'a changing reality [...] in the way those stigmatized saw themselves'.[4] Jennings, too, has focused on these self-adopted roles, writing how the 'post-war notions of femininity afforded women a surprising degree of flexibility in the expression of alternative gender and sexual identities'.[5] This work has been extremely important in examining the origins of self-created identities, and the creation of modern sexual identities in Britain. But it only represents one aspect of those emerging labels. Self-created identities must be seen in the context of other sources of the public discourse surrounding sexuality, which were crucial in establishing both social and group sexual identities. Thus members of the public – homosexual and heterosexual – gained their ideas of what homosexuality was from the public discourse taking place around them, and not simply from a process of self-awareness that, for example, membership of the GLF or a copy of a sexological textbook might have brought.

From the beginning of this period, when the HLRS was created, there have been a plethora of different representations of homosexuality in British society. Indeed, HLRS, with their focus on presenting the discreet and respectable middle-class homosexual through their lobbying efforts, showed that they understood the importance of how the public perceived homosexuality in achieving law reform. Likewise, the MRG had had the same focus on presenting a public face of middle-class respectability. In August 1964, for example, after letters of complaint were written in to *Arena Three*, a motion was debated at their meeting proposing '[t]hat this house considers the wearing of male attire at MRG meetings is inappropriate'.[6] While it was narrowly defeated it reflected what one member described as the view of many *Arena Three* readers:

> 'Butch' working-class lesbians were blatantly sexual and dangerously stupid because they did not care what straight society thought of them. Straight-acting middle-class lesbians were 'decent people', i.e. not 'butch', not working-class and not

CONCLUSION

dangerous. They could not afford to be recognised as lesbians and did not wish to be seen as sharing a common identity with 'butch dykes'.[7]

When the GLF arrived in the United Kingdom this public image of homosexuality changed and became deliberately confrontational, to show the country – and the world – that a gay identity was proud, visible, and in defiance of traditional societal norms. While the early 1980s image of the hedonistic social scene was a continuation of this overt 'difference', the outbreak of HIV/AIDS created an unintended association between homosexuality, death, and disease. These changes in what society perceived as representing a homosexual or gay sexual identity continued to evolve right up to the end of this period. They reflected just one aspect of public perceptions in the creation of these non-static sexual identities in Britain and show how they were deliberately used for, in this case, political ends.

But it was never one single group identity that was being presented to society. Instead, there have been contradictory images being projected by different interests groups – some homosexual, some heterosexual, some opposed to certain kinds of homosexuality, and some opposed to all kinds. This study has sought to use three of the most important arenas for the dissemination of images of and attitudes towards homosexuality, in the creation of broader subjectivities. Politics and the law because they define what is and is not acceptable and legally sanctioned. Media images because they are the most viewed in modern society and have the potential for the greatest influence. And the social lives of gay men and lesbians because they projected a clear discourse on identity (when sexual identities were just emerging). Broadly, these are represented in three distinct time periods. The 'Gay Liberation' period witnessed the emergence of a public identity – given legitimacy through legal reform, nurtured through sympathetic characters in television and film, pitied by the mainstream press, and built up by homosexual publications. By the end of this period, however, things were already changing, with the failure to achieve any significant law reform, and a political, social, and media backlash against homosexuality.

This 'Visible Subculture' period saw the continued expansion of visible representations of homosexuality, contrasting more nuanced portrayals on television and film, and the growth of the gay social scene, with a tabloid, political, and social backlash. The 'Becoming Mainstream' period saw the expansion of legal rights for gay men and lesbians, an improvement in the social attitudes towards homosexuality (albeit with some notable exceptions), and the development of even more diverse characters in television and film, although the tabloids remained broadly negative.

But despite these similarities making the three time periods identifiable, within them this study has shown how the three arenas projected unique images of homosexuality at different times and at different speeds. Thus a gay social and group identity could be built on any one of these different images, depending on an individual's consumption of news, awareness of political/legal changes, interest in programmes and films with a gay plot, or interaction with gay men and lesbians in society. It is clear, however, that it was these public images that defined identity for the majority of people in Britain – especially the heterosexual majority, but also any homosexual man or woman who was just beginning to develop their own sexual identity without first-hand experience of the gay world. Group sexual identity – what it means to define someone as a gay man or a lesbian – was not just a creation of gay men and lesbians themselves, as much as many would like to think. Instead, it was a mixture of all these different aspects of visible ideas being disseminated into the public consciousness. Public perceptions, then, informed and created sexual identity, as the earlier homosexual law reform campaigners were only too aware.

Yet despite the obvious differences between time periods and arenas in projecting public images of homosexuality, there have nonetheless been constants in the post-war history of sexual identity. Homosexuality is, at its very basic level, a label based on same-sex sexual acts. Despite changes in the public's attitude towards those acts, they have nevertheless remained a continuous feature of homosexual identity – whether or not they were subject to moral judgements. For politics and the law, moreover, these sexual acts (and later sexual identities in anti-discrimination legislation) have proved an almost permanent feature of British legal history – outlining a continuous association between homosexuality and the law. So too the minority status of homosexuality has, likewise, remained unbroken. Despite changing attitudes towards homosexuals, they have still remained a minority feature of British society. And throughout this period the social lives of homosexuals have shown an ability to seek out like-minded people for friendship and relationships, despite the risks involved. Although this was not true of all homosexuals, there is clear evidence that coteries of men and women have managed to maintain significant inter-personal relationships, which have in turn contributed to a growing public identity.

Although ostensibly about the creation of a gay group identity in the United Kingdom, this study has also explored the social identities of individuals and how they are constructed. The modern history of sexual identity is in constant flux, as ideas and attitudes change, and as new generations come along unwilling to live in the way the previous generation took for granted. Somewhere in this jumble of identities and ways of living there emerges a dominant discourse, which the majority of people assume represents the homogenous whole. There never was and there never will be a single homosexual social identity, either in a specific time and place, or across history, that accurately reflects the way individuals live their lives and define themselves. Instead, social identity, when present in society (and history shows this is not always the case), is variously modulated by location, class, ethnicity, religious background, and gender.

Indeed, at the beginning of this period the dominant ideas about identity being presented to the public were clearly never representative, and were instead often a deliberate attempt at achieving law reform. Likewise, the youth-orientated counter cultural gay identity that developed in the 1970s was not an identity shared by a middle-aged professional, for example. The image of the gay male 'clone', or the 'butch dyke' from the 1980s social scene did not reflect the identity of a rural worker. Even the 1990s image of the relatively well-adjusted gay man or lesbian living an open life free from discrimination was not representative of the whole. Instead, there have been ideas and images that have defined how people viewed homosexuality, and that have defined what a gay and lesbian group sexual identity meant at particular points in time. There were many people who did not fit this identity, did not want to fit it, or were deliberately excluded, but they were still living lives that could be classified as 'gay'.

Furthermore, the conflicting images being presented reflect a complicated scenario whereby group sexual identity meant more than one thing at one time depending on the forum it was being presented in. It could be that young, male-dominated counter culture, while also being the image of a sad and lonely man and woman. It could be a liberal same-sex family bringing up children, while also being a paedophile intent on indoctrinating children into a homosexual lifestyle. And it could be a man dying from AIDS, while also being one half of a young star-crossed couple falling in love. These examples expose the contradictions in defining anyone based on an identity that is shared by millions of people, even if it is an identity they willingly sign up to. They show that there is no singular gay identity – either in the images being projected in society, or in the groups of people they are said to represent. Instead, there are stereotypes, or characteristics, that need to be understood for the generalisations or fabrications that they were. It was the accessibility of these stereotypes to particular audiences, moreover, as well as their interpretation of them, that ultimately influenced a person's assimilation of them.

This book has sought to understand the construction of sexual identities in post-war Britain. It has shown how images in society have created these representations of identity, which in turn have been adopted as social identities by homosexuals, and as group identities by people in society. The history of homosexuality in Britain during this period cannot be told without reference to the rise of the system of classifying people based on their sexuality, when what you were was as important as what you did. While the history of those who felt excluded from these group identities is equally as significant, it is of fundamental importance that we first understand the nature of these labels. But this book has also been about challenging ideas and assumptions society takes for granted. When we realise that the identities to which people ascribe – in both defining themselves and in defining others – are historical, rather than biological, in origin, we can begin to think about how we really want to be defined, and how we want to define others.

NOTES

Introduction

1. Anthony Grey, *Quest for Justice: Towards Homosexual Emancipation* (London: Sinclair-Stevenson, 1992), p. 183.
2. Author's interview with gay man 'E', 17 July 2012, born 6 March 1985.
3. Jeffrey Weeks, *Coming Out: Homosexual Politics in Britain, from the Nineteenth Century to the Present* (London: Quartet Books, 1977), p. 3.
4. Ibid., p. 18.
5. Jeffrey Weeks, *The World We Have Won: The Remaking of Erotic and Intimate Life* (London: Routledge, 2007), p. (x).
6. Jeffrey Weeks, *Against Nature: Essay on History, Sexuality and Identity* (London: River Oram Press, 1991), p. 87.
7. Weeks, *The World We Have Won*, p. 93.
8. Jeffrey Weeks, *Sex Politics, & Society: The Regulation of Sexuality since 1800* (Harlow: Longman, 1981), preface.
9. Jeffrey Weeks, *Making Sexual History* (Cambridge: Polity Press, 2000), pp. 82–3.
10. Weeks, *Making Sexual History*, p. 8.
11. Rebecca Jennings, *A Lesbian History of Britain: Love and Sex Between Women Since 1500* (Oxford: Greenwood World Publishing, 2007).
12. Rebecca Jennings, *Tomboys and Bachelor Girls: a Lesbian History of Post-War Britain, 1945–1971* (Manchester: Manchester University Press, 2007), p. 173.
13. Hugh David, *On Queer Street: a Social History of British Homosexuality, 1895–1995* (London: HarperCollins, 1997).
14. Ken Plummer, *The Making of the Modern Homosexual* (London: Hutchinson, 1981).
15. Matt Cook, 'From Gay Reform to Gaydar' in *A Gay History of Britain: Love and Sex Between Men Since the Middle Ages*, ed. by Matt Cook (Oxford; Westport, Connecticut: Greenwood World Publishing, 2007).

16. Houlbrook, *Queer London: Perils and Pleasures in the Metropolis, 1918–1957* (Chicago; London: University of Chicago Press, 2005), pp. 236–7.
17. Ibid., p. 226; Jennings, *Tomboys and Bachelor Girls*, p. 2.
18. Dominic Sandbrook, *State of Emergency: The Way We Were: Britain, 1970–1974* (London: Penguin, 2010), p. 10.

Chapter 1   Early Optimism

1. HL Deb, 21 July 1967, vol 285, cols 522–3.
2. Stephen Jeffrey-Poulter, *Peers, Queers and Commons: The Struggle for Gay Law Reform from 1950 to the Present* (London: Routledge, 1991), p. 17.
3. Peter Wildeblood, *Against the Law* (London: Weidenfeld & Nicolson, 1999), p. 11.
4. Police activity against homosexuality intensified after World War II – see for example Houlbrook, *Queer London* and Weeks, *Sex, Politics and Society*.
5. *The Sunday Times*, 28 March 1954.
6. Jeffrey-Poulter, *Peers, Queers and Commons*, p. 16.
7. HL Deb, 19 May 1954, vol 187, cols 737–67.
8. Patrick Higgins, *Heterosexual Dictatorship: Male Homosexuality in Post-War Britain* (London: Fourth Estate, 1996), p. 6.
9. Jeffrey Weeks, *Coming Out*, p. 64; Home Office/Scottish Home Department, *Report of the Committee on Homosexual Offences and Prostitution* (London: Her Majesty's Stationery Office, 1957), p. 25.
10. 'On this day – 1957: Homosexuality 'should not be a crime', *BBC News* [accessed on 23 November 2009]. http://news.bbc.co.uk/onthisday/hi/dates/stories/september/4/newsid_3007000/3007686.stm.
11. Church of England Moral Welfare Council, *Sexual Offenders and Social Punishment* (London: Church Information Board, 1956), p. 27. The report owed its origins to Sherwin Bailey, the Study Secretary of the Church of England Moral Welfare Council, who had been asked to reply to a letter in *Theology* on homosexuality, and did so in an article entitled 'The Problem of Sexual Inversion'. He received a stream of private correspondence in response to the article, and took the matter to the Moral Welfare Council where he asked them to study the subject.
12. 'A.E. Dyson – Obituary', *The Independent* [accessed on 1 March 2011]. http://www.independent.co.uk/news/obituaries/a-e-dyson-748680.html.
13. *The Times*, 7 March 1958.
14. Jeffrey-Poulter, *Peers, Queers and Commons*, p. 38.
15. Wildeblood, *Against the Law*, p. 7.
16. Houlbrook, *Queer London*, p. 243.
17. Home Office/Scottish Home Department, *Report of the Committee on Homosexual Offences and Prostitution* (London: Her Majesty's Stationery Office, 1957), p. 20.
18. Ibid., p. 23.

19. Ibid., p. 32.
20. Antony Grey, *Speaking Out: Writings on Sex, Law, Politics and Society, 1954–95* (London: Cassell, 1997), pp. 32–3.
21. Cook, *From Gay Reform to Gaydar*, p. 174.
22. Jeffrey-Poulter, *Peers, Queers and Commons*, p. 70.
23. *Encounter*, July 1972.
24. Leo Abse, *Private Member* (London: McDonald & Co., 1973), p. 150.
25. Ibid., p. 611
26. HC Deb, 11 February 1966, vol 722, col. 784.
27. HC Deb, 19 December 1966, vol 738, col. 1132.
28. HC Deb, 25 December 1982, vol 29, col. 848–9.
29. Antony Grey, *Quest for Justice*, p. 128.
30. HC Deb, 22 July 1980, vol 989, col. 298.
31. Hall Carpenter Archives, HCA/ALBANY TRUST/2/1. The Homosexual Law Reform Society. Executive Committee meeting minutes 11 October 1967. The Latey Committee had been considering the law relating to minors in England and Wales.
32. Ibid.
33. Jeffrey-Poulter, *Peers, Queers and Commons*, p. 108.
34. Cook, *From Gay Reform to Gaydar*, p. 174.
35. Lucy Robinson, 'Three Revolutionary Years: The Impact of the Counter Culture on the Development of the Gay Liberation Movement', *Cultural and Social History*, 3 (2006), 445–71, p. 452.
36. *Come Together: the Years of Gay Liberation (1970–73)*, ed. by Aubrey Walter (London: Gay Men's Press, 1980), p. 10.
37. Ibid., p. 11.
38. Arthur Marwick, *The Sixties: Cultural Revolution in Britain, France, Italy, and the United States, c.1958–c.1974* (Oxford: Oxford University Press, 1999), p. 553.
39. Walter, *Come Together*, pp. 12–13.
40. Jeffrey Weeks, *Sex, Politics, & Society: The Regulation of Sexuality since 1800* (Harlow: Longman, 1981), p. 286.
41. Walter, *Come Together*, p. 11.
42. Hall Carpenter Archives, HCA/ALBANY TRUST/2/1. The Homosexual Law Reform Society: Constitution and Rules.
43. Gay Liberation Front Manifesto – London 1971, quoted in Lisa Power, *No Bath But Plenty of Bubbles: An Oral History of the Gay Liberation Front 1970–73* (London: Cassell, 1995), p. 328.
44. Weeks,' *Coming Out*, p. 197.
45. Sheila Jeffreys, *Anticlimax: a Feminist Perspective on the Sexual Revolution* (London: The Women's Press, 1990), p. 150.
46. Cook, *From Gay Reform to Gaydar*, p. 182.
47. Power, *No Bath But Plenty of Bubbles*, pp. 139–40.
48. Ibid., p. 179.
49. Ibid., p. 141.

NOTES TO PAGES 30–39   227

50. John Capon, quoted in Power, *No Bath But Plenty of Bubbles*, p. 159.
51. Weeks, *Coming Out*, p. 200.
52. Jeffrey-Poulter, *Peers, Queers and Commons*, p. 107.
53. Hall Carpenter Archives, C456/69. Interview with Nettie Pollard, 13 February 1990; Nettie Pollard, quoted in Power, *No Bath But Plenty of Bubbles*, p. 246.
54. Grey, *Quest for Justice*, p. 183.
55. Hall Carpenter Archives, HCA/ALBANY TRUST/2/1. The Sexual Law Reform Society Constitution.
56. Home Office, Criminal Law Revision Committee, *Fifteenth Report: Sexual Offences* (London: Her Majesty's Stationery Office, 1984), p. 53.
57. Hall Carpenter Archives, HCA/ALBANY TRUST/2/1. Report on Working Party on Sexual Behaviour, Sexual Law Reform Society, 5 September 1974.
58. Jeffrey-Poulter, *Peers, Queers and Commons*, p. 58.
59. Alan Horsfall, quoted in, Jeffrey-Poulter, *Peers, Queers and Commons*, p. 59.
60. Hall Carpenter Archives, HCA/ALBANY TRUST/2/1. Bulletin, North-Western Homosexual Law Reform Committee, April 1968.
61. Hall Carpenter Archives, HCA/CHE/3/2. CHE National Council, An Outline, September 1973.
62. Hall Carpenter Archives, HCA/CHE/1/1. Annual Report, Campaign for Homosexual Equality, 1975.
63. Jeffrey-Poulter, *Peers, Queers and Commons*, p. 112.
64. Ibid.
65. Weeks, *Coming Out*, pp. 210–11.
66. Hall Carpenter Archives, HCA/CHE/1/1. Annual Report, Campaign for Homosexual Equality, 1979.
67. Roy Walmsley and Karen White, *Sexual Offences and Sentencing* Home Office Research Study No. 54 (London: Her Majesty's Stationery Office, 1979), p. 275.
68. Hall Carpenter Archives, HCA/ALBANY TRUST/2/1. Bulletin, North-Western Homosexual Law Reform Committee, April 1968.

Chapter 2 Early Images

1. Significant precedents did exist, however. *The Artist and Journal of Home Culture*, published in the 1890s is discussed for its undercurrent of homoeroticism by Matt Cook in *London and the Culture of Homosexuality, 1885–1914* (Cambridge: Cambridge University Press, 2003).
2. Jennings, *A Lesbian History of Britain*, p. 152.
3. Jennings, *Tomboys and Bachelor Girls*, pp. 134–6.
4. Ibid., p. 137.
5. Jennings, *A Lesbian History of Britain*, p. 154.
6. *Arena Three*, Vol. 8 no. 5. *Arena Three* did not include dates on their publications, making precise dating impossible.

7. Ibid.
8. *Arena Three*, Vol. 9 no. 3.
9. *Arena Three*, Vol. 8 no. 4.
10. *Arena Three*, Vol. 8 no. 7–12.
11. Ibid.
12. *Jeremy*, vol. 1 no. 1, 1969. *Jeremy* did not include dates on their publications, making precise dating impossible.
13. *Daily Mirror*, 5 August 1969.
14. *Jeremy*, vol. 1 no. 2, 1969.
15. *Timm*, no. 18. *Timm* did not include dates on their publications, making precise dating impossible.
16. *Timm*, no. 8.
17. *Timm*, no. 18.
18. Jeffrey-Poulter, *Peers, Queers and Commons*, p. 97.
19. Editor's Letter, *Spartacus*, no. 18.
20. *Spartacus*, no. 25.
21. *Come Together*, Issue 1. *Come Together* did not include dates on their publications, making precise dating impossible.
22. Matt Houlbrook, *Queer London*, p. 222.
23. Hugh Cudlipp, *The Sunday Pictorial*, 1952, quoted in Terry Sanderson, *Mediawatch: The Treatment of Male and Female Homosexuality in the British Media* (London: Cassell, 1995), p. 7.
24. Adrian Bingham, *Family Newspapers? Sex, Private Life, and the British Popular Press 1918–1978* (Oxford: Oxford University Press, 2009), p. 6.
25. Ibid., p. 184.
26. Ibid., p. 188
27. Sanderson, *Mediawatch*, p. 9.
28. Ibid.
29. Ibid.
30. Ibid., p. 10.
31. Bingham, *Family Newspapers?*, p. 194.
32. Ibid., p. 196.
33. *London Evening Standard*, 28 August 1971.
34. *The Observer*, 17 January 1971.
35. *The Observer*, 6 February 1972.
36. *The Daily Telegraph*, 31 May 1976.
37. *The Guardian*, 8 July 1977.
38. Vito Russo, *The Celluloid Closet: Homosexuality in the Movies* (New York: Harper and Row, 1987).
39. *Victim*, dir. by Basil Dearden (The Rank Organisation, 1961).
40. Andy Medhurt, 'In Search of Nebulous Nancies: Looking for Queers in Pre-Gay British film', in *British Queer Cinema,* ed. by Robin Griffiths (London: Routledge, 2006), pp. 21–34 (p. 23).
41. Russo, *The Celluloid Closet*, p. 132.

42. *Daily Express*, 28 July 1961.
43. *London Evening Standard*, 31 August 1961; *The Sunday Times*, 3 September 1961.
44. *The Times Educational Supplement*, 15 September 1961.
45. *Victim*, dir. by Basil Dearden (The Rank Organisation, 1961).
46. Quoted in John Coldstream, *Victim* (London: BFI: Palgrave Macmillan, 2011), p. 100.
47. Ibid., p. 101.
48. Ibid., p. 108.
49. Robin Griffiths, *British Queer Cinema*, p. 11.
50. *The Killing of Sister George,* dir. by Robert Aldrich (The Associates and Aldrich Company, 1968).
51. *Daily Express*, 27 March 1969.
52. Quoted in Stephen Bourne, *Brief Encounters: Lesbian and Gays in British Cinema 1930–1971* (London: Cassell, 1996), p. 213.
53. Quoted in Lizzie Thynne, '"A comic monster of revue": Beryl Reid, *Sister George* and the performance of dykery' in *British Queer Cinema*, ed. by Robin Griffiths (London: Routledge, 2006), pp. 91–103 (pp. 98–9.)
54. Ibid., p. 98.
55. Russo, *The Celluloid Closet*, p. 173.
56. *Man Alive, Consenting Adults: The Men,* dir. by Tom Conway (BBC, 1967).
57. Ibid.
58. Ibid.
59. *Man Alive, Consenting Adults: The Women,* dir. by Adam Clapham (BBC, 1967).
60. Ibid.
61. Ibid.
62. Ibid.
63. Ibid.
64. Ibid.
65. *Birmingham Post*, 10 June 1967.
66. *Reading Evening Post*, 8 June 1967.
67. *Morning Star*, 10 June 1967.
68. *Daily Mail*, 8 June 1967.
69. *Sunday Telegraph*, 11 June 1967.
70. *The Sun*, 15 June 1967.
71. Keith Howes, *Broadcasting It: An Encyclopaedia of Homosexuality on Film, Radio and TV in the UK 1923–1993* (London: Cassell, 1993); 'Girl (1974)', BFI Screenonline [accessed on 24 January 2012]. http://www.screenonline.org.uk/tv/id/1396805/index.htm.
72. *Girl* dir. by Peter Gill (BBC, 1974).
73. *Thirty Minute Theatre: Bermondsey,* dir. by Claude Whatham (BBC, 1972).
74. Ibid.
75. Ibid.

Chapter 3 'Ostentatious Behaviour and Public Flaunting'

1. *Between the Acts: Lives of Homosexual Men 1885–1967*, ed. by Jeffrey Weeks and Kevin Porter (London: Rivers Oram Press, 1998), p. 69.
2. Trevor Thomas in ibid., p. 87.
3. Hall Carpenter Archives, HCA/ALBANY TRUST/2/1. Social Organisations for Homosexuals, 2 May 1968.
4. *Arena Three*, January 1964.
5. Jennings, *A Lesbian History of Britain*, p. 154.
6. Alison Oram and Annmarie Turnball, *The Lesbian History Sourcebook: Love and Sex Between Women in Britain from 1780 to 1970* (London: Routledge, 2001), pp. 237–8.
7. Ibid., pp. 157–8.
8. Ibid., p. 156.
9. Ibid. pp. 163–4.
10. *Arena Three*, vol. 4 no. 7.
11. Hall Carpenter Archives, *Inventing Ourselves: Lesbian Life Stories* (London: Routledge, 1989), p. 55. Interview with Diana Chapman, 10 September 1985.
12. Nina Miller, quoted in Jennings, *A Lesbian History of Britain* p. 167.
13. Hall Carpenter Archives, HCA/ALBANY TRUST/2/1. 'after the Act...'.
14. Hall Carpenter Archives, HCA/ALBANY TRUST/2/1. Bulletin, North-Western Homosexual Law Reform Committee, April 1968.
15. Hall Carpenter Archives, HCA/ALBANY TRUST/2/1. Letter to Professor A.J. Ayer of HLRS, 11 April 1968; Lord Arran quoted in Jeffrey-Poulter, *Peers, Queers and Commons*, p. 95.
16. Hall Carpenter Archives, HCA/ALBANY TRUST/2/1. The Male and Female Homosexual Association of Britain membership form.
17. Grey, *Quest for Justice*, p. 160.
18. Jeffrey-Poulter, *Peers, Queers and Commons*, p. 97.
19. Ibid.; Grey, *Quest for Justice*, p. 160.
20. Jeffrey-Poulter, *Peers, Queers and Commons*, p. 98.
21. Hall Carpenter Archives, HCA/CHE/1/1. Annual Report, Campaign for Homosexual Equality, 1979.
22. Hall Carpenter Archives, HCA/CHE/1/1. Annual Report, Campaign for Homosexual Equality, 1976.
23. Hall Carpenter Archives, HCA/CHE/1/1. Annual Report, Campaign for Homosexual Equality, 1975.
24. Hall Carpenter Archives, HCA/ALBANY TRUST/1/25. Albany Trust: Outline Proposals for Development, 1967–1970.
25. Hall Carpenter Archives, *Inventing Ourselves*, p. 68. Interview with Elisa Beckett, October 1985.

26. Hall Carpenter Archives, C456/003/01–02. Interview with John Alcock, July 1985.
27. *Between the Acts,* p. 101.
28. Hall Carpenter Archives, HCA/CHE/3/1. The Morecombe affair.
29. Ibid.
30. Ibid.
31. Ibid.
32. Hall Carpenter Archives, HCA/CHE/1/1. A change for the future, 1983.
33. *Between the Acts,* p. 170.
34. Hall Carpenter Archives, HCA/CHE/3/2. Women and men in CHE – Discussion paper for the national council, June 1973.
35. See, for example, *Between the Acts,* p. 170.
36. Gay Liberation Front Manifesto – London 1971, quoted in Power, 'No Bath But Plenty of Bubbles', pp. 328–9.
37. Weeks, *Coming Out,* p. 194.
38. Power, *No Bath But Plenty of Bubbles,* p. 35.
39. Weeks, *Coming Out,* p. 194.
40. Hall Carpenter Archives, *Walking After Midnight: Gay Men's Life Stories* (London: Routledge, 1989), p. 72. Interview with Bernard Dobson, September 1985.
41. Andrew Lumsden quoted in Power, *No Bath But Plenty of Bubbles,* p. 67.
42. See, for example, Hall Carpenter Archives, *Walking After Midnight: Gay Men's Life Stories* (London: Routledge, 1989); Hall Carpenter Archives, *Inventing Ourselves.*
43. Marwick, *The Sixties,* p. 7.
44. Ibid., pp. 801–2.
45. Ibid., p. 725.
46. Sandbrook, *State of Emergency,* p. 10.
47. Theodore Roszak, *The Making of a Counter Culture* (London: University of California, 1995), p. 1.
48. Ibid, p. xxvi.
49. Walter, *Come Together,* p. 10.
50. Power, *No Bath But Plenty of Bubbles,* p. 240.
51. Ibid., p. 77; Wimpy had refused to serve unaccompanied women after midnight under fear of prosecution for 'knowingly permitting prostitutes, thieves or drunken and disorderly persons to use their premises under the Late Night Refreshment Houses Act 1969'.
52. Ibid., p. 129.
53. Walter, *Come Together,* p. 14.
54. Ibid.
55. Ibid., p. 25.
56. Ibid., p. 23.
57. Power, *No Bath But Plenty of Bubbles,* p. 54.
58. Matt Cook, '"Gay Times": Identity, Locality, Memory, and the Brixton Squats in 1970's London', *Twentieth Century British History* (2011), pp. 1–26.

59. *Come Together,* Issue 11.
60. Power, *No Bath But Plenty of Bubbles*, p. 236.
61. Ibid., p. 226.
62. Ibid., p. 197.
63. Ibid., p. 181.
64. Ibid., p. 182.
65. Hall Carpenter Archives, *Inventing Ourselves: Lesbian Life Stories* (London: Routledge, 1989), p. 57. Interview with Diana Chapman, September 1985.
66. Hall Carpenter Archives, *Walking After Midnight: Gay Men's Life Stories* (London: Routledge, 1989), p. 120. Interview with Philip Baker, July 1988.
67. Jeffrey Weeks, *The World We Have Won*, p. 81.
68. Power, *No Bath But Plenty of Bubbles*, p. 286.
69. Weeks, *Coming Out*, p. 219.
70. 'About us', *London Lesbian and Gay Switchboard* [accessed on 27 July 2010]. http://www.llgs.org.uk/index.html; L. Trenchard and H. Warren, *Something to Tell You: The Experiences and Needs of Young Lesbians and Gay Men in London* (London, 1984), p. 112.
71. 'Mea Culpa by Rictor Norton', *The Pink Triangle Trust* [accessed on 27 July 2010]. http://www.pinktriangle.org.uk/glh/214/norton.html.
72. Quoted in Alkarim Jivani, *It's Not Unusual*, p. 169.
73. Sheila Jeffreys, *The Lesbian Heresy: A Feminist Perspective on the Lesbian Sexual Revolution* (London: The Women's Press, 1994), p. 143.
74. Quoted in Jennings, *A Lesbian History of Britain*, p. 175
75. Jeffreys, *Anticlimax*, pp. 162–3.
76. Lynne Segal, *Is The Future Female? Troubled Thoughts on Contemporary Feminism* (London: Virago Press, 1987), p. 165.
77. Penny Gulliver, quoted in, Sasha Roseneil, *Common Women, Uncommon Practices: the Queer Feminisms of Greenham* (London: Cassell, 2000), p. 305.
78. Sarah Benham, quoted in ibid., p. 309
79. Leeds Revolutionary Feminist Group, 'Political Lesbianism: The Case Against Heterosexuality', quoted in ibid., p. 177.
80. Segal, *Is The Future Female?*, p. 95.
81. Jennings, *A Lesbian History of Britain*, p. 180.
82. Jeffreys, *The Lesbian Heresy*, p. 179.
83. Ibid.

Chapter 4   Political Backlash

1. Marwick, *The Sixties*, p. 7.
2. HL Deb, 14 June 1977, vol. 384, col. 14.
3. Ibid., col. 12.
4. Ibid., col. 15.

5. Ibid., col. 30.
6. Scottish Offences Act 1976 (c. 67).
7. HC Written Answers, 18 October 1976, vol. 917, col. 264.
8. HC Deb, 3 November 1976, vol. 918, cols 1570–84.
9. Robert Boothby, *Boothby: Recollections of a Rebel* (London: Hutchinson, 1978), p. 212.
10. HL Deb, 10 May 1977, vol. 383, col. 169.
11. HC Deb, 15 July 1977, vol. 935–1, col. 1106; HC Deb, 21 April 1978, vol. 948, col. 959; HC, Deb 28 April 1978, vol. 948, col. 1935.
12. The Standing Advisory Commission on Human Rights had been set up with the purpose of 'Advising the Secretary of State on the Adequacy and effectiveness of the law for the time being in force in preventing discrimination on the grounds of religious belief or political opinion and in providing redress for persons aggrieved by discrimination on either ground.' 'The Good Friday Agreement', BBC News [accessed on 23 July 2012]. http://www.bbc.co.uk/northernireland/schools/agreement/equality/support/er2_c011.shtml.
13. Standing Advisory Commission on Human Rights, *Report on the law in Northern Ireland relating to divorce and homosexuality* (London: Her Majesty's Stationery Office, 1977), pp. 10–11.
14. The National Archives (TNA) CJ4/1507. Memorandum by the Secretary of State for Northern Ireland, June 1977.
15. 'Case of Dudgeon v. The United Kingdom', ECHR Portal [accessed on 15 July 2010]. http://cmiskp.echr.coe.int/tkp197/view.asp?action=html&documentId=695350&portal=hbkm&source=externalbydocnumber&table=F69A27FD8FB86142BF01C1166DEA398649.
16. Michael D. Goldhaber, *A People's History of the European Court of Human Rights* (Piscataway, NJ: Rutgers University Press, 2007), p. 37.
17. HC Deb, 8 March 1979, vol. 963, col. 1486.
18. HC Deb, 2 July 1979, vol. 969, col. 466.
19. *The Guardian*, 8 May 1979.
20. 'Case of Dudgeon v. The United Kingdom (Application no. 7532/76)', *European Court of Human Rights* [accessed on 20 September 2010] http://cmiskp.echr.coe.int/tkp197/view.asp?action=html&documentId=695350&portal=hbkm&source=externalbydocnumber&table=F69A27FD8FB86142BF01C1166DEA398649.
21. HC Deb, 25 October 1982, vol. 29, col. 834.
22. HC Deb, 22 July 1980, vol. 989, col. 286
23. Ibid.
24. Ibid., col. 298.
25. Jeffrey-Poulter, *Peers, Queers and Commons*, p. 147.
26. HL Deb, 21 October 1980, vol. 413, col. 1812.
27. Jeffrey-Poulter, *Peers, Queers and Commons*, p. 202.
28. HCA/CGHE Conservative Group for Homosexual Equality (later Tory Campaign for Homosexual Equality).

29. 'House of Commons Public Information Office Factsheet, No. 16: Statistical Digest of By-Election Results in the 1979–1983 Parliament', UK Parliament Website [accessed on 20 September 2010]. http://www.parliament.uk/documents/commons-information-office/m08.pdf.
30. Peter Tatchell, *The Battle for Bermondsey* (London: Heretic Books, 1983), p. 108.
31. Ibid., p. 109.
32. 'Peter Tatchell: Out and about', *The Independent* [accessed on 16 April 2009]. http://www.independent.co.uk/news/people/profiles/peter-tatchell-out-and-about-524819.html.
33. 'House of Commons Public Information Office Factsheet, No. 16: Statistical Digest of By-Election Results in the 1979–1983 Parliament', UK Parliament Website [accessed on 20 September 2010]. http://www.parliament.uk/documents/commons-information-office/m08.pdf.
34. 'Liberal manifesto 1979', *An Unofficial Site on the Liberal Democrats* [accessed on 3 March 2011]. http://www.libdems.co.uk/manifestos/1979/1979-liberal-manifesto.shtml; Jeffrey-Poulter, *Peers, Queers and Commons*, p. 139.
35. 'The pioneer who changed gay lives', *The Observer* [accessed on 20 September 2010]. http://www.guardian.co.uk/politics/2005/jan/30/uk.aids.
36. Ibid.
37. Jeffrey-Poulter, *Peers, Queers and Commons*, p. 204.
38. '1983 Labour Party Manifesto', *An Unofficial site on the Labour Party* [accessed on 4 March 2011]. http://www.labour-party.org.uk/manifestos/1983/1983-labour-manifesto.shtml.
39. Jeffrey-Poulter, *Peers, Queers and Commons*, pp. 165–6.
40. 'The First Reported AIDS Death' *Brian Deer* [accessed on 26 November 2013]. http://briandeer.com/aids-1981-uk.htm; 'About us: Our history' *Terrence Higgins Trust* [accessed on 21 September 2010]. http://www.tht.org.uk/aboutus/ourhistory/; HC Written Answers, 23 November 1984, vol. 68, col. 326; HC Deb, 11 February 1985, vol. 73, col. 14.
41. HL Deb, 18 March 1985, vol. 461, cols 358–387.
42. Ibid., col. 362.
43. Ibid., col. 387.
44. Quoted in Simon Garfield, *The End of Innocence: Britain in the Time of AIDS* (London: Faber and Faber Limited, 1994), back cover.
45. Jeffrey Weeks, *Making Sexual History*, p. 175.
46. *The Sunday Telegraph*, 20 January 1985.
47. *Daily Express*, 3 February 1985.
48. Author's interview with Waheed Alli, 13 January 2009.
49. Jeffrey-Poulter, *Peers, Queers and Commons*, p. 202.
50. Haringey Labour Party Manifesto 1986, p. 32, quoted in Susan Reinhold, *Local Conflict and Ideological Struggle*, p. 53.
51. Ibid., p. 41.
52. Davina Cooper, *Power in Struggle: Feminism, Sexuality and the State* (Buckingham: Open University Press, 1995), p. 100.

53. Reinhold, *Local Conflict and Ideological Struggle*, p. 60.
54. 'Looney Left' was the term that had been coined regarding the council's earlier response to the death of PC Keith Blakelock during the Broadwater Farm violence, ibid., pp. 47–8.; *The Sun*, 7 July 1986.
55. *Daily Mail*, 9 July 1986.
56. Reinhold, *Local Conflict and Ideological Struggle*, pp. 84–5.
57. *Islington Gazette*, 2 May 1986.
58. *The Sun*, 4 May 1986; *Today*, 7 May 1986.
59. Department of Education and Science circular, DES206/86, 6 August 1986, quoted in Paul Meredith, *Government, schools, and the law* (London: Routledge, 1992), p. 58.
60. 'Fight Back', No. 24, produced by the Tottenham Conservative Party, 1986, quoted in Reinhold, 'Local Conflict and Ideological Struggle', p. 55.
61. HL Deb, 14 June 1977, vol. 384, cols 13–18.
62. HL 1986/1987 Bill 76 Local Government Act 1986 (Amendment) Bill.
63. HL Deb, 14 June 1977, vol. 384, cols 13–18; Throughout its legislative progress, section 28 is variously known as clause 27, clause 28, and, finally, section 28 when it became law.
64. HL Deb, 18 December 1986, vol. 483, col. 316; ibid., col. 320.
65. Lord Graham of Edmonton, ibid., col. 328.
66. HC Deb, 25 November 1974, vol. 882, cols 38–9; HC Deb, 22 July 1966, vol. 732, cols 1099–106
67. HL Deb, 11 February 1987, vol. 484, col. 709; Margaret Thatcher, Conservative Party Conference, 1987, quoted in Alistair Ross, *Curriculum: Construction and Critique* (London: Routledge, 1999), p. 66.
68. 'The Next Move Forward', *Richard Kimber's Political Science Resources* [accessed on 8 May 2009]. http://www.psr.keele.ac.uk/area/uk/man/con87.htm.
69. '1987 Labour Party Manifesto', *An Unofficial site on the Labour Party* [accessed on 4 March 2011]. http://www.labour-party.org.uk/manifestos/1983/1983-labour-manifesto.shtml.
70. Michael Crick, *In Search of Michael Howard* (London: Simon & Schuster, 2005), p. 210; 'Hughes explains his gay admission', *BBC News* [accessed on 1 August 2008]. http://news.bbc.co.uk/1/hi/uk_politics/4649266.stm.
71. Jeffrey Weeks, *Against nature*, p. 139.
72. *Gay Times*, Issue 111, December 1987.
73. Weeks, *Sex, politics, and society*, p. 293.
74. Ibid., pp. 292–4.
75. Margaret Thatcher, *The Downing Street Years* (London: HarperCollins, 1993), pp. 628–9.
76. *The Guardian*, 12 December 1987.
77. Susan Reinhold, *Through the Parliamentary Looking Glass*: 'Real' and 'Pretend' Families in Contemporary British Politics', *Feminist Review*, 48 (1994), 61–79, p. 71.
78. Weeks, *The World We Have Won*, p. 181.

79. 'British Social Attitudes Survey', *British Social Attitudes Information Service* [accessed 8 May 2009]. http://www.britsocat.com/Body.aspx?control=HomePage.
80. Colin Spencer, *Homosexuality: a history* (London: Fourth Estate, 1995), p. 381.
81. Cook, *From Gay Reform to Gaydar*, p. 205, from Geraint John, 'Cock and Bull Story'. *City Limits*, 25 October–1 November 1990.
82. Ibid., p. 206.
83. *Capital Gay*, 11 December 1987.
84. Ibid.
85. *Capital Gay*, 18 December 1987.
86. *Gay Times*, Issue 112, January 1988.
87. Hall Carpenter Archives, HCA/CHE/1/1. Annual Report, Campaign for Homosexual Equality, 1987.
88. Jeffrey-Poulter, *Peers, Queers and Commons*, pp. 156–7.
89. Ibid., p. 214.
90. Grey, *Quest for Justice*, p. 227.
91. Cook, *From Gay Reform to Gaydar*, p. 207.
92. 'Section 28/The Arts Lobby', *Ian McKellen* [accessed on 30 May 2009]. http://www.mckellen.com/activism/section28.htm.
93. *The Times*, 27 January 1988.
94. Hall Carpenter Archives, HCA/WOODS PAPERS/2/21. Stonewall Newsletter, September 1998.
95. 'Stonewall UK', *Ian McKellen* [accessed on 30 May 2009]. http://www.mckellen.com/activism/section28.htm.
96. Hall Carpenter Archives, HCA/WOODS PAPERS/2/21. Annual Report, 1990.
97. Ibid.
98. Ibid.
99. Ibid.
100. Hall Carpenter Archives, HCA/STONEWALL/ANNUAL REPORTS/5. Annual Report, 1991–1992.
101. 'Section 28/The Arts Lobby', *Ian McKellen* [accessed on 30 May 2009]. http://www.mckellen.com/activism/section28.htm; Author's interview with Waheed Alli, 13 January 2009.
102. Weeks, *The World We Have Won*, p. 104.
103. Jeffery-Poulter, *Peers, Queers and Commons*, p. 251.
104. *Capital Gay*, 18 May 1990.
105. 'About OutRage!', *OutRage!* [accessed on 22 October 2010]. http://outrage.org.uk/about/.
106. Ibid.
107. Hall Carpenter Archives, HCA/TATCHELL/1994/2. *Gay Times*, 1994.
108. *The Guardian*, 1 December 1994.
109. *The Daily Telegraph*, 27 November 1994.

110. Hall Carpenter Archives, HCA/TATCHELL/1994/2, '10 Bishops to be named at Synod', Press release, 30 November 1994.
111. *Outright!*, November 1994.
112. 'David Hope's trial of faith', *Yorkshire Post* [accessed on 24 May 2009]. http://www.yorkshirepost.co.uk/features/David-Hope39s-triumph-of-faith.886985.jp.
113. Hall Carpenter Archives, HCA/TATCHELL/1994/2, Outright!, November 1994.
114. *Capital Gay*, 9 December 1994.
115. About OutRage!', *OutRage!* [accessed on 22 October 2010]. http://outrage.org.uk/about/.

Chapter 5 Conflicting Public Images

1. *Gay News*, 1 December 1976; *Gay News*, Issue 1.
2. *Gay News*, Issue 1.
3. *Gay News*, Issue 2.
4. *Gay News*, 21 April 1976.
5. *Gay News*, 23 January 1980.
6. *Gay News*, 14 May 1980.
7. *Gay News*, 2 February 1983.
8. Jeffrey-Poulter, *Peers, Queers and Commons*, p. 167.
9. Anna Durell, 'Cheap at the price', *Capital Gay*, 24 August 1984.
10. *Capital Gay*, 14 May 1982.
11. 'Our freedom too', *Capital Gay*, 1 April 1983.
12. *Capital Gay*, 22 February 1985.
13. *Capital Gay*, 5 February 1986.
14. *Capital Gay*, 5 February 1988.
15. *Gay Times*, May 1995.
16. *Gay Times*, January 1985.
17. *Gay Times*, November 1986.
18. *Gay Times*, January 1989.
19. Ibid.
20. *The Times*, 5 September 1982.
21. *The Sun*, 2 May 1983.
22. *The Sun*, 14 June 1983.
23. Derek Jameson, Radio Four 1994, quoted in Sanderson, *Mediawatch*, p. 34.
24. *The Sunday People*, 20 July 1983.
25. *Daily Mail*, 1 February 1985.
26. Julian Petley, 'Positive and Negative Images', in *Culture Wars: The Media and the British Left*, ed. by James Curran, Ivor Gaber, and Julian Petley (Edinburgh: Edinburgh University Press, 2005), p. 160; *The Daily Telegraph*, 26 April 1983.
27. *The Times*, 1984, quoted in Sanderson, *Mediawatch*, p. 206.

28. Sanderson, *Mediawatch*, p. vi.
29. Richard Dyer, *The Matter of Images: Essays on Representation* (London: Routledge, 1993), p. 1.
30. Derek Jameson, quoted in Sanderson, *Mediawatch*, p. 39.
31. Frank Pierce, 'The British Press and the "placing" of male homosexuality', in Stanley Cohen and Jock Young, eds, *The manufacture of the News: Social Problems, Deviance and the Mass Media* (London: Constable, 1984), p. 307.
32. James Dearing, *Agenda Setting* (Thousand Oaks: Sage Publications, 1996), p. 4.
33. *Islington Gazette*, 2 May 1986.
34. *The Sun*, 4 May 1986; *Today*, 7 May 1986.
35. *The Sun*, 7 July 1986; *Daily Mail*, 9 July 1986.
36. HL Deb, 18 December 1986, vol. 483, col. 310.
37. Ibid., col. 313.
38. Ibid., col. 317.
39. Ibid., col. 318.
40. Ibid., cols 1003–4.
41. A. M. Smith, 'A Symptomology of an Authoritarian Discourse', in *New Foundations: A journal of culture/theory/politics*, 10 (1990), 41–65, p. 44.
42. SC Deb (A), 8 December 1987, cols 1205–6.
43. HC Deb, 15 December 1987, vol. 124, col. 1010.
44. Ibid., col. 1013.
45. *The Sun*, 4 May 1986.
46. The Press Council, quoted in Sanderson, *Mediawatch*, pp. 60–1.
47. *My Beautiful Laundrette*, dir. by Stephen Frears (Mainline Pictures, 1985).
48. Quoted in Russo, *The Celluloid Closet*, p. 309.
49. Kenneth MacKinnon, 'Intermingling under controlled conditions: The queerness of Prick Up Your Ears', in *British Queer Cinema*, ed. by Robin Griffiths (London: Routledge, 2006), pp. 121–32 (p. 122).
50. *Times Educational Supplement*, 10 January 1986.
51. *Gay Times*, May 1988; *Two of Us*, dir. by Roger Tonge (BBC, 1988).
52. *Gay Times*, May 1988.
53. *Two of Us*, dir. by Roger Tonge (BBC, 1988).
54. *Daily Mail*, 13 January 1990.
55. Quoted in *The Guardian*, 31 January 1990.
56. *Gay Times*, May 1988.
57. *London Evening Standard*, 28 March 1988.
58. *The Guardian*, 31 January 1990.
59. *Out on Tuesday*, dir. by Phil Woodward (Channel 4, 1989).
60. *The Daily Telegraph*, 15 January 1989.
61. *London Evening Standard*, 5 April 1989.
62. *The Independent*, 15 February 1989; *The Times*, 24 June 1992.
63. Diane Hamer with Penny Ashbrook, 'OUT: Reflections on British television's first lesbian and gay magazine series', in *The Good, the Bad, and the Gorgeous:*

NOTES TO PAGES 142–153   239

Popular Culture's Romance with Lesbianism, ed. by Diane Hamer and Belinda Budge (London: Pandora, 1994), pp. 166–71 (p. 166).
64. *Oranges Are Not the Only Fruit* dir. by Beeban Kidron (BBC, 1990).
65. Ibid.
66. Ibid.
67. Ibid.
68. Hilary Hinds, 'Oranges Are Not the Only Fruit: reaching audiences other lesbian texts cannot reach', in *Television Times: A Reader*, ed. by John Corner and Sylvia Harvey (London: Arnold, 1996), p. 108.
69. *Financial Times*, 10 January 1990; *The Observer*, 14 January 1990.
70. *Spare Rib*, February 1990.

Chapter 6   Gay Space

1. Houlbrook, *Queer London*, p. 76.
2. Jeffrey-Poulter, *Peers, Queers and Commons*, p. 97.
3. Cook, *From Gay Reform to Gaydar*, p. 184.
4. Cook, *A gay history of Britain*, p. 188; Jeremy Norman, *No Make-Up: Straight Tales from a Queer Life* (London: Elliot and Thompson, 2006), p. 160
5. Norman, *No Make-Up*, p. 160.
6. Ibid., pp. 162–163.
7. Trenchard and Warren, *Something to Tell You*, p. 112.
8. Hall Carpenter Archives, *Walking After Midnight: Gay Men's Life Stories* (London: Routledge, 1989), pp. 182–3. Interview with Eduardo Pereira, December 1987.
9. Frank Mort, *Cultures of Consumption*, p. 168.
10. Ibid., pp. 175–6.
11. Stephen Whittle, 'Consuming differences: the collaboration of the gay body with the cultural state', in *The Margins of the City: Gay Men's Urban Lives*, ed. by Stephen Whittle (Aldershot: Arena, 1994), p. 36.
12. Ibid., p. 27.
13. Weeks, *The World we Have Won*, p. 104.
14. Weeks, *Against Nature*, p. 106.
15. Paul Hindle, 'Gay communities and gay space in the city', in *The Margins of the City*, p. 19.
16. Mort, *Cultures of Consumption*, p. 164.
17. Norman, *No Make-Up*, p. 164.
18. Megan Thomas, Hall Carpenter Archives, *Inventing Ourselves*, p. 142. Interview with Megan Thomas, 22 October 1986.
19. Jennings, *A Lesbian History of Britain*, pp. 147–8.
20. Jeffreys, *The Lesbian Heresy*, p. 142.

21. Hall Carpenter Archives, *Walking After Midnight: Gay Men's Life Stories* (London: Routledge, 1989), p. 155. Interview with Kursad Kahramanoglu, May 1988.
22. Rukus! Federation Ltd, *The Queen's Jewels: a Memory in Progress* (London, 2005), quoted in Cook, *Gay Reform to Gaydar*, p. 187.
23. Hall Carpenter Archives, *Walking After Midnight: Gay Men's Life Stories* (London: Routledge, 1989), pp. 182–3. Interview with Zahid Dar, October 1985.
24. Ibid., p. 183.
25. Ibid., p. 195. Interview with Glenn McKee, January 1988.
26. Ibid., pp. 195–7.
27. 'Pneumocystis Pneumonia – Los Angeles', Centers for Disease Control and Prevention [accessed on 7 August 2008]. http://www.cdc.gov/mmwr/preview/mmwrhtml/june_5.htm.
28. Tim Clarke, quoted in Simon Garfield, *The End of Innocence*, p. 33.
29. 'THT: About us: Our history', THT [accessed on 8 February 2011]. http://www.tht.org.uk/aboutus/ourhistory/
30. 'New homosexual disorder worries officials', *The New York Times*, 11 May 1982.
31. Garfield, *The End of Innocence*, p. 33.
32. Weeks, *Making Sexual History*, p. 146.
33. *The Guardian,* 18 December 1986.
34. Garfield, *The End of Innocence*, p. 281.
35. Quoted in Cook, *From Gay Reform to Gaydar*, p. 199.
36. Quoted in *Positive Lives: Responses to HIV, a Photodocumentary,* ed. by Stephen Mayes and Lyndall Stein (London: Cassell, 1993), p. 77.
37. Hall Carpenter Archives, C456/69. Interview with Nettie Pollard.
38. Quoted in Cook, *From Gay Reform to Gaydar*, p. 200.
39. Weeks, *The World We Have Won*, p. 18.
40. Garfield, *The End of Innocence*, pp. 34–5.
41. Ibid., p. 39.
42. Ibid., p. 38.
43. Ibid., p. 39.
44. Jennings, *A Lesbian History of Britain*, p. 181.
45. Barbara Bell, quoted in ibid.
46. 'Positive Nation: Regulars–Caroline Guinness-McGann: The way we were', Positive Nation [accessed on 8 February 2011]. http://www.positivenation.co.uk/regulars/article.php?article_id=80.
47. Weeks, *The World We Have Won*, p. 102.
48. Garfield, *The End of Innocence*, p. 86.
49. 'Patron', National AIDS Trust [accessed on 17 March 2011]. http://www.nat.org.uk/About-us/Team/Patron.aspx.
50. 'Home', National AIDS Day [accessed on 11 August 2008]. http://www.worldaidsday.org/hivf_wad_twenty.asp; Garfield, *The End of Innocence*, p. 256.
51. Keith Alcorn, *Capital Gay,* 21 May 1993.
52. Garfield, *The End of Innocence*, pp. 181–2.

Chapter 7   'An End to Unjustifiable Discrimination'

1. 'New Labour because Britain deserves better', *An unofficial site on the Labour Party* [accessed on 20 April 2009]. http://www.labour-party.org.uk/manifestos/1997/1997-labour-manifesto.shtml.
2. Criminal Justice and Public Order Act 1994 (c. 33).
3. 'The Election Battles 1945–1997', *BBC News* [accessed on 22 November 2010]. http://news.bbc.co.uk/hi/english/static/vote2001/in_depth/election_battles/1992_results.stm.
4. Hall Carpenter Archives, HCA/STONEWALL/ANNUAL REPORTS/5. Annual Report, 1991–1992.
5. Author's email correspondence with Edwina Currie, 27 September 2010.
6. Ibid.
7. Ibid.
8. Stonewall, *The Case for Change* (London: Stonewall, 1993).
9. Ibid.
10. Hall Carpenter Archives, HCA/STONEWALL/STONEWALL NEWSLETTER/1. Spring 1994 newsletter.
11. HC Deb, 21 February 1994, vol. 238, cols 74–5.
12. HC Deb, 21 February 1994, vol. 238, col. 77.
13. Neil Kinnock, ibid., col. 82.
14. Ibid., col. 85
15. 'British Social Attitudes Survey', *British Social Attitudes Information Service*, [accessed 8 May 2009]. http://www.britsocat.com/Body.aspx?control=HomePage.
16. HC Deb, 21 February 1994, vol. 238, col. 97.
17. Author's email correspondence with Edwina Currie, 27 September 2010.
18. HC Deb, 21 February 1994, vol. 238, col. 98.
19. Ibid., col. 100.
20. Ibid., col. 98.
21. Ibid., col. 104.
22. Criminal Justice and Public Order Act 1994 (c. 33).
23. HC Written Answer, 30 November 1993, vol. 233, col. 528.
24. Hall Carpenter Archives, HCA/STONEWALL/STONEWALL NEWSLETTER/1. Spring 1994 newsletter.
25. Ibid.
26. Hall Carpenter Archives, HCA/TATCHELL/1994/2. *Gay Times*, 1994.
27. 'New Labour because Britain deserves better', *An unofficial site on the Labour Party* [accessed on 20 April 2009]. http://www.labour-party.org.uk/manifestos/1997/1997-labour-manifesto.shtml.
28. Author's interview with Waheed Alli, 13 January 2009.
29. HC Deb, 22 June 1998, vol. 314, col. 756.
30. 'Anne Keen political profile' *BBC News* [accessed on 24 November 2010]. http://news.bbc.co.uk/1/hi/uk_politics/2055642.stm.

31. HC Deb, 22 June 1998, vol. 314, cols 758–9.
32. Ibid., col. 805.
33. 'Profile: Baroness Young', *BBC News* [accessed on 24 November 2010]. http://news.bbc.co.uk/1/hi/uk/1046634.stm.
34. HL Deb, 22 July 1998, vol. 592, col. 938.
35. Ibid., col. 939.
36. Ibid., col. 949.
37. HC Deb, 16 December 1998, vol. 322, col. 985.
38. Author's interview with Ben Summerskill, 25 November 2008.
39. *Sexual Offences (Amendment) Bill parliamentary briefing* (London: Stonewall, 1999).
40. HL Deb, 13 April 1999, vol. 599, cols 650–1.
41. Ibid., col 737.
42. Ibid., col 690.
43. HC Deb, 7 February 2000, vol. 344, col. 83.
44. Ibid., col. 463.
45. HL Deb, 11 April 2000, vol. 612, col. 98.
46. HL Deb, 13 November 2000, vol. 619, col. 21.
47. Ibid., col. 23.
48. 'Blair offers free vote on gay clause', *The Guardian* [accessed on 24 May 2009]. http://www.guardian.co.uk/politics/2000/jan/26/labour.labour1997to992.
49. HL Deb, 7 February 2000, vol. 609, col. 406.
50. Ibid., col. 449.
51. HC Deb, 25 July 2000, vol. 354, col. 1035.
52. 'UK Military Gay Ban Illegal', *BBC News* [accessed on 26 November 2010]. http://news.bbc.co.uk/1/hi/uk/458625.stm.
53. 'Ambitions for Britain', *pixunlimited* [accessed on 28 November 2010]. http://www.pixunlimited.co.uk/pdf/news/election/labourmanifesto1.pdf.
54. HC Deb, 16 May 2002, vol. 385, col. 1004; ibid., col. 1002
55. 'Mapping Britain's Moral Values', *Ipsos Mori 2000* [accessed on 25 May 2009]. http://www.ipsos-mori.com/researchpublications/researcharchive/poll.aspx?oItemId=1875.
56. *Attitude*, May 2005.
57. 'Janet Mary Young', *Oxford Dictionary of National Biography* [accessed on 28 November 2010]. http://www.oxforddnb.com/view/article/77303.
58. Author's interview with Waheed Alli, 13 January 2009.
59. *Repealing Section 28 parliamentary briefing* (London: Stonewall, 2003).
60. Author's interview with Ben Summerskill, 25 November 2008.
61. Ibid.
62. HL Deb, 3 April 2003, vol. 646, col. 1538; 'Polls supports S28 retention', *BBC News* [accessed on 7 March 2011]. http://news.bbc.co.uk/1/hi/scotland/768882.stm.
63. HL Deb, 10 September 2003, vol. 652, col. 389.
64. Author's interview with Waheed Alli, 13 January 2009.
65. Jacqui Smith, *Civil Partnership: A framework for the legal recognition of same-sex couples* (London: Women & Equality Unit, 2003), p. 9.

Notes to Pages 184–194

66. Ibid.
67. Ibid., p. 13.
68. HL Deb, 25 January 2002, vol. 630, col. 1746.
69. 'Lib Dem peer who pushed for civil partnerships calls for gay marriage equality', *Pink News,* [accessed on 28 November 2010]. http://www.pinknews.co.uk/2010/09/09/lib-dem-peer-who-pushed-for-civil-partnerships-supports-gay-marriage/
70. HL Deb, 25 January 2002, vol. 630, col. 1694.
71. Ibid., col. 1718.
72. Ibid., col. 1741.
73. HL Deb, 22 April 2004, vol. 660, col. 388.
74. *Attitude,* May 2005.
75. 'Conservative Election Manifesto 2005' *Conservatives* [accessed on 3 March 2011]. http://www.conservatives.com/pdf/manifesto-uk-2005.pdf.
76. HL Deb, 1 July 2004, vol. 663, col. 398; HL Deb, 24 June 2004, vol. 662, col. 1389.
77. HL Deb, 22 April 2004, vol. 660, col. 407.
78. Anne Widdecombe. HC Deb, 12 October 2004, vol. 425, col. 201.
79. HL Deb, 17 November 2004, vol. 666, col. 1484
80. 'Lib Dem peer who pushed for civil partnerships calls for gay marriage equality', *Pink News* [accessed on 28 November 2010]. http://www.pinknews.co.uk/2010/09/09/lib-dem-peer-who-pushed-for-civil-partnerships-supports-gay-marriage/.
81. Author's interview with Ben Summerskill, 25 November 2008.
82. House of Commons Library, *Same-sex marriage and Civil Partnerships SN/HA/5882* (London: Her Majesty's Stationery Office, 2012), p. 4.
83. Weeks, *The World We Have Won,* p. xiii
84. 'Tony Blair's gay speech in full', *Pink News* [accessed on 2 June 2009]. http://www.pinknews.co.uk/news/articles/2005-3983.html.

Chapter 8   Real Lives in the Media

1. *Attitude*, May 1999.
2. *Attitude,* August 1994.
3. Ibid.
4. Ibid.
5. *Gay Times*, March 2004.
6. *Gay Times,* February 2000.
7. *Gay Times,* December 1991.
8. 'From a queer perspective', *Gay Times*, December 1994.
9. Jane Czyzselska in Ben Summerskill (ed.), *The Way We Are Now: Gay and Lesbian Lives in the 21st Century* (London: Continuum, 2006), p. 19.
10. *Diva,* August 1994.

11. *Diva*, August 1997.
12. 'Wedding Bells', *Diva*, August 1995.
13. *Diva*, October 2002.
14. 'The Sun says out of step, the Government is out of step with the wishes of the people', *The Sun,* 15 July 1997.
15. 'The Lords must not give their consent', *Daily Mail,* 22 July 1998.
16. *Daily Star,* 23 July 1998.
17. *The Observer,* 21 June 1998.
18. 'Coming out for change. The age of homosexual consent should now shift to 16', *The Times,* 22 June 1998.
19. *Daily Mirror,* quoted in *The Independent*, 25 July 1998.
20. *The Sun,* December 2000, quoted in *The Independent,* 2 December 2000.
21. *The Sun*, 30 October 1999.
22. Brain Souter, *The Sun*, 25 January 2000.
23. 'New Labour's insidious love affair with the gay lobby', *Daily Mail,* 3 November 1999.
24. HC Deb, 25 July 2000, vol. 354, col. 1035.
25. 'Bulling of gays 'rife in schools', *The Guardian,* 13 March 1998.
26. *The Independent*, 1 December 2000.
27. *Daily Express*, 9 September 2002.
28. *The Sun*, 15 July 2003.
29. *Daily Mail*, 29 June 2001.
30. *Daily Mail,* 6 September 2001.
31. *London Evening Standard*, 31 August 2001.
32. *The Independent*, 19 August 2001; *The Times,* 30 June 2003.
33. *Daily Mail,* 18 September 2000.
34. *The Daily Telegraph*, 5 December 2005.
35. *Daily Mirror,* 11 November 2005.
36. *Brookside,* dir. by various (Channel 4, 1994).
37. *Beautiful Thing,* dir. by Hettie McDonald (Channel 4 Films, 1996).
38. 'In the eye of the beholder', *The Guardian,* 6 June 1996.
39. *Gay Times,* June 1996.
40. Ros Jennings, 'Beautiful Thing: British queer cinema, positive unoriginality and the everyday', *in British Queer Cinema,* ed. by Robin Griffiths (London: Routledge, 2006), pp. 183–94 (p. 186).
41. Ibid., p. 192.
42. *Gaytime TV,* dir. by various (BBC, 1995).
43. Quoted in *The Observer,* 26 May 1995.
44. *The Guardian,* 8 July 1996.
45. *Queer as Folk,* dir. by Sarah Harding and Charles McDougall (Channel 4, 1999)
46. Mark Aldridge and Andy Murray, *T is for Television: the Small Screen Adventures of Russell T Davies* (London: Reynolds and Hearn Ltd, 2008), p. 99.
47. Russell T. Davies quoted in ibid., pp. 99–100.
48. Quoted in ibid., p. 111.

49. *Daily Mail*, 3 July 1998.
50. *The Sun*, 8 July 1998.
51. *The Daily Telegraph*, 27 February 1999.
52. *The Independent*, 23 January 2000.
53. Mediatheque Archive, BFI, 'Queer as Folk'.

Conclusion

1. David quoted in *Between the acts*, pp. 52–3.
2. Hall Carpenter Archives, *Inventing Ourselves*, p. 49. Interview with Diana Chapman, 10 September 1985.
3. 'Gay Liberation Front Manifesto – London 1971', *Alan Wakeman* [accessed on 28 May 2012]. http://www.awakeman.co.uk/Sense/Books/GLF%20Manifesto%201971.pdf.
4. Weeks, *Coming Out*, p. 3.
5. Jennings, *Tomboys and Bachelor Girls*, p. 173.
6. Quoted in Jennings, *A Lesbian History of Britain*, p. 156.
7. Emily Hamer, quoted in ibid.

BIBLIOGRAPHY

Primary sources

Archives

Hall Carpenter Archives (LSE) – lesbian and gay papers.
HCA/ALBANY TRUST/1/25. Albany Trust: Outline Proposals for Development, 1967–1970.
HCA/ALBANY TRUST/2/1. 'after the Act...'.
———, Bulletin, North-Western Homosexual Law Reform Committee, April 1968.
———, Letter to Professor A.J. Ayer of HLRS, 11 April 1968.
———, Report on Working Party on Sexual Behaviour, Sexual Law Reform Society, 5 September 1974.
———, Social Organisations for Homosexuals, 2 May 1968.
———, The Homosexual Law Reform Society: Constitution and Rules.
———, The Homosexual Law Reform Society. Executive Committee meeting minutes 11 October 1967.
———, The Male and Female Homosexual Association of Britain membership form.
———, The Sexual Law Reform Society Constitution.
HCA/CGHE. Conservative Group for Homosexual Equality (later Tory Campaign for Homosexual Equality).
HCA/CHE/1/1. A change for the future. 1983.
———, Annual Report, Campaign for Homosexual Equality, 1975.
———, Annual Report, Campaign for Homosexual Equality, 1979.
———, Annual Report, Campaign for Homosexual Equality, 1979.
———, Annual Report, Campaign for Homosexual Equality, 1976.
———, Annual Report, Campaign for Homosexual Equality, 1975.
———, Annual Report, Campaign for Homosexual Equality, 1987.
HCA/CHE/3/1. The Morecombe affair.
HCA/CHE/3/2. CHE National Council, An Outline, September 1973.
———, Women and men in CHE – Discussion paper for the national council June 1973.

BIBLIOGRAPHY

HCA/GLF/17. Early GLF dance.
HCA/GLF/3. Gay Day.
HCA/STONEWALL/ANNUAL REPORTS/5. Annual Report, 1991–1992.
HCA/STONEWALL/STONEWALL NEWSLETTER/1. Spring 1994 newsletter.
HCA/TATCHELL/1994/2. '10 Bishops to be named at Synod' – Press release, 30 November 1994.
———, *Gay Times*, 1994.
———, Outright!, November 1994.
HCA/WOODS PAPERS/2/21. Annual Report, 1990.
———, Stonewall Newsletter, September 1998.

Hall Carpenter Archives (British Library) – oral history project
C456/003/01–02. Interview with John Alcock, July 1985.
C456/69. Interview with Nettie Pollard, 13 February 1990.
C1159/104 C1. Interview with Gaye, August 2003.

The National Archives (London)
CJ/1908. Political Outlook in Northern Ireland.
CJ4/1507. Memorandum by the Secretary of State for Northern Ireland, June 1977.
———, Reform in Social Legislation in N.I.
CJ4/1096. Homosexuality: Review of Northern Ireland Law Legislation Medical Matters.
CJ4/2103. European Commission on Human Rights: Northern Ireland Legislation on Homosexuality – Application by Dudgeon; ECHR.

British Film Institute (London) – Mediatheque
Queer as Folk synopsis
Newspapers and Magazines

Arena Three
Attitude
Birmingham Post
Capital Gay
Come Together
Daily Express
Daily Mail
Daily Mirror
Daily Star
Diva
Encounter
Financial Times
Gay News
Gay Times
Islington Gazette
Jeremy

London Evening Standard
Morning Star
Outright!
Reading Evening Post
Spare Rib
Spartacus
The Daily Telegraph
The Guardian
The Independent
The New York Times
The Observer
The Sun
The Sunday People
The Sunday Telegraph
The Sunday Times
The Times Educational Supplement
The Times
Timm
Today
Pink Paper

Printed documents

Government Reports

Department of Health and Social Security, *AIDS: Don't Die of Ignorance* (London: Department of Health and Social Security, 1987).

Home Office, Criminal Law Revision Committee, *Fifteenth Report: Sexual Offences* (London: Her Majesty's Stationery Office, 1984).

Home Office/Scottish Home Department, *Report of the Committee on Homosexual Offences and Prostitution* (London: Her Majesty's Stationery Office, 1957).

House of Commons Library, *Same-sex marriage and civil partnerships SN/HA/5882* (London, Her Majesty's Stationery Office, 2012).

Smith, Jacqui, *Civil Partnership: A framework for the legal recognition of same-sex couples* (London: Women & Equality Unit, 2003).

Standing Advisory Commission on Human Rights, *Report on the law in Northern Ireland relating to divorce and homosexuality* (London: Her Majesty's Stationery Office, 1977).

Walmsley, Roy and White, Karen, *Sexual Offences and Sentencing*. Home Office Research Study No. 54 (London: Her Majesty's Stationery Office, 1979).

Bills and Acts of Parliament

Criminal Justice and Public Order Act 1994 (c. 33)
Education (No. 2) Act 1986 (c.61)
HL 1986/1987 Bill 76 Local Government Act 1986 (Amendment) Bill
Local Government Act 1988 (c.9)
Scottish Offences Act 1976 (c.67)

Bibliography

Non-Government Official Reports

Church of England Moral Welfare Council, *Sexual Offenders and Social Punishment* (London: Church Information Board, 1956).
Colvin, Madeleine, *Section 28: A practical guide to the law and its implications* (London: National Council for Civil Liberties, 1989).
Douglas, Nicola, and others, eds, *Playing It Safe: Responses of Secondary School Teachers to Lesbian, Gay and Bisexual Pupils, Bullying, HIV and AIDS Education and Section 28* (London: Health and Education Research Unit, Institute of Education, University of London, 1997).
Hunt, Ruth and Johan Jensen, *The School Report: The experiences of young gay people in Britain's schools* (London: Stonewall, 2007).
Mitchell, Robert, *Section 28: a guide for schools, teachers, governors* (London: Stop the Clause Education Group, 1989).
Stonewall, *The Case for Change* (London: Stonewall, 1993).
———, *Sexual Offences (Amendment) Bill parliamentary briefing* (London: Stonewall, 1999).
———, *Repealing Section 28 parliamentary briefing* (London: Stonewall, 2003).
Trenchard, L. and H. Warren, *Something to Tell You: The Experiences and Needs of Young Lesbians and Gay Men in London* (London: Gay Teenage Group, 1984).

Hansard

House of Commons Hansard, Series 5, Vols 722, 732, 738, 882, 917, 918, 935–1, 948, 963, and 989.
———, Series 6, Vols 29, 124, 233, 238, 314, 322, 344, 354 and 385.
House of Lords Hansard, Series 5, Vols 187, 285, 384, 383, 413, 461, 483, 484, 592, 599, 609, 612, 619, 630, 646, 652, 660, 662, 663 and 666.

Memoirs

Abse, Leo, *Private Member* (London: McDonald & Co., 1973).
Blair, Tony, *A Journey* (London: Hutchinson, 2010).
Boothby, Robert, *Boothby: Recollections of a Rebel* (London: Hutchinson, 1978).
Campbell, Alastair, *The Blair Years: Extracts from The Alastair Campbell Diaries* (London: Hutchinson, 2007).
Grey, Anthony, *Quest for Justice: Towards Homosexual Emancipation* (London: Sinclair-Stevenson, 1992).
———, *Speaking Out: Writings on Sex, Law, Politics and Society, 1954–95* (London: Cassell, 1997).
Tatchell, Peter, *The Battle for Bermondsey* (London: Heretic Books, 1983).
Thatcher, Margaret, *The Downing Street Years* (London: HarperCollins, 1993).
Walter, Aubrey, ed., *Come Together: the years of gay liberation (1970–73)* (London: Gay Men's Press, 1980).
Wildblood, Peter, *Against the Law* (London: Weidenfeld & Nicolson, 1999).

Interviews

Author's email correspondence with Edwina Currie, 27 September 2010.
Author's interview with Ben Summerskill, 25 November 2008.
———, Waheed Alli, 13 January 2009.

Films and Television Programmes

AIDS: Iceberg/Tombstone, dir. by Nicolas Roeg (Department of Health, 1986).
Beautiful Thing, dir. by Hettie McDonald (Channel 4 Films, 1996).
Brookside, dir. by various (Channel 4, 1994).
Gaytime TV, dir. by various (BBC, 1995).
Girl dir. by Peter Gill (BBC, 1974).
Man Alive, Consenting Adults: The Men, dir. by Tom Conway (BBC, 1967).
Man Alive, Consenting Adults: The Women, dir. by Adam Clapham (BBC, 1967).
My Beautiful Laundrette, dir. by Stephen Frears (Mainline Pictures, 1985).
Oranges Are Not the Only Fruit dir. by Beeban Kidron (BBC, 1990).
Out on Tuesday, dir. by Phil Woodward (Channel 4, 1989).
Queer as Folk, dir. by Sarah Harding and Charles McDougall (Channel 4, 1999).
The Killing of Sister George, dir. by Robert Aldrich (The Associates and Aldrich Company, 1968).
Thirty Minute Theatre: Bermondsey, dir. by Claude Whatham (BBC, 1972).
Two of Us, dir. by Roger Tonge (BBC, 1988).
Victim, dir. by Basil Dearden (The Rank Organisation, 1961).

Websites

'1983 Labour Party Manifesto', *An Unofficial site on the Labour Party*. [accessed on 4 March 2011]. http://www.labour-party.org.uk/manifestos/1983/1983-labour-manifesto.shtml.
'1987 Labour Party Manifesto', *An Unofficial site on the Labour Party* [accessed on 4 March 2011]. http://www.labour-party.org.uk/manifestos/1983/1983-labour-manifesto.shtml.
'A.E. Dyson – Obituary', *The Independent* [accessed on 1 March 2011]. http://www.independent.co.uk/news/obituaries/a-e-dyson-748680.html.
'About OutRage!', *OutRage!* [accessed on 22 October 2010]. http://outrage.org.uk/about/.
'About us: Our history', *Terrence Higgins Trust* [accessed on 21 September 2010]. http://www.tht.org.uk/aboutus/ourhistory/.
'About us', *London Lesbian and Gay Switchboard* [accessed on 27 July 2010]. http://www.llgs.org.uk/index.html.
'Ambitions for Britain', *pixunlimited* [accessed on 28 November 2010]. http://www.pixunlimited.co.uk/pdf/news/election/labourmanifesto1.pdf.
'Anne Keen political profile', *BBC News* [accessed on 24 November 2010]. http://news.bbc.co.uk/1/hi/uk_politics/2055642.stm.
'Blair offers free vote on gay clause', *The Guardian* [accessed on 24 May 2009]. http://www.guardian.co.uk/politics/2000/jan/26/labour.labour1997to992.
'British Social Attitudes Survey', *British Social Attitudes Information Service* [accessed on 8 May 2009]. http://www.britsocat.com/Body.aspx?control=HomePage.
'Canal Street, Manchester', *Google Maps* [accessed on 7 June 2012]. http://maps.google.co.uk/.
'Case of Dudgeon v. The United Kingdom', ECHR Portal [accessed on 15 July 2010]. http://cmiskp.echr.coe.int/tkp197/view.asp?action=html&documentId=695350&portal=hbkm&source=externalbydocnumber&table=F69A27FD8FB86142BF01C1166DEA398649.

Bibliography

'Conservative Election Manifesto 2005', *Conservatives* [accessed on 3 March 2011]. http://www.conservatives.com/pdf/manifesto-uk-2005.pdf.

'David Cameron says sorry over Section 28 gay law', *The Telegraph* [accessed on 6 August 2009]. http://www.telegraph.co.uk/news/newstopics/politics/david-cameron/5710650/David-Cameron-says-sorry-over-Section-28-gay-law.html.

'David Hope's trial of faith', *Yorkshire Post* [accessed on 24 May 2009]. http://www.yorkshirepost.co.uk/features/David-Hope39s-triumph-of-faith.886985.jp.

'Gay Liberation Front Manifesto – London 1971', *Alan Wakeman* [accessed on 28 May 2012]. http://www.awakeman.co.uk/Sense/Books/GLF%20Manifesto%201971.pdf.

'Girl (1974)', BFI Screenonline [accessed on 24 January 2012]. http://www.screenonline.org.uk/tv/id/1396805/index.htm.

'Home', National AIDS Day [accessed on 11 August 2008]. http://www.worldaidsday.org/hivf_wad_twenty.asp.

'House of Commons Public Information Office Factsheet, No. 16: Statistical Digest of By-Election Results in the 1979–1983 Parliament', UK Parliament Website, [accessed on 20 September 2010]. http://www.parliament.uk/documents/commons-information-office/m08.pdf.

'Hughes explains his gay admission', *BBC News* [accessed on 1 August 2008]. http://news.bbc.co.uk/1/hi/uk_politics/4649266.stm.

'Interview: Henry Badenhorst, the Gaydar guy', *Pink News* [accessed on 18 July 2012]. http://www.pinknews.co.uk/2011/06/21/interview-henry-badenhorst-the-gaydar-guy/.

'Janet Mary Young', *Oxford Dictionary of National Biography* [accessed on 28 November 2010]. http://www.oxforddnb.com/view/article/77303.

'Lib Dem peer who pushed for civil partnerships calls for gay marriage equality', *Pink News* [accessed on 28 November 2010]. http://www.pinknews.co.uk/2010/09/09/lib-dem-peer-who-pushed-for-civil-partnerships-supports-gay-marriage/.

'Liberal manifesto 1979', *An Unofficial Site on the Liberal Democrats* [accessed on 3 March 2011]. http://www.libdems.co.uk/manifestos/1979/1979-liberal-manifesto.shtml.

'Mapping Britain's Moral Values', *Ipsos Mori 2000* [accessed on 25 May 2009]. http://www.ipsos-mori.com/researchpublications/researcharchive/poll.aspx?oItemId=1875.

'Mea Culpa by Rictor Norton', *The Pink Triangle Trust* [accessed on 27 July 2010]. http://www.pinktriangle.org.uk/glh/214/norton.html.

'Men jailed for gay barman murder', *BBC News* [accessed on 16 May 2012]. http://news.bbc.co.uk/1/hi/england/london/5087286.stm.

'New Labour because Britain deserves better', *An unofficial site on the Labour Party*, [accessed on 20 April 2009], http://www.labour-party.org.uk/manifestos/1997/1997-labour-manifesto.shtml.

'On this day – 1957: Homosexuality should not be a crime', *BBC News* [accessed on 23 November 2009]. http://news.bbc.co.uk/onthisday/hi/dates/stories/september/4/newsid_3007000/3007686.stm.

'Patron', National AIDS Trust [accessed on 17 March 2011]. http://www.nat.org.uk/About-us/Team/Patron.aspx.

'Peter Tatchell: Out and about', *The Independent* [accessed on 16 April 2009]. http://www.independent.co.uk/news/people/profiles/peter-tatchell-out-and-about-524819.html.
Politicsresources.net. http://www.psr.keele.ac.uk/area/uk/man/con87.htm.
'Pneumocystis Pneumonia – Los Angeles', Centers for Disease Control and Prevention [accessed on 7 August 2008]. http://www.cdc.gov/mmwr/preview/mmwrhtml/june_5.htm.
'Polls supports S28 retention', *BBC News* [accessed on 7 March 2011]. http://news.bbc.co.uk/1/hi/scotland/768882.stm.
'Positive Nation: Regulars–Caroline Guinness-McGann: The way we were', Positive Nation [accessed on 8 February 2011]. http://www.positivenation.co.uk/regulars/article.php?article_id=80.
'Profile: Baroness Young', *BBC News* [accessed on 24 November 2010]. http://news.bbc.co.uk/1/hi/uk/1046634.stm.
'Section 28/The Arts Lobby', *Ian McKellen* [accessed on 30 May 2009]. http://www.mckellen.com/activism/section28.htm.
———, [accessed on 30 May 2009]. http://www.mckellen.com/activism/section28.htm; Author's interview with Waheed Alli, 13 January 2009.
'Stonewall UK', *Ian McKellen* [accessed on 30 May 2009]. http://www.mckellen.com/activism/section28.htm.
'The Election Battles 1945–1997', *BBC News* [accessed on 22 November 2010]. http://news.bbc.co.uk/hi/english/static/vote2001/in_depth/election_battles/1992_results.stm.
'The Good Friday Agreement', BBC News [accessed on 23 July 2012]. http://www.bbc.co.uk/northernireland/schools/agreement/equality/support/er2_c011.shtml.
'The Next Move Forward', *Richard Kimber's Political Science Resources* [accessed on 8 May 2009]. http://www.psr.keele.ac.uk/area/uk/man/con87.htm.
'The pioneer who changed gay lives', *The Observer* [accessed on 20 September 2010]. http://www.guardian.co.uk/politics/2005/jan/30/uk.aids.
'THT: About us: Our history', THT [accessed on 8 February 2011]. http://www.tht.org.uk/aboutus/ourhistory/.
'Tony Blair's gay speech in full', *Pink News* [accessed on 2 June 2009]. http://www.pinknews.co.uk/news/articles/2005-3983.html.
'UK Military Gay Ban Illegal', *BBC News* [accessed on 26 November 2010]. http://news.bbc.co.uk/1/hi/uk/458625.stm.

Secondary Sources
Books

Abelove, Henry, Michèle Aina Barale and David M. Halperin, eds, *The lesbian and gay studies reader* (London: Routledge, 1993).
Ainley, Rosa, *What is she like? Lesbian identities from the 1950s to the 1990s* (London: Cassell, 1995).
Aldridge, Mark and Andy Murray, *T is for Television: the small screen adventures of Russell T Davies* (London: Reynolds and Hearn Ltd, 2008).
Bingham, Adrian, *Family Newspapers? Sex, Private Life, and the British Popular Press 1918–1978* (Oxford: Oxford University Press, 2009).

BIBLIOGRAPHY

Blank, Joani and Marcia Quackenbush, eds, *The Playbook for Kids About Sex* (London: Sheba Feminist Publishers, 1982).
Bosche, Susanne, *Jenny Lives with Eric and Martin* (London: Gay Men's Press: 1983).
Boswell, John, *Christianity, social tolerance, and homosexuality* (Chicago: University of Chicago Press, 1980).
Bourne, Stephen, *Brief Encounters: Lesbian and Gays in British Cinema 1930–1971* (London: Cassell, 1996).
Butler, Judith, *Gender Trouble: feminism and the subversion of identity* (New York: Routledge, 1990).
Cant, Bob and Susan Hemmings, eds, *Radical Records – Thirty Years of Lesbian and Gay History* (London: Routledge, 1988).
Chasin, Alexandra, *Selling Out: The Gay and Lesbian Movement Goes to Market* (New York: Palgrave Macmillan, 2001).
Chauncey, George. *Gay New York: Gender, Urban Culture, and the Making of the Gay Male World 1890–1940* (New York: Basic Books, 1994).
Clark, Anna, *Desire: a history of European sexuality* (London: Routledge, 2008).
Cohen, Stanley and Jock Young, eds, *The manufacture of the news: social problems, deviance and the mass media* (London: Constable, 1984).
Coldstream, John, *Victim* (London: BFI: Palgrave Macmillan, 2011).
Conekin, Beck, Frank Mort and Chris Waters, eds, *Moments of Modernity: Restructuring Britain 1945–1964* (London: River Oram Press:, 1999).
Cook, Matt, *London and the Culture of Homosexuality, 1885–1914* (Cambridge: Cambridge University Press, 2003).
——— ed. *A gay history of Britain: love and sex between men since the middle ages* (Oxford; Westport, Connecticut: Greenwood World Publishing, 2007).
Cooper, Davina, *Power in Struggle: Feminism, Sexuality and the State* (Buckingham: Open University Press, 1995).
Coote, Anna, *Sweet freedom: the struggle for women's liberation* (London: Pan, 1982).
Cretney, Stephen, *Same Sex Relationships: From 'Odious Crime' to 'Gay Marriage'* (Oxford: Oxford University Press, 2006).
Crick, Michael, *In Search of Michael Howard* (London: Simon & Schuster, 2005).
Curran, James, Ivor Gaber, and Julian Petley, eds, *Culture Wars: The Media and the British Left* (Edinburgh: Edinburgh University Press, 2005).
D'Emilio, John, *Making trouble: essays on gay history, politics and the university* (New York: Routledge, 1992).
Davenport-Hines, Richard and Peter Treadwell, *Sex, death and punishment: attitudes to sex and sexuality in Britain since the Renaissance* (London: Collins, 1990).
David, Hugh, *On Queer Street: a social history of British homosexuality, 1895–1995* (London: HarperCollins, 1997).
Davies, Christie, *The Strange Death of Moral Britain* (London: Transaction Publishers, 2004).
Davis, Glynn and Gary Needham, *Queer TV: Theories, Histories, Politics* (London: Routledge, 2009).
De Lauretis, Teresa, *Queer theory: lesbian and gay sexualities: an introduction* (Providence: Differences, 1991).
Dearing, James, *Agenda Setting* (Thousand Oaks: Sage Publications, 1996).
Doan, Laura, *Fashioning Sapphism: the origins of a modern English lesbian culture* (New York: Columbia University Press, 2001).

Durham, Martin, *Sex and Politics: The Family and Morality in the Thatcher Years* (Basingstoke: MacMillan Education, 1991).
Dyer, Richard, *The Matter of Images: Essays on Representation* (London: Routledge, 1993).
———, *The culture of queers* (London: Routledge, 2002).
Engel, Stephen M., *Unfinished Revolution: Social movement theory and the gay and lesbian movement* (Cambridge: Cambridge University Press, 2001).
Epstein, Debbie, ed., *Challenging Lesbian and Gay Inequalities in Education* (Buckingham: Open University Press, 1994).
Foucault, Michel, *The History of Sexuality: An Introduction* (London: Penguin, 1990).
Garfield, Simon, *The End of Innocence: Britain in the Time of AIDS* (London: Faber and Faber Limited, 1994).
Gay Left Collective, eds, *Homosexuality: Power & Politics* (London: Allison and Busby, 1980).
Gill, John, *Queer Noises* (London: Cassell, 1995).
Goldhaber, Michael D., *A People's History of the European Court of Human Rights* (Piscataway, NJ: Rutgers University Press, 2007).
Griffiths, Robin, *British Queer Cinema* (London: Routledge, 2006).
Hall Carpenter Archives, *Inventing Ourselves: Lesbian Life Stories* (London: Routledge, 1989).
———, *Walking After Midnight: Gay Men's Life Stories* (London: Routledge, 1989).
Halperin, David, *One Hundred Years of Homosexuality: and other essays on Greek love* (London: Routledge, 1990).
Haste, Cate, *Rules of Desire: Sex in Britain: World War 1 to the Present* (London: Pimlico, 1994).
Healey, Emma and Angela Mason, eds, *Stonewall 25: The making of the lesbian and gay community in Britain* (London: Virago Press Ltd, 1994).
Hekma, Gert, ed., *Volume 6: A Cultural History of Sexuality in the Modern Age* (London: A & C Black Publishers Ltd, 2012).
Higgins, Patrick, *Heterosexual Dictatorship: male homosexuality in post-war Britain* (London: Fourth Estate, 1996).
Hogg, Michael A. and Graham M. Vaughan, *Social Psychology* (Harlow: Pearson Education, 2011).
Houlbrook, Matt, *Queer London: perils and pleasures in the metropolis, 1918–1957* (Chicago; London: University of Chicago Press, 2005).
Howes, Keith, *Broadcasting It: An Encyclopaedia of Homosexuality on Film, Radio and TV in the UK 1923–1993* (London: Cassell, 1993).
Jeffrey-Poulter, Stephen, *Peers, queers and commons: the struggle for gay law reform from 1950 to the present* (London: Routledge, 1991).
Jeffreys, Sheila, *Anticlimax: a feminist perspective on the sexual revolution* (London: The Women's Press, 1990).
———, *The Lesbian Heresy: A feminist perspective on the lesbian sexual revolution* (London: The Women's Press, 1994).
Jennings, Rebecca, *A Lesbian History of Britain: Love and Sex Between Women Since 1500* (Oxford: Greenwood World Publishing, 2007).
———, *Tomboys and Bachelor Girls: a lesbian history of post-war Britain, 1945–1971* (Manchester: Manchester University Press, 2007).
Jivani, Alkarim, *It's Not Unusual: A History of Lesbian and Gay Britain in the Twentieth Century* (London: Michael O'Mara Books Limited, 1997).

BIBLIOGRAPHY

Katz, Jonathan Ned, *The Invention of Heterosexuality* (London: University of Chicago Press, Ltd., 2007).
Kinsey, A.C., W.B. Pomeroy, and C.E. Martin, *Sexual Behaviour in the Human Male* (Philadelphia: W.B. Saunders Company, 1948).
Kirsch, Max H., *Queer Theory and Social Change* (London: Routledge, 2000).
Kosofsky Sedgwick, Eve, *Epistemology of the Closet* (London: Harvester Wheatsheaf, 1991).
Kraft-Ebing, Richard von, *Psychopathia Sexualis: with especial reference to contrary sexual instinct, a medico-legal study* (Philadelphia: F.A. Davis, 1896).
Marwick, Arthur, *The Sixties: cultural revolution in Britain, France, Italy, and the United States, c.1958–c.1974* (Oxford: Oxford University Press, 1999).
Mayes, Stephen and Lyndall Stein, eds, *Positive Lives: Responses to HIV, a photodocumentary* (London: Cassell, 1993).
McLaren, Angus, *Twentieth-Century Sexuality: A History* (Oxford: Blackwell, 1999).
Meredith, Paul, *Government, schools, and the law* (London: Routledge, 1992).
Moran, Leslie, *The Homosexuality of the Law* (London: Routledge, 1996).
Mort, Frank, *Cultures of Consumption: masculinities and social space in late twentieth-century Britain* (London: Routledge, 1996).
Norman, Jeremy, *No Make-Up: straight tales from a queer life* (London: Elliot and Thompson, 2006).
Oram, Alison and Annmarie Turnball, *The Lesbian History Sourcebook: love and sex between women in Britain from 1780 to 1970* (London: Routledge, 2001).
Peele, Thomas, *Queer Popular Culture: Literature, Media, Film, and Television* (New York: Palgrave Macmillan, 2007).
Plummer, Ken, *The Making of the Modern Homosexual* (London: Hutchinson, 1981).
——— ed., *Modern Homosexualities: fragments of lesbian and gay experience* (London: Routledge, 1992).
Power, Lisa, *No Bath But Plenty of Bubbles: An Oral History of the Gay Liberation Front 1970–73* (London: Cassell, 1995).
Rees, David, *The Milkman's on his Way* (London: Gay Men's Press, 1982).
Richardson, Diane, *Rethinking sexuality* (London: Sage, 2000).
Roseneil, Sasha, *Common Women, Uncommon Practices: the queer feminisms of greenham* (London: Cassell, 2000).
Roszak, Theodore, *The Making of a Counter Culture* (London: University of California, 1995).
Ross, Alistair, *Curriculum: Construction and Critique* (London: Routledge, 1999).
Russo, Vito, *The celluloid closet: homosexuality in the movies* (New York: Harper and Row, 1987).
Sandbrook, Dominic, *Never Had It So Good: A History of Britain from Suez to the Beatles* (London: Abacus, 2005).
———, *State of Emergency: The Way We Were: Britain, 1970–1974* (London: Penguin, 2010).
Sanderson, Terry, *Mediawatch: The Treatment of Male and Female Homosexuality in the British Media* (London: Cassell, 1995).
Segal, Lynne, *Is The Future Female? Troubled Thoughts on Contemporary Feminism* (London: Virago Press, 1987).
Sinfield, Alan, *Gay and After* (London: Serpent's Tail, 1998).
Smith, Anna Marie, *New right discourse on race and sexuality: Britain, 1968–1990* (Cambridge: Cambridge University Press, 1994).

Smith, Patricia Juliana, ed., *The Queer Sixties* (London: Routledge, 1999).
Spencer, Colin, *Homosexuality: a history* (London: Fourth Estate, 1995).
Stein, Edward ed., *Forms of Desire: Sexual Orientation and the Social Constructionist Controvers* (London: Routledge, 1992).
Summerskill, Ben, ed., *The way we are now: gay and lesbian lives in the 21st century* (London: Continuum, 2006).
Tajfel, Henri, *Differentiation between Social Groups: studies in the social psychology of intergroup relations* (London: Academic Press, 1978).
Turner, John, *Rediscovering the Social Group: A Self-Categorization Theory* (Oxford: Basil Blackwell, 1987).
Warner, Michael, ed., *Fear of a Queer Planet: Queer Politics and Social theory* (Minneapolis: University of Minnesota Press, 1993).
Watney, Simon, *Imagine Hope: AIDS and gay identity* (London: Routledge, 2000).
Weeks, Jeffrey, *Coming Out: Homosexual Politics in Britain, from the Nineteenth Century to the Present* (London: Quartet Books, 1977).
———, *Sex Politics, & Society: The regulation of sexuality since 1800* (Harlow: Longman, 1981).
———, *Against Nature: Essay on history, sexuality and identity* (London: River Oram Press, 1991).
———, *Making Sexual History* (Cambridge: Polity Press, 2000).
———, *The World We Have Won: The Remaking of Erotic and Intimate Life* (London: Routledge, 2007).
Weeks, Jeffrey and Kevin Porter, eds, *Between the acts: lives of homosexual men 1885–1967* (London: River Oram Press, 1998).
———, Brian Heaphy and Catherine Donovan, *Same Sex Intimacies: Families of Choice and Other Life Experiments* (London: Routledge, 2001).
Whisman, Vera, *Queer by choice: lesbians, gay men, and the politics of identity* (Routledge: London, 1996).
Whittle, Stephen, ed., *The margins of the city: gay men's urban lives* (Aldershot: Arena, 1994).
Wittig, Monique, *The straight mind and other essays* (New York: Harvester-Wheatsheaf, 1992).

Journals and Chapters

Andersson, Johan, 'East End Localism and Urban Decay: Shoreditch's Re-Emerging Gay Scene', *The London Journal*, 34, 1 (2009), 55–71.
Anon., 'Crime and Sin: Sir John Wolfenden At Winchester', *The British Medical Journal*, 2, 5192 (1960), 140–2.
Bell, David and Jon Binnie, 'Authenticating Queer Space: Citizenship, Urbanism and Governance', *Urban Studies*, 41 (2004), 1807–20.
Blasius, Mark, 'An Ethos of Lesbian and Gay Existence', *Political Theory*, 20, 4 (1992), 642–71.
Bristow, Joseph, 'Remapping the Sites of Modern Gay History: Legal Reform, Medico-Legal Thought, Homosexual Scandal, Erotic Geography', *Journal of British Studies*, 46, 1 (2007), 116–42.
Cocks, H.G., 'Modernity and the Self in the History of Sexuality', *The Historical Journal*, 49 (2006), 1211–27.

———, 'The History of Sexuality Meets Evolutionary Psychology', *Contemporary British History*, 24, 1 (2010), 109–29.
Connolly, Clara, 'Splintered Sisterhood: Antiracism in a Young Women's Project', *Feminist Review*, 36 (1990), 45–54.
Cook, Matt, '"Gay Times": Identity, Locality, Memory, and the Brixton Squats in 1970s London', *Twentieth Century British History* (2011), 1–26.
Davidson, Roger, and Gayle Davis, '"A Field for Private Members": The Wolfenden Committee and Scottish Homosexual Law Reform, 1950–67', *Twentieth Century British History*, 15, 2 (2004), 174–201.
Durham, Martin, 'Abortion, Gay Rights and Politics in Britain and America: A Comparison', *Parliamentary Affairs*, 58, 1 (2005), 89–103.
England, L.R., 'Little Kinsey: An Outline of Sex Attitudes in Britain', *The Public Opinion Quarterly*, 13, 4 (1949–1950), 587–600.
Hallam, Julia, and Margaret Marshment, 'Framing experience: case studies in the reception of *Oranges are Not the Only Fruit*', *Screen*, 36, 1 (1995), 1–15.
Halperin, David, M., 'The Normalization of Queer Theory', *Journal of Homosexuality*, 45, 2–4 (2003), 339–43.
Hamer, Diane with Penny Ashbrook, 'OUT: Reflections on British television's first lesbian and gay magazine series', in *The good, the bad, and the gorgeous: popular culture's romance with lesbianism*, ed. by Diane Hamer and Belinda Budge (London: Pandora, 1994).
Hauser, Gerard, 'Vernacular dialogue and the theatricality of public opinion', *Communication Monographs*, 65, 2 (1998), 83–107.
Hinds, Hilary, 'Oranges Are Not the Only Fruit: reaching audiences other lesbian texts cannot reach', in *Television Times: A Reader*, ed. by John Corner and Sylvia Harvey (London: Arnold, 1996).
Jenness, Valerie, 'Coming out: Lesbian identities and the categorization problem' in *Modern Homosexualities: fragments of lesbian and gay experience*, ed. by Ken Plumber (London: Routledge, 1992).
Jennings, Rebecca, '"The Most Uninhibited Party They'd Ever Been to": The Postwar Encounter between Psychiatry and the British Lesbian, 1945–1971', *The Journal of British Studies*, 47 (2008), 883–904.
Medhurt, Andy, 'In search of nebulous nancies: Looking for queers in pre-gay British film', in *British Queer Cinema*, ed. by Robin Griffiths (London: Routledge, 2006).
Moscovici, Serge, 'The phenomenon of social representations', in *Social Representations* ed. by R.M. Farr and S. Moscovici (Cambridge: Cambridge University Press, 1983).
Nayak, Anoop and Mary Jane Kehily, 'Playing it Straight: Masculinities, Homophobias and Schooling', *Journal of Feminist Studies*, 5 (1996), 211–230.
Rayside, David M., 'Homophobia, Class and Party in England', *Canadian Journal of Political Science*, 25, 1 (1992), 121–49.
Reinhold, Susan, 'Through the Parliamentary Looking Glass: "Real" and "Pretend" Families in Contemporary British Politics', *Feminist Review*, 48 (1994), 61–79.
Robinson, Lucy, 'Three Revolutionary Years: The Impact of the Counter Culture on the Development of the Gay Liberation Movement', *Cultural and Social History*, 3, (2006), 445–71.
Smith, A.M., 'A Symptomology of an Authoritarian Discourse', in *New Foundations: A journal of culture/theory/politics*, 10 (1990), 41–65.

Sontag, Susan, 'Notes on Camp', *Partisan Review* (1964), 515–30.
Turner, Georgina, 'Catching the Wave', *Journalism Studies*, 10, 6 (2009), 769–88.
Waites, Matthew, 'Homosexuality and the New Right: The Legacy of the 1980s for New Delineations of Homophobia', *Sociological Research Online*, 5, 1 (2000).
——, 'Inventing a 'lesbian age of consent'? The history of the minimum age for sex between women in the UK', *Social & Legal Studies*, 11 (2002), 323–42.
——, 'Equality at Last? Homosexuality, Heterosexuality and the Age of Consent in the United Kingdom', *Sociology*, 37 (2003), 637–55.

Theses
Reinhold, Susan, *Local Conflict and Ideological Struggle: 'Positive Images' and Section 28* (unpublished doctoral thesis, University of Sussex, 1994).

INDEX

Abse, Leo, 23–26, 71, 94, 96. *See also* Sexual Offences Act 1967
Adair, James, 26. *See also* Wolfenden Report
Adoption and Children Bill, 181–182
AIDS Coalition to Unleash Power (Act-Up), 160
Alli, Waheed, 102, 114, 173, 176, 179, 182, 184. *See also* Section 28
Arena Three, 38–41, 68, 69, 70, 218. *See also* Minorities Research Group.
Arran, Lord, 17, 22–25, 71, 92–93. *See also* Sexual Offences Act 1967
Attitude magazine, 182, 185, 190–192

Beautiful Thing, 206–208
Berkeley, Humphry, 24
Bermondsey (drama), 63–64
Bermondsey election, 97–98
Birmingham Post, 61
Black Panthers, 27
Blair, Tony, 169–170, 173, 182, 187–188, 200, 201. *See also* Labour Party
Blatch, Baroness, 178, 182–183
Bogarde, Dirk, 54
Boothby, Lord, 19, 93, 96

British Social Attitudes Survey, 109, 185–186
Brookside, 205–206

Campaign for Homosexual Equality (CHE) formally Committee for Homosexual Equality, 10, 33, 34, 72–78, 81, 92, 111, 114, 147, 152. *See also* Homosexual Law Reform Society
Capital Gay, 115, 118, 123–126
Chapman, Diana, 38, 70
Christian Festival of Light, 29–30
Church of England, 19, 32, 116–117
civil partnerships, 184–187, 203
Class, 1, 2, 18–19, 22, 36, 39–41, 43, 56, 63, 68, 69–70, 114, 153, 215, 218
clone, 149, 154, 161, 221
clubs, 146–156
COC, 22, 72
Come Together, 45, 81, 121. *See also* Gay Liberation Front
commercialism, 74, 83, 101, 120–121, 127, 129, 144, 146–156, 190–191
Conservative Party, 92, 93, 95, 97, 101–102, 104–105, 107–108,

114, 125–126, 135, 166–167, 169, 179, 182–183, 185–186
Cook, Robin, 93, 96
Crime and Disorder Bill, 173–179
Criminal Justice and Immigration Act 2008, 187
Criminal Justice and Public Order Act 1994, 165–173
Criminal Law Revision Committee, 25, 31–32, 34, 43, 111
Currie, Edwina, 165–171, 198

Daily Express, 48, 54, 57, 102, 135, 140, 201
Daily Mail, 48, 61, 103, 133, 135, 139, 197, 200, 202, 203, 208, 210
Daily Mirror, 41, 48, 130, 198, 201, 203
Daily Star, 197
Daily Telegraph, The, 48, 51, 130, 134, 137, 141, 197, 201, 203, 210
Disability, 102–103, 154–155
Diva, 194–196
Dudgeon, Jeff, 94–95. *See also* Northern Ireland
Dunkley, Paddy, 38. *See also* Minorities Research Group
Dyson, A.E., 20. *See also* Homosexual Law Reform Society

EastEnders, 204–205

feminism, 29, 78–79, 84–86
Financial Times, 143

Gay Liberation Front (GLF)
    clubs, 76–77
    Come Together magazine, 45
    communes, 81–82
    counter culture, 8, 27–29, 77–78, 79
    criminality, 82
    ethnicity, 83
    feminism, 78–79, 84–85
    friction, 30–31

gay days, 79–80
gay identity, 1, 6, 28, 36, 39, 49–50, 79
London Lesbian and Gay Switchboard, 84
protests, 29–30, 76, 80–81
Gay Men Fighting AIDS (GMFA), 160
Gay Men's Press, 84
Gay News, 45, 52, 73, 75, 84, 121–123
Gay pride, 29, 76
Gay Times, 57, 108, 111, 123, 126–128, 140, 172, 192–193, 207
Gaytime TV, 208–209
Gemma, 155
Girl, 10, 62–63
Greater London Council (GLC), 101–103
Greenham Common, 85–86
Grey, Antony, 1, 22, 38, 39, 69, 71. *See also* Sexual Offences Act and Homosexual Law Reform Society
Guardian, The, 95, 109, 140, 200, 207, 208–209

Halsbury, Lord, 92–93, 105–106, 133. *See also* Section 28
Haringey, 102–105, 125, 133, 141. *See also* Section 28
HIM exclusive, 123, 126
HIV/AIDS, 91, 99–102, 127–132, 148–149, 155–161, 167, 194
Homosexual Law Reform Society (HLRS), 1, 17–18, 20–25, 31, 32, 38, 71, 215. *See also* Campaign for Homosexual Equality
Horsfall, Allan, 32, 72. *See also* Campaign for Homosexual Equality
Howard, Michael, 169, 185. *See also* Conservative Party
Hughes, Simon, 97–98, 107–108. *See also* Liberal Democrats

Independent, The, 142, 200–201, 202–203, 210

INDEX

Inner London Education Authority (ILEA), 104, 134–135. *See also* Section 28
Islington Gazette, 104

Jenkins, Roy, 31, 34
Jenny Lives with Eric and Martin, 84, 104, 135, 200. *See also* Section 28
Jeremy, 41–42, 45

Kenric, 70
Killing of Sister George, The, 55–58
Knight, Jill, 106

Labouchere Amendment 1885, 66–67
Labour Party, 24–25, 96–98, 99, 101–102, 106–107, 114, 165, 173, 179–182, 199
Langley, Esme, 38, 70. *See also* Minorities Research Group
Legislation for Lesbian and Gay Rights Campaign (LLGRC), 111
Liberal Democrats (formally the Liberal Party), 97–98, 180, 181, 203
Livingstone, Ken, 101–102, 134–135, 202
Local Government Bill 2000, 179–180
London Evening Standard, 48, 49–50, 54, 133, 140, 202
London Lesbian and Gay Switchboard, 84, 148

Male and Female Homosexual Association of Great Britain (MANDFHAB), 71, 147
Man Alive, 58–62
Manchester Guardian, The, 48
Maxwell-Fyfe, David, 19, 47. *See also* Wolfenden Report
McKellen, Ian, 111–115, 166. *See also* Stonewall (charity)
Mellors, Bob, 27. *See also* Gay Liberation Front

Milkman's on His Way, The, 104
Minorities Research Group (MRG), 38, 60, 67–70, 218–219. *See also* Grey, Antony
Montagu, Lord, 18–19, 48. *See also* Wolfenden Report
Morning Star, 61
My Beautiful Laundrette, 137–139

New Statesman, 47–48
Northern Ireland, 18, 24, 26, 93–95
North-Western Homosexual Law Reform Committee (NWHLRC), 32, 71

Observer, The, 47–48, 50, 51, 143, 197–198
Oranges Are Not The Only Fruit, 11, 142–144
Organisation for Lesbian and Gay Action (OLGA), 111, 115. *See also* Section 28
Out on Tuesday, 140–142
OutRage!, 98, 115–118, 151, 172, 192–193, 203

paedophilia, 21–22, 36, 46, 48, 49, 105–106, 118, 136, 174–175, 177, 178, 196–197, 199, 202, 204, 210
Paisley, Ian, 94. *See also* Northern Ireland
Pitt-Rivers, Michael, 18. *See also* Wolfenden Report

Queer as Folk, 209–211

Racism, 153–155
Reading Evening Post, 61
Reid, Cynthia, 38, 60. *See also* Minorities Research Group
Rowe, Dilys, 38. *See also* Minorities Research Group.

Scotland, 17, 25–26, 93, 95–97, 180, 183, 200
Scottish Minorities Group (SMG), 33, 92
Section 28
  introduction, 21, 36, 84, 99, 104–115, 125–126, 128, 132–136, 138, 140, 141
  repeal, 179–184, 185, 199–204
Sexual Law Reform Society (SLRS), 31–32
Sexual Offences Act 1967, 17–21, 24–25, 27, 35–36, 43, 51, 55, 58, 67, 76, 93–94, 106, 110, 167–172
Sexual Offences Act 2004, 187
Sexual Orientation Regulations 2006, 183–184, 187
Smith, Chris, 98–99
Spare Rib, 143–144
Spartacus, 43–45
St James Gazette, 46
Stonewall (charity),
  campaigns, 166–167, 171–172, 175, 176, 181, 182–183, 185, 186–188
  formation, 112–115, 116, 118
Stonewall (riots), 27, 42
Summerskill, Ben, 176, 183, 186. *See also* Stonewall (charity)
Sun, The, 18–19, 62, 97, 103, 104, 129–130, 133, 135, 136, 140, 196, 199–200, 201, 202, 210
Sunday Express, 48
Sunday People, The, 48, 130
Sunday Pictorial, The, 46
Sunday Telegraph, The, 61–62, 101
Sunday Times, The, 18, 54
Switsur, Julie, 38, 60

Tatchell, Peter, 97–99, 116–117, 172, 186. *See also* OutRage!
Terrence Higgins Trust (THT), 157–158, 190
Thatcher, Margaret, 106–107, 108, 183. *See also* Conservative Party
The Times, 20, 48, 54, 112, 129, 130, 133, 142, 198, 203
Times Educational Supplement, The, 54, 138
Timm, 42–43
Today, 104, 133
Tory Campaign for Homosexual Equality (previously The Conservative Group for Homosexual Equality) (TORCHE), 97, 114, 167
Trades Union Congress (TUC), 99
Troops Out, 78
Two of Us, 138–140

Union for Sexual Freedoms in Ireland (USFI), 92

Victim, 53–55

Walter, Aubrey, 27, 79, 84. *See also* Gay Liberation Front
Whitehouse, Mary, 52
Wilde, Oscar, 46
Wildeblood, Peter, 18, 20–22
Wilshire, David, 107–109, 134, 141. *See also* Section 28
Wolfenden Report, 19–21, 26, 46–48, 67
Women's Liberation Movement (WLM), 84–85

Young, Baroness, 174, 176–179, 182